Support Your RV Lifestyle!

An Insider's Guide to Working on the Road

Support Your RV Lifestyle!
An Insider's Guide to Working on the Road

By Jaimie Hall

Pine Country Publishing

Grateful acknowledgment is made for the use of the following material:
* For survey data found in *Over the Next Hill: An Enthnography of RVing Seniors in North America* by Dorothy Ayers Counts and David E. Counts, published by Broadview Press, Ontario, Canada, 1996 and 2001.
* For the budget worksheet developed by Stephanie Bernhagen for the Life on Wheels Conference, assistance with the online budget survey, and "Working with the Mouse." © 2001
* For an updated version of *Whistle While We Work* by Janice Lasko, published originally in the February 1994 *Camperways;* and for *Janice's Grocery Shopping List.*

Other contributions:
* For "Family Volunteering" and "Hope's Story and Advice" from Hope Sykes.
* For "Desert Ecology," by Chuck Wright, originally published in the Boomer newsletter.
* For "Working Tales" by Lou Schneider.
* Graphics in the text ©2002 *www.ArtToday.com.*

In order to protect privacy, some names have been changed.

Cover Design and Photo by Paul Jones

Library of Congress Cataloging-in-Publication Data

Hall, Jaimie.
    Support Your RV lifestyle! : an insider's guide to working on the road / by Jaimie Hall.
    p. cm.
    Includes bibliographical references and index.
    LCCN 2001099204
    ISBN 0-9716777-0-0
    1. Recreational vehicle living--United States.
2. Temporary employment--United States. I. Title.
TX1110.H35 2002   796.7'9'0973
                           QBI02-200025

This book is dedicated to my
husband, Bill.
Without his support,
encouragement and patience this
book might never have been
completed.

Table of Contents

SECTION IV. RV LIFESTYLE CONSIDERATIONS

SECTION V. APPENDICES

SECTION V. RESOURCES

Acknowledgments

This book is the culmination of ten years on the road and many experiences and sharing. Two incidents were instrumental in even conceiving of the idea of *Support Your RV Lifestyle! An Insider's Guide to Working on the Road*:

✔ The first was when we pulled Grand Teton National Park for our first seasonal jobs. Snow still covered the ground and the jagged Teton peaks. Being there was a dream come true. Both Bill and I were excited. We had actually gotten seasonal jobs with the National Park Service. I wanted to share how we had done it with anyone else who wanted to know.

✔ The second took place at a "Boomerang" in October of 1994 in Pena Blanca, Arizona. Alice Zyetz invited several women RVers to participate in writing exercises a la Natalie Goldberg's *Writing Down the Bones*. Little did I suspect that day that this book would result. Alice's book, *You Shoulda Listened to Your Mother: 36 Timeless Success Tips for Working Women,* was yet to be written also.

Besides the hours of personal time, this book would not have been completed without the generous help of many people.

I would especially like to acknowledge and thank Alice Zyetz, my editor and friend, for her tireless work. I actually got a package deal. Chuck Zyetz, too, spent considerable time editing, the book benefitting from his logical, engineering mind.

Also giving editorial assistance and encouragement were Stephanie Bernhagen, Phyllis Frey, Judith Waite Allee, Janice Lasko, Joe and Kay Peterson, Greg and Debbie Robus, Paul Bernhagen, and Hope Sykes. Carol Richards, David Loring, Alfred Lutz and Ron Chance provided invaluable assistance with the chapters on legal and financial issues facing working RVers and managing RV expenses. Friends Shaneen and DeAnna willingly shared valuable information they have gathered in dealing with health issues on the road. Heidi Young assisted with the chapter on e-mail. Jodi Carroll helped with fact checking.

Stephanie Bernhagen, author of *Take Back Your Life! Travel Full-Time in an RV*, wrote her book on the road and gave invaluable assistance and encouragement with the publishing process. Stephanie has also generously shared the Web site she developed with me, RV Hometown. com.

I also owe a big thanks to Paul Jones for the striking Utah scene and cover of this book. After I saw Stephanie's cover for *Take Back Your Life!*, I never considered anyone else to do this one. He spent hours making it just right.

Several individuals contributed pieces to the book: Hope Sykes, Stephanie Bernhagen, Janice Lasko, Virginia Heitman, Lou Schneider, and Chuck Wright. Their experiences and contributions added valuable information.

It would be impossible to list all who helped. I thank the many working RVers who have shared their stories with me over the years; you will see many of their names throughout the book. Ron and Val Jones deserve special mention. They are the consummate working RVers; their work experiences are mentioned in several chapters. They represent what this adventure is all about, having expertly used working on the road to achieve their travel and life goals. Terry and Joe Sweeney are another special couple. Their skill and determination in making this lifestyle work has been an inspiration too.

And finally, I would like to thank you, dear readers, for your openness and willingness to create your own lives!

Jaimie Hall

Preface

Support Your RV Lifestyle! is written for three groups of readers:

✔ You're new to RVing and are considering working on the road.
✔ You've had some work experience on the road and you're not entirely satisfied.
✔ You're experienced working RVers who would like some new ideas and tools for making money on the road.

When we first became full-time RVers in 1992, my husband Bill and I knew we would need to work on the road to support our RV lifestyle. Could we do it? Where could we find jobs? Could we find jobs to make enough money to live on? Unfortunately, there was no manual to help us answer these questions.

Because of this void, I began listening for and collecting information about working on the road. For the last ten years I have been sharing this information with other working RVers through articles, newsletters, seminars and personal contact.

Support Your RV Lifestyle! is the result of ten years of research and sharing. This is the "how-to" manual that we wished we had when we started out. *Support Your RV Lifestyle! An Insider's Guide to Working on the Road* provides the necessary tools and resources to find jobs that pay well and enhance your experiences on the road.

Why you need this book:
14 mistakes working RVers can avoid

Talk to RV workers about their work experiences and you'll find many who have had at least one job doing things they didn't like. Others have paid out more money than they earned or quit their jobs mid-season because it was nothing like what they expected. Contrast these with other RV workers who always seem to get wonderful jobs. They get free tickets to area attractions, see things that only locals know about, and save more money now than before they hit the road. I want to help you become part of the second group of working RVers.

This book provides the tools to:

✔ make the money you need or want to

✔ get the most out of your RV lifestyle

Too many RV workers are not achieving these goals because they make one or more of the following avoidable mistakes:

MISTAKE #1: TAKE THE FIRST JOB YOU ARE OFFERED.

RV workers have told me they talked to one employer and got hired. They were so excited about getting a job, they jumped at it. Later on they confessed that it wasn't what they were expecting. It is a piece of cake to find a job. The trick is finding a job that makes the money you want and adds to your travel experiences.

To do this you will examine your income needs and wants. You'll identify what you want to do and what you don't want to do. You'll find out how to prepare for an interview to find out about a job before taking it.

MISTAKE #2: UNDERVALUE YOUR SKILLS AND WHAT YOU HAVE TO OFFER.

If you are new to a field, you may have no idea what the going rate for a position is or how your skills compare to those of other RV workers. Many RV parks and other seasonal employers advertise very low wages so you figure that's what you must accept, even if you bring more value to the job. This often goes with Mistake #1, grabbing the first job offer.

You will learn how to do your research to enable you to negotiate from strength and knowledge.

MISTAKE #3: NEED A JOB SUDDENLY.

Suddenly needing a job could happen for any number of reasons: an expected job falls through, the stock market declines, or you have unexpected expenses like vehicle repairs or a medical emergency. Being in a position where you need a job and have nothing lined up does not put you in a good bargaining position.

You'll learn how to have several options, how to develop your job contacts, and what to do to find a last-minute position.

MISTAKE #4: WORK 20 HOURS/WEEK FOR A "FREE" RV SITE.

You may get an RV site as all or part of your compensation. Remember, your time is valuable. The site is not free. Depending on the monthly rate, you may be "earning" the equivalent of $2 or $3 an hour.

You'll learn several ways to value your "free site" to determine if you are working for a fair amount.

MISTAKE #5: PAY TAXES ON YOUR "FREE" RV SITE.

You could end up owing income taxes on your "free" RV site. The IRS looks at your site as income unless certain conditions are met.

You will learn about the letter you must get from your employer to avoid such taxes.

MISTAKE #6: GET CHARGED OUTRAGEOUS AMOUNTS FOR YOUR "FREE" SITE.

You may have an employer tell you the site you are getting is worth $750 dollars a month. However, the employer based it on the daily rate of $25 per night. You are entitled to the much-reduced monthly rate.

You'll learn how to determine a fair value for your RV site, even if the employer does not have a published rate.

MISTAKE #7: WORK 50-60 HOURS, GET PAID FOR 40.

Salaried employees are usually expected to work beyond the standard work week. Accepting a salary for your work instead of an hourly rate is inviting trouble. If you are not paid for extra hours you can find yourself donating lots of time to an employer.

You'll learn how to set limits and make sure you get paid appropriately for your work.

MISTAKE #8: WORK FOR THE "BOSS FROM HELL."

Let's face it, some bosses are wonderful and working for them can be a joy. Others are not. They make you wonder how they ever stayed in business this long.

You'll learn how to use networking, sharp interview techniques, communication skills and a good sense of self-worth to avoid being victimized by a difficult boss.

MISTAKE #9: OWE BIG BUCKS IN STATE INCOME TAX.

In each state where you have earned W-2 income, you must file a state income tax return — if that state requires it. What you may not know is that some states want a proportional share of all of your income based on the length of time you spent there. If you worked for six months in such a state, for example, then they would consider that you earned half of your total income (counting retirement, investments, etc.) in that state and tax you accordingly. Don't get surprised at tax time.

You'll learn why you should check your tax situation before accepting a job offer and how to do so.

MISTAKE #10: SPEND MORE MONEY THAN YOU MAKE BY TAKING A JOB.

More than one RV worker has driven hundreds of miles to a job, earned barely minimum wage, and then realized this was a losing proposition. Expenses were higher than income, especially considering the travel costs to get there.

You'll learn to make a good estimate of your expenses and learn how to evaluate the true income from your work.

MISTAKE #11: RETURN TO THE SAME PLACE, SAME JOB EVERY YEAR.

Inertia, staying in your comfort zone, can find you going back to the same place year after year. It may be your best choice, but is it? You are missing out on the very reasons that most people RV — to have new experiences and see new places. You may be underpaid and overworked and never know it. And you could be suddenly left with no job if there is a change of ownership or management, or if the business folds.

You'll have many more possibilities to consider after reading this book.

MISTAKE #12: COUNT ON A "SURE" THING.

The employer told you he wanted you back next year. Then he changes his mind, dies or sells the business. You are left without a job.

You'll learn the importance of keeping abreast of the job market and how to do it.

MISTAKE #13: PURSUE MONEYMAKING OPPORTUNITIES WHERE YOU LOSE YOUR SHIRT.

A business opportunity can sound like you will rake in the dough yet end up costing you money. If you only look at the income side and fail to consider your expenses, it could be a disaster.

You'll learn factors to consider in starting an enterprise and how to determine if you can "afford" this business.

MISTAKE #14: HAVE NO TIME TO PLAY.

One RV worker and her husband accepted a job requiring 24 hours/ week each, then found out after they arrived, they'd be working six four-hour days. They didn't have time to explore the area since they had to drive a long way to get anywhere. Other couples have said they didn't get two days off back-to-back, or their days off weren't the same. Some employers expect 6-day weeks during the busy parts of the season. One day off when you have grocery shopping and laundry to do leaves very little time for adventures.

You'll learn to ask the right questions and negotiate what is important to you.

Whether you have made any of these mistakes, are new to RV work, or are looking for new ideas for earning or making money, the chapters ahead will position you to avoid these mistakes. You'll find more than 300 job and moneymaking categories and a whole world of possibilities.

How to use this book

HOW THIS BOOK IS DIVIDED

Section I: Know Yourself

Introduces possibilities for working and volunteering on the road. You'll determine how much income you need, think about the kind of work you are qualified to do on the road, and decide what types of jobs you'd like to do.

Section II: Nitty-gritty of getting work to support your RVing

Gives you the tools for getting a well-paying job. You'll find out:

✔ How to locate seasonal and temporary job openings and volunteer positions
✔ How to write a résumé for working on the road
✔ How to prepare for an interview
✔ How to negotiate for good pay and perks

Section III: Job List and more than 300 moneymaking opportunities

Starts with a job list that lists actual jobs, job categories, volunteer and moneymaking opportunities that dovetail with the RV lifestyle. You'll learn where to locate them and what they entail. You'll read the stories of working RVers doing many of these jobs.

In each chapter you'll see several partial ads in boxes. These are ads from actual publications or jobs that working RVers have had.

Included are chapters on:

✔ How to get jobs with a campsite
✔ How to get jobs traveling in your RV
✔ How to get jobs within the RV industry
✔ How to get seasonal federal jobs
✔ How to get jobs working in the outdoors

✔ How to get jobs at resorts and travel destinations
✔ How to get temporary jobs and work at special events
✔ How to be your own boss
✔ How to help your budget by volunteering

Section IV: RV lifestyle considerations
Covers managing RV expenses and additional issues you may face on the road.

Section IV: Appendixes
Appendix 1: State tourism offices
Appendix 2: National Park Service regional offices
Appendix 3: U.S. National Forest regional offices
Appendix 4: State parks
Appendix 5: State revenue offices and tax information
Appendix 6: State motor vehicle and driver's licensing bureaus
Appendix 7: Janice's grocery shopping list
Appendix 8: Budget worksheet
Appendix 9: Stephanie Bernhagen's budget worksheet
Appendix10: Three RV worker stories

Section V: Resources
Lists resources by chapter. Included in resources are:

✔ Specific job search sites
✔ Employers
✔ Resources for locating job openings

HOW TO GET THE MOST OUT OF THIS BOOK

Planning stage
If you are still in the planning stage, go through the entire book. You will have a clearer picture of what you are getting into and be able to make better plans. For example, you might want to begin now to develop a current job or business, or even a new one, that will support you as you travel. You could take classes to sharpen or acquire skills that will make you more valuable.

Before you begin full-timing, subscribe to *Workamper News,* check Web sites listed in **Resources** for Chapter 9, look at ads, and talk to potential employers to get an idea of what you can make per hour. Read RV publications and talk to any RVers you meet. If you have not already done so, I recommend also that you read at least one general book on full-time RVing to use in conjunction with *Support Your RV Lifestyle!* See the beginning of **Resources**.

On the road but limited or no work experience

If you are already on the road and haven't worked, or are not satisfied with your current work experience, start with **Section I** also. You'll take a look at work ideas and what it is you would like to get out of working or volunteering. Take advantage of the knowledge other workers have shared. Make sure you read "Why you need this book:14 mistakes Working RVers Can Avoid." Also, begin getting familiar with the job market. Subscribe to *Workamper News* and check Web sites listed in **Resources**.

Seasoned RV workers

You may have experience and be looking for some new ideas. Look at **Section III** with more than 300 job categories and moneymaking opportunities that fellow working RVers are already doing. If you haven't done so, be sure to use "Why you need this book:14 Mistakes Working RVers Can Avoid" as a checklist and review the appropriate chapters in **Sections I and II** if needed. You may pick up helpful ideas and information. You'll have a handy reference you can turn to whenever you are job hunting.

Volunteers

If you are thinking of volunteering, or would like additional ideas, read Chapter 22. Since highly desirable volunteer positions can be competitive, you'll benefit from information in other chapters that will help you locate and obtain positions.

HOW TO MAKE THIS BOOK YOURS

You'll see **Your turn!** in many of the chapters in the first two sections. Here you can apply the chapter information to your unique situation. I know many of us hate exercises, but to get the most out of this book, do them!

Start a **Job Notebook** to keep job and volunteer information in one place. A three-ring binder is ideal so you can add additional pages or even job applications easily. I recommend these sections:

Section 1:
Your turn! Keep your answers here.

Section 2:
Contacts: Include contacts you make. Any time you meet people who are working or volunteering on the road, jot down their names, contact information, and what you learned. Include contacts you have gotten from RV-related discussion forums on the Internet, newsletters, and mutual friends.

Section 3:
Potential Employers: As you travel and see areas you'd like to work in, or if you stay at an RV park you enjoy, write down contact information and the date you were there. Introduce yourself to potential employers during your visit and find out about the application process. Take notes so if you later apply for a job with those employers, you can remind them of your visit. If you pick up an application, file it here along with your notes. Include ads in *Workamper News* and other publications. Don't forget to write down employers mentioned in discussions with other working RVers.

Go for it!
We have met lots of RVers in our travels. Most have one regret: They didn't hit the road sooner!

The author's work story

HOW WE GOT STARTED

In 1991, Bill and I took a typical tourist vacation, a three-week whirlwind trip from Pennsylvania out west and back. This trip took us as far as Yellowstone, south to the Grand Canyon, then back home by way of Colorado. We drove 14 hours the first day. Once we slowed down a bit we started meeting full-time RVers. We knew people vacationed in RVs. But live in one?

Some of these full-timers were working. We were tent camping out of our Chevy Cavalier station wagon in Custer State Park, South Dakota. Ward came up and started talking to us and insisted on showing us his RV. He and his wife were working there and living in their motorhome, which was set up to be totally self-contained. When not working, they could park on BLM (Bureau of Land Management) or Forest Service land without hookups, lowering their yearly expenses drastically. Ward also introduced us to *Workamper News,* a publication with employment ads for RVers. Intrigued, I copied down the address.

At Old Faithful in Yellowstone, we met two more full-time RVers, salesladies in the gift shop who started telling Bill all about this lifestyle, their work experiences and the Escapees RV Club. Escapees? From what? We wrote that address down too.

Some of our work and volunteer experiences:

- worked at seven national parks
- volunteered at one national forest and one national park for our site
- volunteered at one national park to get experience
- provided tax season help
- sold Christmas trees
- remodeled houses
- worked at tourist businesses in Alaska

In the Grand Tetons we met a couple headed back for their third season in Yellowstone. We also talked to a seasonal maintenance worker for the National Park Service about her job and how she got it. She was a college student with no real maintenance background. Fascinated, we stopped in Personnel to find out how to apply. Maybe we could work at a beautiful place like this.

All the way back across Kansas, Indiana, Ohio and western Pennsylvania, we talked about the pros and cons of this lifestyle. In Kansas we were leaning towards giving it a try, in Indiana how could we think of such a thing. By the time we got home, we had decided to send for books on full-time RVing by Joe and Kay Peterson (founders of the Escapees RV Club), order a sample issue of *Workamper News,* and call our realtor.

We went back and forth. Could we get jobs that paid enough? How would we handle banking and getting cash? Would we get a motorhome, a 5th wheel or pull trailer? We went to RV shows, visited RV dealers and answered RV ads. We put our house on the market. If it sold, that would decide it. We were meant to go. Houses in our area usually took a year or more to sell, yet the first person who looked fell in love with it. "I've been looking for this house for five years," she exclaimed. Sold!

We had found a barely used Pace Arrow Motorhome that came with a CJ7 Jeep, which the owners agreed to hold until the house sold. We moved in with a recently separated friend I worked with, saved some more money and held yard sales. The big day came Election Day, 1992. We voted and left!

That winter, when the announcements came out for maintenance workers at the Tetons, we worked our way through the tedious application process for jobs there as well as at ten or eleven other national parks. We got our wish. We were both hired to work at the Tetons and set off on our odyssey.

Since then we have also worked at national parks in Colorado, Utah, California, Arizona and Alaska. We've had a variety of other work and volunteer experiences as well.

FLEXIBILITY

What this lifestyle has given us is a great deal of flexibility. When my mother was terminally ill with cancer, we were able to drive our motorhome to California to help her and my dad. We stayed for seven months. We could never have done that in our old way of life.

Unless we have made another commitment, we can stay as long as we like if we are enjoying an area. The weather gets bad? Want a new view? Move our rig somewhere else. It's wonderful.

While Bill and I see this as a wonderful lifestyle and are passionate about RVing, we aren't evangelical about it. What we love is that each of us defines our own lives. And, if it doesn't work or isn't fun anymore, we can make new choices. For example, we recently opted to buy a winter home base instead of purchasing a new RV. We still plan to travel and work in national parks during the summers.

THE RV LIFESTYLE

On the road, we've had some wonderful experiences and great adventures. Bill used to watch old World War II movies and think how exciting it would be to see Pearl Harbor or the mothball fleet near San Francisco. He has seen them both. Alaska was my special dream. We spent a fantastic summer in Skagway. On a weekend trip to Glacier Bay we kayaked among the dolphins and whales. Things we never in our wildest dreams thought we'd do, we've seen and done.

We have made countless friends through RVing and working and have quite a support network. We have found RVers to be accepting and to judge people for what kind of person they are rather than by their material possessions.

As working RVers, we have a community of friends and new adventures as well as freedom and control of our lives. We demonstrate continually that we create our own lives. If there is something we want to do, we'll find a way to do it. For us, it doesn't get much better than this.

SUPPORT YOUR RV LIFESTYLE!

You, too, can live the life you dream. Working can keep you on the road and take you to places you want to visit. It can give you the freedom and flexibility to be where you want, when you want. There is no right or wrong way. *Support Your RV Lifestyle!* will give you the resources and tools to create the future of your choosing.

Warning - Disclaimer

This book is designed to provide information on making money and working on the road as a full-time RVer. It is sold with the understanding that the publisher and author and contributors are not engaged in rendering legal, financial or other professional services. If legal or expert assistance is needed, the services of a competent professional should be sought.

It is not the purpose of this book to reprint all the information that is otherwise available, but to complement, amplify and supplement other books and resources. You are urged to read all the available material, print and Internet, and learn as much as possible about full-time RVing and working on the road and to tailor the information to your individual needs. For more resources, see Resources at the end of this book and the appendices.

Every effort has been made to make this book as complete and accurate as possible. However, there *may be mistakes,* both typographical and in content. Therefore, this book should be used only as a general guide and not the ultimate source for making a major lifestyle change. Furthermore, this book only contains information on making money and working on the road up to the printing date.

The purpose of this book is to educate and entertain. The author and Pine Country Publishing shall have neither liability nor responsibility to any person or entity with respect to loss or damage caused, or alleged to be caused, directly or indirectly by the information contained in this book.

If you do not wish to be bound by the above, you may return this book to the publisher for a full refund.

Section I. KNOW YOURSELF

Chapter 1
What do you bring to the job market?

You will be amazed at what you already bring to the job market. Attitude and perseverance, not experience, are the main keys to job success on the road. Employers are crying for responsible workers and increasingly prefer retired or semi-retired people. Therefore, they advertise in publications and Web sites aimed at RVers.

Working at Lake Powell one summer, we heard a college-aged woman complain to her co-worker, *"I have to go back to school in three weeks and I haven't even had a chance to see my friends."* She quit the first part of August. For many employers, this is all too typical. Is it any wonder that many prefer RV workers who don't have school commitments and will honor their agreements?

This chapter will help you identify what you bring to the RV job market, but first, let's look at some of the things you could do.

HOW CAN YOU MAKE MONEY ON THE ROAD?

Working and making money on the road usually fall into one of the following categories. Which ones interest you?

Seasonal temporary work

If you want to work only part of the year, many seasonal and temporary positions are tailor-made for you. Resort areas have RV parks that need help. What better source of labor than RVers who understand the needs of their visitors?

> There are any number of ways to make money on the road.

In national parks, concessionaires hire hundreds of seasonal workers to run hotels, stores, restaurants, and other tourist activities and services. They've learned that RVers are good workers. About one-third of the workers for Yellowstone National Park Lodges are "mature" workers (meaning not college-aged kids), many living in their RVs. In fact, many openings occur in mid-season. A retired couple stopped by Flagg Ranch, between Yellowstone and the Grand Tetons, just to check it out. They were asked to start work the next day.

Jobs that include travel

"Home is where you park it," reads an Escapees RV Club bumper sticker on the back of our motorhome. RV workers bring their houses with them so jobs that require moving from site to site are natural for them. Working at craft fairs or shows, checking gas pipelines, house-sitting, or leading caravans are just a few possibilities.

Your own business

If you have the entrepreneurial spirit, you can have your own business as you travel. From making money on the Internet to supplying and servicing the burgeoning RV subculture, there are many ways to make a buck. Some RV entrepreneurs use their creative abilities like writing, performing, making arts and crafts to earn money.

Skills from your former life

You may be able to take skills from your previous work life and use them to earn money on the road. RVers have gone back and worked a few months a year for former employers, started consulting businesses, or given seminars. Handy people and mechanics can pick up jobs wherever they find RVers parked. Some of these options take planning before you leave if you want to earn money right away.

> **Acquire jobs skills for the road by volunteering.**

Volunteering and exchange of services

Reducing your expenses is money in the bank. Volunteers for federal and state agencies generally get a full hookup site in exchange for their efforts. You won't be spending money on gas to travel or for a space in an RV park, two of the largest items in most RVers' budgets.

You could work out an exchange of services for a place to park. Some options are to provide security by your presence, housesit, take care of mail, plants or pets. For example, Ardith and Page worked ten hours a week for their site in Anchorage, Alaska, having plenty of time for paying jobs and exploring.

If you want a paying job in a new field, volunteering is an excellent way to get experience and references. Jim worked as a volunteer at Acadia National Park in Maine, doing the same tasks that rangers did. After volunteering two seasons, the rangers encouraged him to apply and he was hired for the following year. Nick and Joanne were campground hosts at a state park. They asked for a letter of reference that they used to get paying jobs at a state park in another state.

WHAT DO I HAVE TO OFFER?

I bet you are qualified for more seasonal jobs than you would imagine. Your skills and abilities can translate to cash in your pocket. Remember, you have life experience! That counts for a great deal.

Most seasonal jobs are front-line jobs, like cash register operation or registering campers. These skills can be learned on the job. Employers will want to train you in "their way."

Key attributes needed for nearly all jobs are ones you probably have:

✔ People skills — with customers, co-workers, management
✔ Willingness to follow directions
✔ Sense of responsibility
✔ Common sense
✔ Flexibility
✔ Reliability

> **Include non-paid as well as paid experience on your application.**

For positions requiring a trade, you must show that you have the necessary skills, but they don't need to be from paid experience. For example, Bill had worked in steel fabrication and management. He was applying for maintenance positions where skills in several trades were needed — carpentry, plumbing, etc. On applications, Bill listed the house he remodeled and the addition he built, plus high school summer jobs as a plumber's helper. He received several job offers in maintenance.

I applied for maintenance worker and motor vehicle operator positions for my first seasonal job. My background was in teaching, sales, and customer service. However, I had done many aspects of the job. As a teenager, I had driven trucks pulling horse trailers. I'd been driving both our motorhome and 4-wheel drive Jeep. I am an excellent assistant, having helped Bill and my dad with their projects. Because I highlighted my *relevant* experience, I was hired.

As you inventory your skills, knowledge, and abilities, be sure to consider all your activities outside work as well as past jobs. Hobbies, home maintenance, travel, and community activities should be evaluated and included.

YOUR TURN!

Start your **Job Notebook** now. (Refer to instructions in "How to use this book.") Record your answers to **Your Turn!** in section one of your three-ring binder, beginning with the activity below. You could also put your **Job Notebook** answers on your computer. *Caution: Make sure you back up your computer periodically.*

Now it's your turn to identify what you can bring to the job market. Be specific. Brainstorm to uncover all the skills and abilities you have. Don't edit. This will help you focus your job search. We'll be returning to this list several times. If you have a spouse or travel partner, each of you should make a separate list.

My skills and abilities:

List jobs you've had, including part time and summer jobs and the main skills you used. Then do the same for the other categories. Three examples are provided: one for jobs, one for home maintenance, and one for community activities.

Activity	Skills
Receptionist:	Used people skills for handling complaints. Followed company procedures.
Remodel house:	Hung drywall and kitchen cabinets, installed dishwasher, rewired, painted.
Lions Club:	In charge of annual fund-raiser, over $10,000 raised. Sold refreshments, collected money.

Jobs:

Hobbies:

Volunteer and Community activities:

Home and vehicle maintenance:

RV maintenance:

Tools/equipment I can use:

People skills:

Skills that could be taken on the road: computer skills, management skills, selling, writing, art, teaching a skill, nursing, massage, hairdressing.

BEGIN FOCUSING:

Start getting acquainted with the job market for RVers. I suggest you look at the **Job List** in the beginning of **Section III** (page 127). You can also scan through chapters in **Section III** that interest you. Looking at issues of *Workamper News* and looking on the Internet at employer and job-search Web sites listed in **Resources** can also give you ideas.

- In your **Job Notebook**, list two or three jobs you could do on the road.
- List another two or three jobs you *would like* to do.
- As you come across specific jobs or employers that interest you, record them in Section 3, Potential Employers.

Finding a job will not be a problem. To take advantage of the opportunities and flexibility this lifestyle affords, you need to stop and think about your dreams and goals. What have you always dreamed of doing? What kind of work would you like to do? Where would you like to work? In the next chapter, we'll focus on identifying your dreams and goals.

Key points

✍ **Attitude and perseverance are keys to job success on the road.**

✍ **RV workers have many different options for earning money.**

✍ **Most seasonal jobs require good people skills, responsibility, and common sense.**

✍ **You have acquired marketable skills in all aspects of your life: jobs, hobbies, community activities, and chores.**

Notes

"Do what you can, with what you
have with where you are."
Theodore Roosevelt

"Would you tell me, please, which way I ought to go from here?" asked Alice. "That depends a great deal on where you want to get to," said the Cheshire Cat.
Alice in Wonderland

Chapter 2
What do you want to do for the rest of your life?

If you want to earn top dollar, you would probably do better staying put in your 9 to 5 job with a two- or three-week vacation. However, you are considering, or have chosen the RV lifestyle because you want freedom and adventures.

WORKER ADVENTURES

As a working RVer you will have the opportunity for experiences you never would have had in your old life. I encourage you to look at job opportunities not only in terms of your former skills, but what you want to accomplish in your travels. Let's look at some adventures other workers have had on the road.

A chance to really see it

Llorene and her husband worked several months one winter at Death Valley National Park. Death Valley has many fascinating and wondrous spots but they are miles and miles apart. Most tourists visit Furnace Creek and Scotty's Castle, but usually have to skip remote or less accessible sites like the Ubehebe Crater, the race track or Titus

> **Is there a place you have always dreamed of seeing?**

Canyon, to name a few. Since Llorene and her husband worked there, they could visit one location at a time on their days off.

"Pristine Death Valley has many different moods. Sunrises and sunsets transform it like a kaleidoscope. Overall, it was our most enjoyable job and one we will never forget," says Llorene.

Is there a place you have always dreamed of seeing or wanted to explore?

Experience the unusual

An extended stay often gives workers and volunteers opportunities to experience the unusual. Sue and Coby volunteered at Yosemite National Park. Sue's assignment was Search and Rescue (SAR).

> **An extended stay often gives workers and volunteers opportunities to experience the unusual.**

One time Sue's team was called on to rescue a man suffering from abdominal problems. Suited up in flight suit, helmet, earplugs, goggles and leather gloves, Sue was helicoptered from the valley floor to the top of Nevada Falls — a spectacular ride. That rescue was barely completed when two more hikers in the same area required evacuation. Sue ended up being helicoptered off the valley floor, flying alongside the rugged cliffs, and landing at the top of the waterfall three times in one day! Since planes are not allowed to fly low over the park, this was an experience a park visitor could not buy. Coby, not to be outdone, assisted in the release of a bear that was being relocated. It will take quite a bit to top these adventures.

Does experiencing the unusual appeal to you?

Beautiful places

Working can take you to beautiful places and enhance your experience. Betty and Lin worked as freelance photographers and took photos to accompany Betty's articles. They once visited Bryce Canyon in the dead of winter to photograph the snow on the red rocks. They enjoyed the winter solitude and left with spectacular photos and memories.

For Betty and Lin, writing and photography dovetailed with RV travel. They sought places that have scenic beauty and interesting history, both natural and human. Says Betty, "The writing and photography enhance these places and help fix them in our minds." Article and photo sales rewarded their efforts with income and allowed for tax deductions as they traveled.

Would you like to capture beautiful places in a creative way and be paid to do so?

Perks of the job

Workers and volunteers in tourist areas may have the opportunity to experience expensive area attractions at little or no cost. Ron and Val worked at an RV park in Haines, Alaska. Local tour operators offered them free or reduced-rate tours, providing direct experience with area attractions. This enabled them to better advise campers staying at their park. As a result, Ron and Val rafted down the Valley of the Eagles, rode the White Pass and Yukon narrow gauge railroad, and flew over Glacier Bay National Park. These experiences certainly added to their summer's memories.

Do your travel dreams include taking special excursions like these?

YOUR DREAMS AND GOALS

If you stop to think about it, there are probably things you have always wanted to do but have not done. You could see Niagara Falls, visit Alaska, paint a picture, be in a play, volunteer for a national park, or work at Disney World.

YOUR TURN!

Using your **Job Notebook**, brainstorm about things you'd like to do. List them with no thought to their importance or whether they are realistic. Just focus on getting them written down.

Take several days to add to your list. You might want to compare lists with your spouse or travel partner after you have exhausted your own ideas. Then, identify those items you want to focus on.

Don't underestimate the power of writing down your goals. Coach Lou Holtz read *The Magic of Thinking Big* by David Schwartz at age 28. Inspired, he wrote down 107 goals he wanted to achieve in his lifetime; many were lofty goals like having dinner at the White House, meeting the Pope, becoming the head coach at Notre Dame, and jumping out of an airplane. He has achieved 81 of those goals — so far. (See *www.louholtz.com* for photos.)

> **Don't underestimate the power of writing down your goals.**

Why are you working?

Work can enable you to achieve your goals and enhance your RV travels. How will working or volunteering fit into your RV lifestyle? Here are some reasons working RVers mention:

✔ **Maximize money earned:** Earning the most money in the least amount of time is a goal often mentioned. If you can work for $10.00/hour rather than $5.00/hour, it will take half the time to meet your income goal. For example, Wally & Patsy have chosen sales because they have found it makes the most money per hour for them.

✔ **Work as a way to see the country or a location:** Lester and Audrea make it a point to never work in the same location twice. In six years, they have worked in eight different states. Sometimes working RVers take less pay to work in an area they have always wanted to experience.

> **Lester and Audrea never work in the same location twice.**

✔ **Time for an avocation:** Love boats and fishing? Work at a lake or marina. Jerry loves golf. He has taken several lower paying jobs at golf courses so he has golf privileges. Paul went back to the Grand Tetons to work year after year because of the excellent fishing in Jackson Lake and other lakes in the nearby national forests.

✔ **New experiences:** Ron was a policeman in his former work life. The RV lifestyle has given him the opportunity to work at a marina and at two NASCAR races. He's done maintenance at campgrounds and sold Christmas trees. Page and Ardith explain they look for jobs that "…give us a chance to live in different places and meet different people; we like learning new things and doing different types of work."

✔ **Renewed purpose in life:** Having a sense of purpose and contributing something to the world is important for many people. Al always leaves an area better than he found it. For example, he will haul rocks to fill potholes and pick up litter. Many of our RV friends participate regularly in Habitat for Humanity builds, constructing decent affordable homes for low-income families.

✔ **Reduce expenses:** Gas and campground fees are big expenses for most RVers. Working and volunteering can reduce both. While you are in one place, your fuel costs for traveling will be zero. The money you spend on fuel will depend on how much you explore. You may get your site as part of the job or pay a reduced rate. Some employers supply shirts or entire uniforms, allowing you to save on clothing.

In addition, you may receive free or discounted propane, laundry, recreation, meals and other items. This effectively adds to your income.

✔ **Be your own boss:** Some people prefer to set their own schedules and do things their own way. They often seek ways to be entrepreneurs or independent contractors on the road.

✔**Be near family:** Working or volunteering in an area near your family can work well. You have time for visits with grandchildren or other special people while having a place to park in the area. Parking in a relative's driveway for a summer may be too close. Roy and Pat volunteer many summers at a state park not far from their daughter so they can spend time with their grandchildren.

✔**Obtain perks:** Sometimes the perks you receive on a job can help you experience an area. Besides the wonderful perks they got while working in Alaska, Ron and Val took jobs in Branson, Missouri, where they received free or reduced-price tickets for any show they wanted to see. They saw more than 20 shows in their month in Branson.

✔ **Provide for extras:** A job, or even a volunteer position, can provide money to supplement your regular income. Some RVers work for extras like a new tow vehicle or a special trip, or work when unexpected expenses leave a dent in the budget.

YOUR TURN!

Using the above reasons for working as a starting point, add your own reasons to your **Job Notebook.**

Consider also: Are you comfortable working for someone else or do you want to be your own boss?

Look at your lists. Are there any travel destinations you can achieve by meeting your goals for work? You will probably find overlap. If you do, that's great.

How long do any of us have to travel? Think about it and get cracking!

Key points

✍ **As a working or volunteering RVer you can have unique and wonderful experiences.**

✍ **To focus on what is important to you, write down your dreams and goals.**

✍ **Working as an RVer can help you achieve your dreams and goals.**

✍ **You are in control of your life.**

Chapter 3
How much money will you need?

That's a good question. The answer is *very* individual. However, chances are you will need less money on the road than you did previously. While it is difficult to know exactly what your budget will be until you get out there and get some RVing time under your belt, this chapter will give you the tools to estimate how much money you will need.

WHAT RVERS SPEND

Dorothy and David Counts, Canadian anthropologists, spent several years in the early 1990s studying the RV lifestyle and completing an ethnography. They recorded their observations and interviews during one year of travel and collected information by way of a questionnaire from almost 300 RVers. Results were published in *Over the Hill: An Ethnography of RVing Seniors in North America*. They reported that 60.2 percent of those surveyed spent between $700 and $1999 a month. It would be difficult to spend less than $700 a month and still travel, and you can surely spend more than $1999. But this is a good range to consider.

In 2001, Stephanie Bernhagen and I polled full-time RVers, asking what they spend on average per month on the road. Results were spread out but were similar for the 324 respondents. Our poll showed that 58 percent live on less than

As a full-time RVer, how much money do you spend on average in a month?

Under $700	11%
$700 -$1400	21%
$1500 -$1999	27%
$2000 - $2499	17%
$2500 - $2900	5%
Over $3000	18%

Poll taken online Jan-April 2001

$2,000 a month. Page 42 shows two different budgets that were shared with us by respondents.

MAJOR BUDGET CATEGORIES

The following are the categories I suggest you use to estimate your expenses on the road.

RV payment

Costs for an RV can range from a few thousand dollars (secondhand) to more than half a million dollars. I recommend you talk to your tax consultant about the implications of financing versus buying your RV outright. While an RV payment may decrease your flexibility, the tax benefits could make financing a better choice for you.

Food, including restaurant meals

There are two basic ways you spend money on food: eating out or buying groceries to prepare meals in your rig. (You do have cooking facilities!) The best way to control your expense is to limit restaurant meals. Your grocery bill will probably be similar to what you spent prior to full-time RVing. However, there are factors to consider. You will not be able to buy in bulk due to lack of storage space. Grocery prices and availability will vary depending on where you are.

> **Some RVers go without any health insurance while others have complete coverage.**

Health insurance

If you are currently covered by your employer, you can continue coverage under COBRA for at least 18 months after you leave your job. You can use this COBRA amount as a starting point to calculate your budget. If you will not have coverage, you must research what is available to you. Some RVers go without any insurance while others have complete coverage. Health care expenses vary widely because they are dependent on many factors:

✔ Your age
✔ The state where you have coverage
✔ Amount of your deductible

✔ Your pre-existing conditions and general health
✔ Smoker or nonsmoker
✔ Type of coverage

In this budget category also include any out-of-pocket expenses for items such as prescription drugs, dental work, eyeglasses, your deductible, and co-payments.

For additional information and references, see Chapter 23, and **Resources.** I also recommend reading Chapter 12 of *Take Back Your Life! Travel Full-time in an RV* by Stephanie Bernhagen.

Camping fees

Private RV parks charge $20-25/night, a killer on a limited budget. You can decrease this expense in several ways. If you stay a week or more, you should be able to get a reduced weekly or monthly rate. You can work for an employer who provides a free or low-cost campsite as part of the job. Two other ways to reduce this budget item are staying at federal or state campgrounds and boondocking (camping without hookups).

Some RVers purchase a membership in an RV park organization to reduce their camping fees. After the initial purchase, they pay annual dues and then reduced daily fees each time they stay at one of their member parks. I recommend waiting to join a membership park until you know your travel patterns. If you are working, you may not be able to use it enough to justify the expense. Also, before you purchase, make sure their parks are located where you plan to travel. If you are seriously considering a membership, Bernhagen's book has a good discussion on this subject.

> **Wait to join a membership park until you know your travel patterns.**

However you plan to camp, make sure you list all your fees, whether annual, monthly or daily. (See Chapter 23.)

Transportation

✔ **Fuel:** Your fuel costs will be directly proportional to how many miles you drive. Take the mileage you expect to drive and divide it by your RV's miles per gallon (mpg). Take that result and multiply by an average price per gallon. If you don't know your mileage, figure that an RV with a gasoline engine gets about 5 mpg and one with a diesel engine gets about 8. For example: You have a motorhome with a gasoline engine and will travel 1000 miles per month. You expect the purchase price of gasoline to average $1.50/gal. The calculations would be the following: 1000 ÷ 5 = 200 x $1.50 = $300 per month for fuel.

When you are working in one location for several months, you will probably do less driving, and your fuel costs will be reduced.

✔ **Insurance:** Insurance will be higher for your RV than for a car. If you no longer own a house, you will need insurance designed for full-timers that covers your RV as well as its contents. If you do not have your RV yet, you can still get estimates from insurance companies on the type of rig you want. Be sure to check prices in all the states you are considering for your domicile. (See Chapter 13) Two companies listed in **Resources** for this chapter give "quick quotes" at their Web sites. If your policy does not include a road service or towing package, you can purchase these coverages separately.

✔ **License and registration:** Fees for license and registration vary widely from state to state. See **Appendix 6** for contact information for all state motor vehicle departments.

✔ **Maintenance and repairs:** Be sure to set aside money for maintenance and repairs. The amount of money you spend will vary based on the age and condition of your rig, as well as your ability to maintain and repair it. Your driving habits also have an effect. The best way to minimize this expense is to take care of anything that goes wrong right away and follow your manufacturer's instructions for periodic preventative maintenance.

Communication

For potential employers to reach you, at a minimum you need a mailing address ("snail mail"), voice mail for messages, and long distance calling cards. Occasional Internet access (free at public libraries) is almost a requirement nowadays for obtaining jobs. Cellular phones and regular e-mail capability are convenient but will add to your expenses. Not only is there the cost of buying these devices, but each has a monthly fee that will add up. You may want to look at your travel and spending patterns before purchasing these extras. See Chapters 5 and 6 for a complete discussion of communication and alternatives.

> **Occasional Internet access is almost a requirement nowadays for obtaining jobs.**

Other

All other expenses go here. These can include federal and state taxes, life insurance, clothing, propane, cable or satellite TV, gifts, entertainment, membership in clubs, laundry and other miscellaneous expenses. List your anticipated expenses for each item. Your RV lifestyle may decrease your costs for some of these. For example, since many jobs provide uniforms or allow you to wear casual clothes, you will save the expense of dress clothes and dry cleaning. If your RV site will be near your work place, you can walk or bicycle instead of drive, eliminating commuting expense. Because of limited space, you will buy fewer souvenirs and knickknacks, thus spending less. In addition, you can eliminate state income tax by working in a state that has none. (See Chapter 13.)

> **RVers buy fewer souvenirs and knickknacks.**

Some comments from RVers about expenses:

✔ It costs me more money sitting in one spot than it does on the road, mainly because of the electricity and phone hookups.

✔ We work to save up one year's money. When we get down to six month's worth, we get jobs again.

✔ House-sitting for a month saved us money.

✔ If we stay in one place for awhile, we eat out more. When we travel, fuel consumption goes up.

✔ Camping fees can vary: a monthly rate is cheaper than daily and if we volunteer, we get a free site.

✔ We have (and pay for) a storage shed for all the household items I refuse to give up!

Two sample budgets

To help you estimate your own budget, on the next page are two different budgets that are broken down into the seven categories we have been discussing. These budgets were submitted by two RVing couples who had responded to our poll. They illustrate two different spending levels. Neither couple has an RV payment. If you have one, it could add a considerable amount to your budget.

Two sample budgets

Budget between	$1500-$1999 month	$3,000-$3500 month
RV payment/housing	$ 0	$ 0
Food, including restaurants	$ 160	$ 760
Health		
Medical insurance	$ 124	$ 377
Other medical expenses	$ 118	-
Camping Fees		
Membership parks & campground fees	$ 300	$ 392
Transportation		
Fuel	$ 150	$ 116
Insurance, incl. towing	$ 157	$ 244
License & reg.	$ 17	-
Maintenance	$ 200	$ 271
Communication		
Telephone and Internet	$ 20	$ 135
Mail service	$ 17	$ 38
Other		
Clothing	-	$ 135
Gifts	$ 0	$ 105
Laundry	$ 20	-
Life insurance	$ 47	-
Memberships- clubs	$ 20	-
Federal/state taxes	$ 21	-
Propane	-	-
TV/satellite	$ 36	$ 60
Misc.	$ 20	$ 589
Total	**$ 1,653**	**$ 3,168**

Note: Not each couple specified the same budget categories. Where you see a "dash," the couple did not break out an amount for that particular category. I suspect that Couple 2 lumped spending on several categories under "Miscellaneous."

YOUR TURN! DEVELOP A BUDGET FOR WORKING ON THE ROAD

A budget is essential for knowing how much money you require. This, in turn, will determine how much you need to work. (See instructions on the next page.)

(Per month)	Now	Full-timing
RV payment/housing	$	$
Food, including restaurants	$	$
Health		
Medical insurance	$	$
Other medical expenses	$	$
Camping Fees		
Membership parks & campground fees	$	$
Transportation		
Fuel	$	$
Insurance, incl. towing	$	$
License & reg.	$	$
Maintenance	$	$
Communication		
Telephone and Internet	$	$
Mail service	$	$
Other		
Clothing	$	$
Gifts	$	$
Laundry	$	$
Life insurance	$	$
Memberships- clubs	$	$
Federal/state taxes	$	$
Propane	$	$
TV/satellite	$	$
Misc.	$	$
Total	$	$
	X 12 = _____/yr	x12=_____/yr

YOUR TURN!

Instructions for developing a budget for working on the road: To develop your budget, complete the chart on the preceding page. In column one, use figures for what you are currently spending per month. Use estimates if you don't have exact figures. Next, refer to the budget categories on the previous pages to estimate what your full-time RVing expenses will be and enter them in the second column. If you don't have a firm number for a budget item, use a range based on your research to date and spending patterns from column one. *Hint:* One RV couple noted, "We kept track of our expenses for 18 months and found that the minor things we hadn't thought about are what add up in expenses." (Some examples would be postage, newspapers, and snacks.)

Note: If you want a more detailed budget or further explanation see **Resources.** An additional Budget Worksheet is provided in **Appendix 8. Appendix 9** is a comprehensive budget worksheet Stephanie Bernhagen used in her seminar for Life on Wheels. Full-time RVing books cover budgeting for RVing in more detail as well.

HOW MUCH DO YOU NEED TO MAKE PER HOUR? WORK 25 INSTEAD OF 50 WEEKS A YEAR

An almost universal goal for working RVers is to have more time off than the standard two-week vacation. In fact, most RVers would like to only work 25 weeks a year. There are three factors to consider to achieve that goal: amount of annual income needed, hourly rate earned, and number of weeks worked.

Now that you have an estimate of how much money you need, let's look at the **Earning Charts** on the following page that show the relationship between the hourly rate and the number of weeks worked. The amounts in the first chart are based on one worker; the second shows the amounts for two workers.

Earning chart: One person working				
Hourly rate	1 week	25 weeks	37 weeks	50 weeks
$6.00/hr	$240	$6,000	$8,880	$12,000
$7.00/hr	$280	$7,000	$10,360	$14,000
$8.00/hr	$320	$8,000	$11,840	$16,000
$9.00/hr	$360	$9,000	$13,320	$18,000
$10.00/hr	$400	$10,000	$14,800	$20,000

Earning chart: Two people working				
Hourly rate	1 week	25 weeks	37 weeks	50 weeks
$6.00/hr	$480	$12,000	$17,760	$24,000
$7.00/hr	$560	$14,000	$20,720	$28,000
$8.00/hr	$640	$16,000	$23,680	$32,000
$9.00/hr	$720	$18,000	$26,640	$36,000
$10.00/hr	$800	$20,000	$29,600	$40,000

Suppose you have determined that the two of you will need to earn $18,000 a year. Looking at the above chart for two people working, you can earn this amount by each working for about $6.00/hour for 37 weeks, or by each working for $9.00/hour for 25 weeks.

If the chart does not fit your exact situation, here are three methods you can use. Substitute your own numbers for the ones used below.

I want to work 25 weeks. How do I figure the hourly rate I will need?
1. Divide your total income needed by 2 to figure the amount each person will need to earn. ($18,000 ÷ 2 = $9,000 each)
2. Divide by the number of weeks you want to work. ($9000 ÷ 25 weeks = $360 per week)
3. Divide that result by 40 hours. ($360 ÷ 40 hours/week = $9.00/hour)
4. You will each need to earn $9.00/hour.

We each have job offers earning $7.50/hour. How many weeks will we need to work to earn $15,000?

1. Divide your total income by 2 to figure the amount each person will need to earn. ($7,500)
2. Divide by the hourly rate. ($7,500 ÷ $7.50 = 1,000 hours)
3. Divide by 40 hours/week. (1,000 hours ÷ 40 = 25 weeks)
4. You will need to work 25 weeks or half a year.

We each have job offers earning $6.50/hour. If we work 21 weeks, how much will we earn?

1. Multiply the hourly rate by 40. ($6.50 x 40 = $260/week)
2. Multiply the result by the number of weeks you will work. ($260 x 21 = $5,460)
3. Double the amount to get the total for two. ($5,460 x 2 = $10,920)
4. Together you will earn $10,920 at these jobs.

You can earn the amount you need from one job or work at two or more jobs for shorter amounts of time. Or, throw in an extra short-term job. For example, we sold Christmas trees for three weeks and made a quick $3,000. Our other jobs provided the rest of what we needed to earn for the year.

YOU CAN DO IT!

This chapter demonstrates that you have many options. A reasonable budget doesn't mean you can't have any fun. One couple who spends about $1500 a month parked a week in Tucson taking in a concert, a play, the movies, eating Thai, Chinese, Middle Eastern, Ethiopian and Italian food. After they left, they boondocked out in the desert to bring their budget back into balance.

If you want to take a job that pays a bit less because it fulfills a dream, work a little longer. Or, you might settle in for awhile and work at a higher-paying job to build up your savings or to take a special trip. You may want to work a few hours a day or just a couple of days a week so you have plenty of time to relax or explore. The beauty of this lifestyle is the flexibility. There is no right or wrong way. If you don't like a job or a location, you can leave. If you are having fun, you can stay longer. Put together the life that works for you.

Key points

- More than half of full-time RVers live on $700-$1999 a month.
- You can control or reduce expenses in all budget categories.
- How much you earn is a function of how much per hour you make and how many weeks a year you work.

Notes

"Money is better than poverty,
if only for financial reasons."
Woody Allen

SECTION II. NITTY GRITTY OF GETTING WORK TO SUPPORT YOUR RVING

Chapter 4
Finding jobs that fit your lives: Getting started

I want you to you to have the money you need while making the most of your RV lifestyle. That means finding well-paying jobs or moneymaking opportunities located in areas where you want to be so you can explore or do the things you enjoy. Working and volunteering should add to the enjoyment of your lifestyle.

The first step is to know what you want or need. If you have skipped the first three chapters and haven't identified what you want out of your travels, you may end up disappointed in your RV lifestyle. As Ben Stein (writer/actor/game show host) said, "The indispensable first step to getting the things you want out of this life is this: decide what you want."

YOUR TURN! FOCUSING EXERCISE

Look at your income goal, your dreams and your skills that you identified in **Section I.** Select the ones that are most important to you in each category. To focus your thinking, in your **Job Notebook,** consolidate this information into a short chart:

Type of work you can do	
Type of work you want to do	
Travel goals: hobbies	
Travel goals: places	
Income: annual amount	
Number of weeks to work	

A JOB THAT FITS YOUR LIVES

Finding a job on the road is easy if you will take any job. Getting a job that fits all your needs and goals will take effort on your part, but can be done. You may not satisfy all your goals in your first job, especially if you need to earn more than minimum wage; however, if you work at it, you can eventually achieve the goals you summarized in the above chart.

> **"We wanted a job that fit around our lives."**

Rob and June's search for employment illustrates this process. Both were very definite about what they wanted to do. They figured the income they needed each year, what parts of the country they wanted to be in, and what dates they wanted to be there. Then they contacted many, many companies before they found a match. "There is a ton of work out there," says June, "but many jobs were in locations where we didn't want to be or at times that were inconvenient for us. More often than not, the companies wanted a greater time commitment from us than we wanted to give." They did find a match. Adds June, "After having spent years in corporate America making our lives fit around a job, we wanted a job that fit around our lives."

Focus:

✔ *Is there a particular job or location you want to focus on next season? Circle or highlight your choices on your chart.*

If you still aren't clear on what you'd like to focus on, spend some additional time familiarizing your self with the job market. Use the **Job List** and examples in the chapters in **Section III**. Also look through *Workamper News* and take a look at Web sites listed in **Resources** (Chapter 9). You will get the most benefit from the next chapters in this section if you select one job to focus on.

✔ *Is there a match between what you want to do and what your skills support?*

Yes, you have a match: For example, if you want to work in maintenance and have done these types of tasks in maintaining your own home, then *someone* will hire you as a maintenance person. If you'd like to deliver RVs with your pickup truck and you have some road time, you will find job opportunities.

No, you don't have a match yet: You may want to do something that you don't have the qualifications, training or experience for. You can still get started on the path to earning money and getting that job. Some companies provide training. For example, Princess Land Tours and Gray Line Bus Tours provide training for their bus drivers each year. If you would like to deliver RVs and do not have enough experience pulling an RV, you can get another driving job, one without hauling, while you acquire road time. Do some investigating. Courses in the skill you need may be available. **Section III** includes information about a number of training courses available.

Getting started

To find a job that meets your goals, you want to apply to enough jobs so you have two or three job offers to choose from. Look at the process of finding a job like an inverted pyramid or funnel:

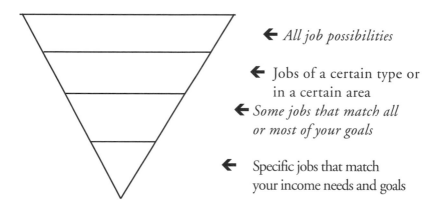

← *All job possibilities*

← Jobs of a certain type or in a certain area
← *Some jobs that match all or most of your goals*

← Specific jobs that match your income needs and goals

In order to get the job you want, you must set criteria and then narrow down the available jobs to find ones that match you goals and income needs. As you work through job possibilities, most will fall by the wayside because they don't meet one or more of your criteria. Remember, employers go through a similar selection process, screening out employees who aren't a match to find the best candidate.

You must start with many job prospects to make this process work so that you have two or more good job offers to consider. The next story illustrates the importance of having many options and what can happen if you don't.

OUR DREAM JOB: THE JOB THAT FIT AROUND OUR LIVES

When Bill and I hit the road, we began looking for summer jobs in December. Our dream job was to work in maintenance for the National Park Service (NPS) at Grand Teton National Park. Our second choice was to work in a national park in any location.

We figured that the larger parks with campgrounds would hire more seasonal maintenance workers, so using AAA trip planning books, we identified 20 western national parks with campgrounds. I made up a chart, listing each park and their telephone numbers. I started calling to find out if they hired seasonal maintenance workers and when they put out their job announcements. I recorded the date to call back, crossing those off who weren't hiring. As I followed up, I recorded the action I took and the step of the process we were in. (Now job announcements for the National Park Service can be found USAJOBS Web site, *www.usajobs.opm.gov.*)

> **Our dream job was to work in Grand Teton National Park.**

At the same time, we subscribed to *Workamper News.* For any job that looked like it might pay more than $6/hour, we followed up with either a résumé or telephone call. We also participated in the Workamper Referral System, making our résumé available to employers through *Workamper News,* and received several calls as a result. We contacted and screened an additional 30-plus employers. We narrowed this list down to acceptable job offers at two locations in case a park job didn't come through.

As each job announcement from a national park came, I completed the paperwork. We applied to twelve parks. We both got offers at the same two parks and one of them was the Tetons!

Year 2

Our second year on the road, we learned the hard way why lots of contacts are important. We assumed we would go back to the Tetons so we applied to only two other parks. We missed a step in the re-hire process and there were changes in management. We weren't going back.

Then it was a mad scramble. We applied to employers advertising in *Workamper News* and checked their hotline. We had a number of offers but not in the same pay range we had made our first summer. We took a position in Minnesota, driving all the way from California. It didn't work out. Right after we quit, Bill was offered a position in a national park in Colorado. We spent a lot of money driving half way across the country twice, as well as losing time traveling and working for lower wages.

How much effort you need to put into your job search depends on how closely your experience matches the job requirements, how important your goals are, and how much you need to earn. In our case, with no experience working for the government, and determined to get positions with the National Park Service, we were willing to put in a lot of effort. We had offers at state parks and RV parks that first year, but the pay wasn't as good and those locations weren't our first choice. Now that we have experience with NPS, getting positions is much easier. However, we have learned to never count on just one possibility.

The rest of **Section II: Nitty Gritty of Getting Work to Support Your RVing,** will prepare you to obtain the position you want and cover the mechanics of getting a job on the road.

Key points

✍   **Apply for many jobs that meet your criteria so you have a better chance of getting job offers to choose from.**

✍   **Start with jobs that meet both your income and your travel goals.**

✍   **Keep your options open.**

Notes

*"Persistence is what makes the impossible possible, the
possible likely, and the likely definite."*
Robert Hall

"For every obstacle there is a solution — over,
under, around or through."
Dan Zadra

Chapter 5
How employers and family can reach you:
Getting mail and phone calls on the road

To get jobs, you must be able to contact and be contacted by employers. You'll need to be able to receive employment information and applications in a timely manner.

RECEIVING MAIL ON THE ROAD

How do you get your mail when traveling? RV clubs as well as private businesses provide mail forwarding services to RVers.

Mail forwarding

While some RVers have family members forward their mail, many prefer a professional mail forwarding service so that mail is sent out the day requested, rather than at a family member's convenience. You pay a fee for the service as well as for postage and supplies.

When you sign up for a mail forwarding service, you have all your mail sent to their address with your personal mailbox number (PMB) on it. You then instruct the service where and when to send your accumulated mail.

> **Several RV clubs provide mail forwarding for their members.**

Mail forwarding services vary. Some forwarding services send out mail according to a set schedule. Others require one or two days' notice. More personalized services will check at your request to see if certain pieces of mail have arrived or even read that letter to you.

RV clubs like Family Motor Coach Association (FMCA), Good Sam, and Escapees RV Club provide mail forwarding for members. Private mail box providers like Mail Boxes, Etc. will also forward mail, but are usually more expensive than services set up exclusively for this task. You can find advertisements in RV publications for other mail forwarding services geared to full-time RVers.

Before signing up for a mail service, compare costs and services. Talk to RVers using them and see if they are doing a good job. Consider also the state you will choose as your domicile. This address will be part of establishing your domicile.

Where do you pick up your mail?

If you will be in a location long enough for your mail to reach you, you can have your mail forwarded to the nearest post office in care of General Delivery. If you are working there for the season, you may need to rent a post office box or find an alternative place for mail delivery. Post offices vary on how long you can receive General Delivery mail; it can be as little as 10 days to more than 30 days. You might be able to have mail

> **When traveling, forward your mail to the nearest post office in care of General Delivery.**

delivered to your employer or the RV park where you are staying, with their permission. Unless the RV park or employer has separate renter or employee mail boxes, we prefer renting a mail box at the post office so we receive our mail as soon as it arrives, rather than have to track down our mail each week.

If you are traveling and decide to have your mail forwarded to you, figure out where you'll be in five to seven days and have it sent to that post office in care of General Delivery. Verify whether that post office accepts general delivery mail by calling the location or the toll-free U.S.P.S. number below. Some don't. If a town has several zip codes, only one will accept general delivery mail. To obtain the correct zip code, or verify that a post office accepts general delivery mail, call the U.S.P.S. toll-free number, 800/275-8777.

If your travel plans change and you can't be at that town when you expected, call or drop the Postmaster a card so that post office holds your mail until you arrive. We have had mail returned to sender because the mail handler didn't recognize our names or we didn't pick it up in a few days. If your mail forwarding service has already sent out your mail and now you won't be going to that location, or, you will not be able to wait for its arrival, complete and turn in a change of address card. Your mail will be forwarded to the new address. Unfortunately, it may take a couple of weeks or more for your mail to catch up with you when you do this.

Mail at best can be iffy, as I'm sure we've all experienced. Be prepared for frustrating waits. If you are on a tight time schedule and waiting for something important, you may want to pay extra to have it sent Express Mail, Federal Express, or by another overnight carrier. Be aware that Express Mail can take two days to arrive at many rural locations.

To use Federal Express, UPS or other carrier, you need a physical address. You could use an RV park or perhaps a relative's address. A mail store, like Mail Boxes, Etc., might accept it also, perhaps charging a fee. In small towns, the general store may agree to accept your package. And if there is a UPS or FedEx office in that town, make arrangements to have your parcel sent to that office and held until your arrival. You will need to have the package properly labeled. Contact the local office or call their toll-free number. (See **Resources.**) In any case, make sure it is expected so the delivery isn't refused and returned to sender.

> **The general store may agree to accept your UPS or FedEx package.**

If time is important, have mail sent from an employer directly to your current location or to a location where you will arrive in a few days. Going through your mail service could delay your mail for up to two weeks, taking you out of contention for a position.

For an even quicker response to a job opening, you could have the application faxed. For a fee, you can receive a fax at businesses like Kinkos or Mail Boxes Etc. Or, receive the faxed application via the Internet if you have occasional access or can stop at a public library with Internet access. Sign up for e-Fax *(www.efax.com)* or other free fax services that provide you with a personal fax number. You receive the fax as an e-mail attachment. Another option is receiving an e-mail directly from the employer, which is even faster if you can get online. (See Chapter 6 for information about e-mail on the road.)

Make it easy for employers to send applications or information to you. However you get employment information or applications from an employer, be very clear about where to send it, spelling out anything that might get misspelled. If mail is being sent to general delivery, don't apologize. Explain that you are traveling and that you will get it more quickly this way. Make sure you return applications or other requested materials as soon as possible. Clear communication is a way to sell yourself to an employer.

RECEIVING TELEPHONE MESSAGES AND CALLS

The two main options for working RVers for getting messages from potential employers are voice mail and cellular telephones. Cellular service can also provide direct communication that is more immediate and convenient, but also more expensive. If you are trying to keep your costs down, voice mail is much more economical and can work almost as well.

> **There are several options for receiving voice mail.**

Voice mail

Most RVers want a way for family members to contact them in case of emergency. A voice mail service works for family and friends and can also be used for employment purposes. Several RV clubs like Escapees RV Club and FMCA offer voice mail to members for a fee. You can also look for advertisements in RV publications, financial publications like Money Magazine, and search the Internet for "voice mail." Ask other RVers what service they are using and what their costs average per month.

There are four types of services available.

✔ **Toll-free personal voice mail:** (800, 888, 877 or other toll-free exchange)
✔ **Toll-free voice mail number:** Caller inputs a box number or extension to access your voice mail box.
✔ **Voice messaging associated with a cellular telephone:** Not toll-free to the caller. (See next section.)
✔ **Local voice mail service:** May have a box number, long distance for non-local callers.

The first two have a toll-free number, which has two key advantages. One, your family and friends will more likely call and leave a message if the call is free. Second, employers who aren't used to RVers, or who need a worker quickly, won't know where you are located. If your area code is

520, for example, a Massachusetts employer might assume you are in Arizona and won't be available right away.

To the caller, a personal toll-free number sounds the same as reaching an answering machine. With the toll-free personal voice mail, the caller hears a personal greeting in your own voice. With the toll-free voice mail number, the caller will be asked to input the box number or extension before hearing your recorded greeting. (Note: a few services do not allow for a personal greeting.) No matter which service you choose, if you are job hunting, it is best to have a short, professional greeting such as:

"You have reached Tom and Nancy Kampers. Please leave your name, telephone number, and a short message and we will get back to you. We check our messages once a day."

> **To the caller, a personal toll-free number sounds the same as reaching an answering machine.**

A personal toll-free number, or voice mail service with a four- or five-digit mail box, is best. If your voice mail has a number of menus or steps to work through, it increases the chances that an employer or other caller will get discouraged or make an error. You may miss a message and a job offer or important personal message.

For example, members of FMCA can use their voice mail system for a relatively low charge. However, the system is complicated and not designed for business use. Members are limited in the number of calls they can receive each month. The caller does not hear your voice so is never sure that you got the message.

Other things to consider in a voice mail service

✔ **Monthly fees:** Most services charge a monthly fee, plus so much per minute. Remember, the per-minute fee is charged both when the caller leaves the message and again when you retrieve it. The charges for a 2-minute message will actually be for 4-minutes, 6-minutes if you listen twice. Other services have only a per-minute charge, but it is usually higher than those that also charge a monthly fee. Do some comparison-shopping.

✔ **Per minute charge:** To figure out the actual charge per minute, divide the total bill by the number of minutes you used in the month. Many companies do not itemize your calls, but most will list the total number of minutes you used during the month.

✔ **Six-second increments:** You will pay less if the company charges in six-second increments starting from the first second rather than billing for the whole minute. Example: your call lasts one minute and 5 seconds at $.10/minute. With six second increments, you are billed $.11. If you get charged by the full minute, the charge will be $.20.

✔ **Service in Canada:** Not all services allow you or the caller to call your toll-free number from Canada.

✔ **Special features:** One service saves the box holder money by ringing if there are no messages. If the box has messages, it goes right to the greeting with no rings. Another service does not start timing until the caller begins leaving a message so there is no charge for listening to the greeting. (This particular service has a 10-14 digit box number code, however.) Voice Mail Connect, the service we use, allows you to check to see if you have any calls at a Web site, a savings if you have computer access. (See **Resources.**)

> **Billing in six-second increments is a big money-saver.**

✔ **Your greeting:** Most services charge you for the time the caller is listening to the greeting. Keep your greeting short and save money.

Cellular telephone service

Companies like AT&T, Sprint and Verizon have one-rate plans that allow you to call anywhere in the U.S. for a low rate per minute. You may have to buy a large quantity of minutes to get the best rates. Some things to keep in mind:

✔ **Your budget:** Do you spend (or plan to spend) at least the minimum required for long distance calls each month? If you are on a tight budget, the answer may be no. Long distance calls are a controllable expense. Take advantage of that. Use calling cards instead (costs on these can also vary.)

✔ **Voice mail:** Is voice mail messaging included or extra? If not, you may still need a voice mail service.

✔ **Roaming charges:** With the monthly plans that allow so many minutes anywhere in the U.S. with no long distance or roaming fees, be aware that there may be limitations. Calls that cannot be completed on the supplier's network may have roaming charges so find out when and if you will be charged for roaming. Calls made on an affiliate network may not be billed in the month made, thus reducing your available minutes the following month when they are reported. Read the fine print.

✔ **Analog versus digital service:** If you plan to use your cellular phone for retrieving e-mail and getting on the Internet, you want a provider with maximum digital service areas. You will also need to buy a phone with this capability and a Web connectivity kit.

✔ **Service area:** Will you be traveling and working primarily in areas that have service? RVers who work or travel a lot in remote locations may find they have to drive a distance or climb hills to make calls or retrieve messages. Many plans require a year or two contract. Make sure you can suspend your plan in the event you spend several months working in an area with no coverage.

✔ **Actual experience:** If $30-90 a month is in your budget for long distance telephone calls, talk to RVers who are using these services.

Make it easy for employers to reach you. If other applicants are easier to reach, some employers may give up trying to reach you. Whatever method you decide upon should be easy to use and sound professional. Make sure you check your messages daily and return calls promptly. How you handle calls

> **Make it easy for employers to reach you.**

and messages gives an employer an impression about the kind of employee you will be. Make sure the impression you leave is a positive one — don't make your potential employer listen to your directions for Aunt Martha or other personal messages.

Key points

✍ **Have a professional-sounding way employers can leave a message for you.**

✍ **Comparison shop and talk to other RVers about voice mail, cell phone, and mail forwarding services.**

✍ **Prices and service vary considerably.**

Notes

*"We are what we repeatedly do. Excellence
then, is not an act but a habit."*
The Goals Guy at www.goalsguy.com

"A computer lets you make more mistakes faster than any invention in human history — with the possible exceptions of handguns and tequila."
Mitch Ratcliffe

Chapter 6
How to use a computer in your job search

Do you need a computer to find and get jobs on the road? The answer is both yes and no. Yes, it will make the job search process easier and no, you can get by without your own computer. While paper and pen can work if you decide not to get one right away, it is a real asset in organizing and tracking information as well as enhancing the materials you send out to employers.

ADVANTAGES OF USING A COMPUTER

Professional looking résumés and cover letters

While you could use a typewriter to type your résumé and cover letter, computers make it much easier. You can easily update your information and tailor your résumé and cover letter for a particular job without having to retype the entire document again or pay someone to do it. Since your documents are saved, you simply make the revisions you want and print out the revised document. You can print out a fresh-looking résumé whenever you need one.

> **You can revise your résumé easily without having to retype it.**

Error reduction

The spell-check feature of most word processors reduces errors and typos. You still need to proofread carefully so that *there* isn't a *their* or *they're*. When the spelling is correct, but the word is wrong, your spell checker will not catch it.

Time-saving software

You can purchase résumé software programs at computer or office supply stores that provide templates for résumés. A résumé template may come with your word processing program. If you are applying for federal jobs, you can purchase software that will allow you to store your OF-612 application or government résumé. You can easily update it for specific jobs. This is a BIG time saver. (See **Resources,** Chapter 17.)

Internet job searches

If you are hooked up to a telephone for a time, you can subscribe to an Internet provider and use your own computer for job searches. (See Chapter 9.)

COMPUTER LITERACY—KEY TO MANY JOBS

The companion question to "Do I need a computer?" is "Do I need to be computer literate?" Again, the answer is no, but you have an advantage in the job market. Not only does the ability to use a computer open up new and effective job search techniques, but it can also improve your marketability and help you get many jobs.

> **51 percent of those surveyed use a computer to do their jobs.**

In Zogby's Real America, a 1998 survey found that 51 percent of those surveyed use a computer to do their jobs. Of those earning under $15,000 a year, one-third use computers on the job.

Many jobs now require the use of a computer, computerized machines or data input devices, where they didn't a few years ago.

Computer programs are easier to learn now. Microsoft's Windows has become the industry standard. Software programs written for Windows have the same menus and toolbars. Once you've learned one program, others will be easier to learn. Having your own computer allows you to learn software programs at your own pace.

Other ways you can learn about computers or specific software packages:

✔ **Use built-in tutorials** that come with some software. Books and videos for specific software are often available at computer stores.

✔ **Take any company-offered training** that is available.

✔ **Ask a fellow employee** to help you learn a computer application for work when it won't interfere with productivity.

✔ **Volunteer** where you will be able to pick up new skills

✔ **Check with your temporary agency.** Larger agencies offer courses to employees working for their agency.

✔ **Check at a community college** if you will be in the area for the length of a course. Some community colleges offer no- or reduced-tuition courses for seniors. That age may be as low as 55 .

✔ **Investigate training through State Job Service offices.** Every state has a Job Service. Counselors may be able to connect you with training classes to upgrade your skills, particularly if you are on unemployment.

✔ **Locate a Senior Net Center.** Senior Net is a nonprofit organization that provides adults aged 50 and over with education for and access to computer technology. The organization has 160 Learning Centers in 36 states.

✔ **Ask your computer vendor** if they offer any free or low-cost computer training if you purchase a new computer.

Other uses

These computer applications can make your traveling easier or more enjoyable.

- **Mapping programs** like Street Atlas USA will map out routes, compute mileage and help you if you turn down the wrong street in a town.

- **Data bases** or listings of free places to park have been developed by RVers. Instead of carrying reams of paper or a book, it is all on the computer and is easily updated.

- **Financial programs** such as *Quicken* keep records of money you spend.

- **Software for hobbies** like genealogy and photography store and organize your information.

- **Correspondence** with family and friends is easier with a computer. Some RVers produce family newsletters.

- **Writing or graphics programs** could be used to earn money, for example designing and printing business cards.

- **Save photos** with the right computer. You can store a vast amount of photos instead of in albums. You can even post your photos in a personal Web site for family and friends to view.

CHOOSING A COMPUTER

With so many kinds and models of computers, how do you choose one?

PCs or MacIntosh computers?

Both PCs (personal computers) and Macs have their advantages. There are more programs written for PCs than Macs, though Macs are easier to learn. Most employers, however, use PCs, which tend to be cheaper.

Laptop v desktop computers

Laptop computers are portable and take up little space. You can also send and receive e-mail on a regular basis with a laptop. (See next section.) Desktop computers take up more space and need to be anchored down while traveling. However, a desktop is significantly cheaper to buy and has a larger screen that is much easier to read. As of this writing, you can buy an excellent desktop computer for under $1,000.

Power needed to operate your computer is a consideration, especially if you are boondocking. You will need to use an inverter or run your generator to operate your desktop. The size inverter needed will depend on the power draw of your computer. Make sure the inventor supplies adequate power or you can damage your computer. A laptop can be run off its

> **A desktop is significantly cheaper ...**

battery(s). But it must be periodically charged. Charging can be accomplished by plugging the laptop into a small inverter while traveling, or with any 110 volt electrical source. If you plan to boondock frequently, you may want a second battery(s).

Selecting a model

Choosing your first computer can be overwhelming. A good resource for RVers needing some basic knowledge about computers and what to consider in your purchase is *Camping on the Internet* by Loren Eyrich.

Computers are being improved so quickly that even if you buy a new one, it may be only a matter of weeks before there are new bells and whistles you could buy. If you mainly do word processing and perhaps e-mail, you don't need anything fancy so an older model will be adequate. If you plan to use a digital camera or work with graphics, you will need more of everything, especially hard drive space and memory. Since what is considered minimum in the way of hard drive and memory changes rapidly, it would be a good plan to check with a reputable dealer, review some of the computer magazines that rate computers, and to have a knowledgeable friend help you make your decision.

Many RVers have gotten started with computers by purchasing an older model from an RV friend who was upgrading to a better computer. Purchasing an older model lowers your investment while learning. On the other hand, you might inherit some problems and you'll have no guarantee.

Before you buy

The decision to purchase a computer is an individual one. If you don't have one and have never used one, I'd suggest waiting. Use the computers in libraries to see how that works and find out if you are "computer-compatible." You can also use computers at full-service copy and computer chains such as Kinkos for a small fee. Talk to others and see what features you might use and what fits your budget. You might pick up just what you need at a very low cost. If you get hooked, you'll undoubtedly want to upgrade, but by then you will have some experience and knowledge under your belt and can make a more informed decision.

> **Before you buy, find out if you are "computer compatible."**

If you decide not to buy a computer right away, simple supplies like a pen, paper and a box of floppy diskettes will work. You can store your résumé on a diskette and then use a computer at a library or copy shop to print out copies as you need them.

USING YOUR COMPUTER FOR E-MAIL

E-mail is a low-cost way to keep in touch and another method for communicating with employers that are online. If you have a laptop computer, you can get e-mail on the road. Many truck stops and RV parks provide data ports to plug in your computer to send and receive e-mail or now have a Wif-Fi "hotspot." If you are within few hundred yards or so of a hot spot, you can connect to the Internet. There are fees to use some WiFi hotspots, others are free.

Services like America Online (AOL), Earthlink, and AT&T, which have low-cost monthly plans for those who only spend a short time per month on the Internet, work well for RVers. You can write all your e-mail off-line in your RV ahead of time. You plug in, dial up either a local number or a toll-free number (which costs you an additional $.10/minute) and in a minute or so, your e-mail is sent and any messages waiting for you are retrieved. You can read and reply to your messages at your leisure. Free e-mail services exist (such as Juno) but if you aren't in a location where there is a local access number, you will incur long distance charges.

With the digital cellular telephones, you can send and retrieve e-mail on your laptop computer using your cell phone. You need a cellular-capable modem and an adapter, or a connectivity kit. Many laptops already have a cellular-capable modem card. If not, it may run as high as $300, though you can find one for less by shopping on the Web. The adapter or cable could range from $30 to $100.

Newer PCS or tri-mode phones can connect digitally to the Web and retrieve e-mail, with or without a computer. The phone acts as the modem so your computer does not have to have one.

Handhelds like the Palm and Handspring products were developed so people could have an easily-carried portable device for storing and accessing their contact information, calendar and memos. The wireless versions can send and receive e-mail and retrieve specially formatted Web pages.

> **PocketMail seems designed for RVers.**

Usually transmission time with cellular phones and handhelds is slow, but new technology is speeding that up.

High-speed, two-way satellite Internet, DataStorm, has been developed that includes automatic targeting software. It is still very expensive.

Wireless technology is continually improving and coverage expanding but currently each method has limitations so do your research before buying.

PocketMail

One service that seems designed for RVers is PocketMail. With a choice between two e-mail devices or an adapter for a Palm Pilot, you can write, send and retrieve e-mail. You dial a toll-free number, hold the device against the receiver of the telephone, and send and retrieve your e-mail. You can read your e-mail later then write replies. Message size is restricted, though now you can divide longer messages into two or more parts. It works on most phones, pay phones included. The PocketMail appliances cost between $100 and $150. PocketMail Service is about $15 per month for unlimited calls.

There are some disadvantages to PocketMail. The keyboard is slow and small so writing your e-mail takes longer than using a computer. Send and receive times are also long, and you cannot receive attachments. E-mails with attachments or that are longer than the PocketMail message size limit can be viewed at their Web site. Despite these limitations, they work well for many RVers. However, if you receive a lot of e-mail, PocketMail may not be your best choice.

COMPUTER WORK AREA

While newer RVs often come with computer work areas, ours did not. We modified our motorhome to accommodate our desktop computer. We removed (and sold) the dinette and replaced it with a desk made of Formica placed on two two-drawer file cabinets. I have a nice place to work and file cabinets to store our records. A side benefit is more space in the kitchen-dining area. In addition, we sold the couch and put a La-Z-Boy recliner in its place. These modifications have made our motorhome more comfortable and give it a homey feeling. Our RV reflects our personality rather than the assembly-line look.

The other modification we made was to install several 12-volt fluorescent lights. They are much brighter for computer use and for reading and pull less power. We also installed a 110-volt fluorescent light above my computer to use when our RV is plugged into an electric source.

Key Points
- Make your job search easier with a computer by storing résumés and cover letters that can easily be revised, updated and printed out as needed.
- Evaluate your needs before buying. A computer is not a necessity.

Notes

*"There are no shortcuts to
any place worth going."*
Bevery Sills

*"Efforts and courage are not enough
without purpose and direction."*
John F. Kennedy

Chapter 7
How to prepare résumés and cover letters for working on the road

Résumés

Although it is unlikely you will need a fancy, detailed résumé, you'll will still need a written summary to show the employer why you are the right person for the job.

You can prepare a résumé on a computer or typewriter that will work for most positions and look professional, or you can have one professionally done. You can purchase résumé software and books with models or templates to use. (See **Resources,** or save money by checking out books at the public library.) A model for a functional résumé is on page 77.

Before sending out your résumé, be sure to check it over carefully for errors. Misspellings and grammatical errors indicate sloppy work habits to a prospective employer. Ask a friend or spouse to proofread your résumé.

Résumé categories

Categories you often see on résumés,

In a survey of human resource managers, respondents gave this advice for résumés:

♦ Grammar and spelling 100% correct
♦ No typos
♦ Personalized cover letter
♦ No more than two pages
♦ Emphasize accomplishments
♦ Concise and well-written

1999 Résumé Survey Report

usually in capital letters and bold type, are:

✔ Objective
✔ Work Experience
✔ Skills (or Computer Skills)
✔ Education
✔ Remarks or Interests
✔ Foreign Languages
✔ References

Choose the categories that match the position and your background. For most jobs on the road, I recommend omitting "Education" unless it directly correlates to the job at hand. Having a Master's degree in Science is not relevant to working as a cashier in a retail establishment and might make the employer wonder whether you'd be happy doing such work. On the other hand, a college degree in accounting should be listed if you are applying for a bookkeeping or accounting position. Other categories like Foreign Languages would be appropriate if you might be dealing with customers speaking this language in this particular position; otherwise omit it. Sign language skills make you more valuable and should be noted.

Objective

Start with your objective:

> *"Work as a maintenance man, using skills from a variety of trades."*
> *"Work as cashier or sales staff in a retail establishment."*

For a couple seeking a position together, *"Couple seeks assistant manager position at an RV park or campground."*

> **Use a chronological résumé when your work experience matches the position.**

If you are having someone else prepare your résumé and won't be able to customize it to fit each job, leave the objective rather general, unless you will only be applying for one type of job.

Chronological or functional résumé

There are two types of résumés: chronological and functional. Use a chronological résumé when your work experience showcases or matches the skills you need for the position. For example, you are applying for a night auditor position and you have worked for an accounting firm or other establishments in the accounting department. Or, you are applying for a campground manager position and you have several years of working on the road as manager or assistant manager.

With a chronological résumé, "Work Experience" would be your next category. List your work experience from most recent back at least ten years. Key accomplishments are listed or briefly described. Include relevant experience even if it was more than ten years ago.

> **Use a functional résumé when your work experience does not match the position.**

If, however, your work experience does not match the type of position you are seeking, a functional résumé can showcase your abilities to your advantage. Some examples where a functional résumé would be better:

- ✔ You are seeking a maintenance position but have never held one. You have done the upkeep on your house, added on a room, and completed all the repairs. You helped your neighbor build his garage.
- ✔ You have no experience working in a campground office, but you have worked in customer service. You are familiar with computers and get along with people.

In a functional résumé, the category "Skills" would follow your objective. List your skills in a bullet list or use the skills needed for the position as your categories or headings, such as "Communication Skills" or "Maintenance Skills" and describe how you have used these skills. Perhaps you used them in your hobby or in a community activity. That experience is valid and will be considered, but a chronological résumé will not point this out as effectively. To pick out logical categories, use your knowledge of the job or the job description.

In a functional résumé, skills should be followed by a brief listing of employers for the last ten years.

You can also list relevant skills in a chronological résumé after your work experience. If you have knowledge of certain computer programs or can operate equipment listed in the job description, this would be the place to name them.

Volunteer or unpaid experience

Volunteer experience and unpaid experience related to the position are valuable and should be included. They will sound more impressive if you state your jobs or skills, rather than "volunteer."

"Fund-raiser, Non-profit agency, 1996-1998."

Remarks or Interests

In the "Remarks" or "Interests" category you can include hobbies, civic activities or other information that might show your good character or relevant experience. For example, if applying to an RV park, "RVer for fifteen years" would show you are familiar with RVs even if you have only recently begun full-time RVing. "Member of the Kiwanis" indicates time spent in community service and implies that you like dealing with people.

References

For references, you can either list at least three references, or write "References on request." If you chose the latter, you should have a type-written list ready to send off as soon as an employer requests it. If possible, have more than three employers lined up to use as references, especially if you will be applying to many jobs. That way they won't get overwhelmed with telephone calls from potential employers.

To speed up the process, you could request letters of reference in advance and include copies with your résumé. When I left my last job before we began full-time RVing, I requested a letter of reference. My boss even suggested I write it. I wrote two: one detailing the tasks I did in case I wanted a similar position, and a second one stressing my good work habits. My boss happily signed them both. I copy and include the appropriate one with my résumé.

> **Always ask permission to use someone as a reference.**

Always get permission to use someone as a reference. Pick references who will speak well of you and remember who you are. Employers have told me they called a reference who had no memory of the applicant. If you are short on space, omit "References on request." If employers would like references, they will request them.

One page

Stick to one page, unless you are applying for a technical or professional position and have a lot of relevant experience. For a couple, send both of your individual résumés, each limited to a page. Often for seasonal work, even if you are asked to send a résumé, the employer will have you complete an application. The résumé is a screening device.

Electronic résumés

At this writing, few Web sites for seasonal or temporary work post résumés. If you are searching for a position in your former industry, you might want to post your electronic résumé at a job search site that has similar listings.

Résumés for the Internet are formatted differently. With literally millions of résumés posted on the Web (Anderson Consulting alone receives four million résumés a year), employers now search databases of résumés by keywords. These terms, including industry terms, buzz words, professional jargon, skill-focused words and commonly used trade terms for that industry are listed in a separate category at the top. Look at the larger job search sites for articles and tips for online résumés. (See **Resources.**)

THE COVER LETTER

When you mail your résumé to a prospective employer, always include a cover letter. The cover letter expresses your interest in the position and highlights how your experience and skills match the employer's needs. You also ask for an interview and let the employer know how you can be reached. If you have a gap in employment, such as in the model résumé on page 77, you can explain. For example, "We began full-time RVing in 1999 and, after traveling for a year and one-half, we are now seeking summer employment."

The cover letter should be one page, in business format, typed or word processed, if possible. If you must hand write it, write or print neatly in ink.

Photos

If you are applying to a private employer, you could also enclose a recent photo of yourselves. Include a photo of your rig too, if your rig will be parked on the premises. Some employers will request them. We took photos of the two of us and our motorhome and made 20 copies of each to include with our applications and résumés. Do not include a photo when applying for a government position.

TELEPHONE RESPONSE

If a telephone number is given in the ad instead of an address, your call will be similar to a cover letter. The employer is probably using the telephone call to pre-screen potential employees or needs to hire someone fairly quickly. In this situation you want to find out the next step. And it may be an opportunity to get more information to see if the position is a match.

A sample functional résumé and a cover letter follow.

Key points

✍ **The purpose of a résumé is to get you an interview or to be considered.**

✍ **Résumés can be chronological or functional, depending on your experience.**

✍ **The cover letter introduces you, highlights your experience and asks for an interview.**

Example of a functional résumé

JOHN E. WORKER
PO BOX 321
ANYWHERE TX 77388
800/609-4892
worker5@aol.com

OBJECTIVE: Work in an RV park or campground in maintenance

SKILLS:

Maintenance

Maintained factory equipment and machinery on the job. Used a variety of skills to maintain house and property including plumbing, carpentry, appliances, and simple electrical repairs. Also landscaped yard, mowed one acre of lawn using riding mower, trimmed grass and plants, planted and cared for large vegetable garden and flower gardens. Did all maintenance on own vehicles including cars and motorhome. Added a wooden deck to front of house and remodeled bathroom and bedroom.

Communication

Dealt with customers; determined needs as well as problem solving and handling complaints. Supervised and trained eight workers. Organized and oversaw fund raising event for community service club.

Operate equipment
- Forklift
- Backhoe
- Riding mowers

WORK EXPERIENCE

1990-99 Acme Widget Factory, San Antonio, TX - Supervisor
- Supervised eight assembly workers.
- Trained new-hires.

1983-90 Widget's Deluxe, San Antonio, TX - Factory sales rep.
- Called on industrial clients.
- Planned projects.
- Customer service: troubleshooting, expediting orders, resolving complaints.

Other: Worked as plumber's helper, Christmas tree lot worker, sales and customer service.

REMARKS: Member, Lions Club. Den leader for Cub Scouts. Full-time RVer since July 1999.

REFERENCES: Available on request.

Sample cover letter

JOHN E. WORKER
PO BOX 321
ANYWHERE TX 77388
800/609-4892

January 14, 2XXX

Sam Johnson
Happy Valley RV Park
PO Box 431
Happy Valley, CA 92042

Dear Mr. Johnson:

I am responding to your ad in RV Magazine for a maintenance worker to work in your RV park this summer. Enclosed please find my résumé.

My wife and I began full-time RVing in 1999, and after traveling for a year and a half, are now seeking summer employment. I have excellent maintenance skills and have maintained buildings and grounds. I have worked extensively with the public and enjoy people. I am a responsible worker and will do whatever it takes to get the job done.

I would like the opportunity to talk to you about the position. I can be reached with a message at the above number or by e-mail. I check telephone messages once a day and e-mail about every three days.

I look forward to hearing from you.

Sincerely,

John E. Worker

"Find a job you like and you add
five days to every week."
H. Jackson Brown

Chapter 8
How to do a job search

Now that you have your résumé prepared, let's get on with the job search. Follow these three rules for a successful job search. A successful job search will result in two or more job offers for you to choose from.

THREE RULES FOR JOB FINDING SUCCESS

Rule 1: **The more jobs you apply for, the better chance that you will have choices when you have gone through the job search process. If it all works as planned, you will have two or more job offers to consider that meet your criteria.**

Rule 2: **Each contact is an opportunity to show your good work qualities and professionalism and sell yourself.**

Rule 3: **Keep your options open.**

FIVE STEPS TO LOCATING A JOB

1. **Identify** at least twenty employers who meet your criteria for type of work and location(s).
2. **Contact each one.** Send your résumé and cover letter or contact the employer by telephone or e-mail. When you find an employer who is not hiring, you can add another to take its place. For a job that has potential, even if the employer is not currently hiring, ask if you may send your résumé for consideration if an opening occurs in the future.
3. **Follow up** with each employer providing whatever is requested. Also follow up after mailing your résumé to make sure it was received and

after the interview to thank the interviewer, keeping in mind Rule Two: *Each contact is an opportunity to sell yourself.*

4. **Use each step of the process** — résumé or application, interview, follow up calls, negotiations — as a screening process to eliminate employers who are not a match, keeping in mind Rule Three: *Keep your options open.*

5. **Choose** the best overall job offer.

> **You do not need to see a help-wanted ad before contacting an employer.**

In this chapter and the next we will look at the various sources for finding job leads and potential employers. Remember, you do not need to see a help-wanted advertisement before contacting an employer. Some of the best-paying jobs are uncovered by contacting an employer directly. It shows initiative on your part, which many employers value. Follow up on anything that looks promising. If a job offer doesn't result for the upcoming season, tuck it away for future reference.

PRINT RESOURCES FOR LOCATION JOBS

Section III, Job List and More Than 300 Moneymaking Opportunities, lists dozens of employers and refers you to specific resources for similar employers. A few key sources are listed below.

Seasonal jobs

✔ ***Workamper News:*** Lists hundreds of jobs for RVers. Includes private and public employers, and paid and unpaid positions. Listings are grouped by regions of the country. You'll find listings for RV parks and resorts, positions working for national forest concessionaires, amusement parks and an assortment of other opportunities. A variety of state, county and federal agencies list volunteer opportunities. Articles on workamping©, job fairs and a bookstore are excellent resources too. A subscription is helpful to keep a finger on what's available and what employers are willing to pay.

✔ ***Caretaker Gazette:*** Lists a variety of site-sitting jobs, from exchange for site to house couple positions that pay as much as $100,000 a year with benefits. Includes overseas listings.

✔ **RV publications:** General RV magazines occasionally have employment and volunteer listings. Check their classified section.

Geographic job search

Useful sources if you are looking for a job in a specific area:

✔ **Campground directories:** *Woodall's* and *Trailer Life* are two of several available that have listings of RV parks throughout the U.S. and Canada. If an RV park has more than 100 sites, you can be sure they will need extra help during their busy season, but don't rule out smaller parks. Parks with fewer sites but lots of amenities may still be hiring, though they are more likely to offer a site in trade for hours worked. Contact them directly or stop by. Use these directories to supplement print ads for locating other RV parks in the area.

✔ **Classified employment ads in newspapers:** Local newspapers are a source of temporary and seasonal jobs. You will find job fairs listed there too. If you won't stay long enough to work, check the Sunday paper anyway. Some seasonal employers schedule interviews during the winter in southern cities like Phoenix and Los Angeles for summer positions in other areas and advertise in the classifieds.

✔ **Tourist publications:** Annual state and regional travel guides list resorts, RV parks, and major tourist attractions in the area. You can pick these up at Information Centers along the Interstate highways as you enter a state, or call the state's tourist bureau (See **Appendix 1.**) Browse through travel magazines at the library or newsstands for ideas and phone numbers.

✔ **Free employment publications:** Metropolitan areas often have free job or career publications in newspaper dispensers and at public libraries. These weekly magazines have job listings and announce local job fairs.

✔ **Lists of local employers:** State employment service job centers, located in many cities throughout a state, as well as local chambers of commerce often have print lists of major employers. Look in the government pages of your telephone book to locate these centers.

> **Be creative!**

Be creative. A job that requires travel or work at different locations may dovetail with the RV lifestyle. Check it out. A phone call may uncover an excellent opportunity. Dean and Judy saw an ad in a Phoenix paper for a job installing bathtub liners. They traveled from hotel to hotel around the country making about $70,000 a year, with benefits and generous time off.

NETWORKING

The old adage "It's not what you know but WHO you know that counts" applies to working on the road as well. It can mean the difference in finding well-paying, pleasant situations versus getting stuck in a position that seems to last forever and loses money overall. Most situations aren't that black and white, but developing a network saves time and money. In fact, even with the use of the Internet added as a job search tool, making a personal connection is vital. Says JoAnne Smith, consultant with career-management firm Drak Beam Morin of Boston, "… the majority of jobs are still found through networking."

What is networking?

In her book, *You Shoulda Listened to Your Mother,* Alice Zyetz defines networking as "the development of contacts or exchange of information to help you build, maintain or change your career." Alice advises "Don't overlook any activity that involves people" as a chance to network.

> **360,000 people are only one contact away.**

At a sales conference I attended, the instructor said most people have casual contact with at least 600 people. Each of these knows 600 more people, which means 360,000 people are only one contact away. An astounding 216 million people are only two contacts away. Most anyone in the U.S. is reachable in just a few contacts — but you have to ask.

Informational interviews

How can we network while traveling from spot to spot? One way to develop your network while learning about jobs on the road is to set up an "informational" interview. You interview an employer with the purpose of finding out more about the job. For example, you are considering working at an RV park, but you don't know that much about it. You make an appointment at the park you are staying in to find out about jobs at RV parks. Most people are delighted to share information.

Interestingly enough, an informational interview often leads to a job offer. "While one out of every 200 résumés — some studies put the number as high as 1,500 résumés — results in a job offer, one out of every 12 informational interviews results in a job offer," says Katharine Hansen, author of *A Foot in the Door: Networking Your Way Into the Hidden Job Market*. "That's why informational interviewing is the ultimate networking technique, especially considering that the purpose of informational interviewing is not to get job offers."

Others are willing to help

Alice Zyetz continues: "When you network with other people, you find out what jobs are available, what's happening in the industry. When you're new to the job, you want to know what jobs pay, what kind of work people do on the job, where the jobs really are, who has available jobs and names of additional contacts. You shouldn't be ashamed or embarrassed to do this," admonishes Alice. "Others have been in your shoes and are willing to help you as they were helped themselves."

She adds, when you identify someone who might lead to a contact, ask "WHO DO YOU KNOW WHO....? (sells X product, works in Blank City, works for X company or in X industry)."

> **Others are willing to help.**

As I related in our RV Work Story, before we hit the road, we took a trip out from Pennsylvania out west and back. We met a young maintenance worker at Grand Teton National Park and asked her how she got her job. After talking to her we stopped at the personnel office and learned we'd need to apply in January for summer jobs. Job announcements are only open for two to three weeks so we might very well have missed the opportunity to apply without this prior knowledge. Two summers later, we too were working in maintenance at the Grand Tetons with an RV site overlooking Jackson Lake, reflecting the snow-capped peaks that towered behind.

By building your network, you'll acquire contacts for both employers and other RV workers willing to give you job leads. Ray and Pat decided to look for a job mid-summer. They posted a note on an RV discussion board on the Internet asking if anyone knew of employers looking for workers to finish the season. Within a few days they had received several possibilities. They called one of the suggested employers and were both offered jobs working for the concessionaire at Mesa Verde National Park.

Don't give up!

If you don't get a certain position that first season, don't give up. Most sales of products to a business result after a minimum of seven contacts. You are selling yourself, so keep in touch. If at all possible, meet the person who makes the hiring decision, or at least keep in phone contact. When there is an opening, either later in the season, or the following year, you will have a decided advantage.

Find out about moneymaking opportunities

On several occasions, we had talked to RVers about their experiences selling Christmas trees. It didn't sound appealing. One couple had sold trees in the frigid Midwest and had electricity for only an hour a day. Then friends told us about their experience managing a lot in Texas. Kathy had heard about it from "Frenchy," an RVer she met in the laundry room. The word spread through our group of friends. That next winter, six couples who had talked to Kathy and husband Gene sold Christmas trees for the same owner.

From talking to Kathy and Gene we knew this owner followed through on his promises. We also knew questions to ask like, "Will we have hookups?" From talking to others as well, we could evaluate this owner's compensation offer and know that being paid a salary plus $1.00 per tree sold was above average pay.

> **Kathy had heard about selling Christmas trees from "Frenchy," an RVer she met in the laundry room.**

Working for any small business owner has its frustrations. Many RVers have years of business experience and don't always agree with business practices and decisions they see. We've heard of two owners we would not work for. Christmas tree selling has some of its own built-in frustrations, like delivery trucks from Christmas tree farms that don't arrive on time. With Gene and Kathy as our mentors, we had more realistic expectations.

Each communication with a working RVer can lead to contacts and job ideas. By talking to others you can also learn about both the good and the bad aspects of a job or employer and thus better evaluate whether a job is a good match for you. Take advantage of this resource.

Finding the perfect job

Ron and Val are very effective at using networking. They enjoy working in RV parks. They use contacts they make in one RV park to line up jobs in areas they want to work or jobs they'd like to do. They are able to find and check out potential employers through other RV workers they meet on the job. On their off-season, they stop at potential employers if their travels take them nearby.

These meetings give Ron and Val a chance to meet the employer and check out working conditions. More importantly, it gives them an advantage if they decide to apply. If they are not offered a job on the spot, (although they frequently are), they are no longer an unknown quantity to that employer. If Ron and Val can't visit, they might have a mutual acquaintance who would tell the employer about them, raising them above the other unknown applicants. In 1996, Ron and Val spent a month at Silver Dollar City in Branson, Missouri with co-workers from their summer job who were returning to Silver Dollar City for another stint. The biggest perk? Free tickets to all the shows!

> **They stop at potential employers if their travels take them nearby.**

John and Wanda have found that selling a product at fairs and home shows gives them the kind of schedule they like. They have developed contacts with other vendors, and according to Wanda, "There are lots and lots of opportunities out there." These contacts have enabled them to research other products and job possibilities that are more compatible with what they want in a job. They were looking for a vendor willing to ship the product to the shows, rather than having to transport it themselves. Some products like Swedish Back Massage machines were over-saturated at shows, which would limit their income. As a result of talking to others, they found a new product to represent that was a match for their goals.

Practical networking tips:

✔ **Talk to other RVers about their jobs:** Make it a practice to ask other working RVers about their jobs. Keep your antenna out. If someone is working at a job that looks interesting or has potential, or you overhear someone talking about a job in the laundry room or repair shop, ask them about it. Most RVers are very willing to help others. And let others you meet know about the places you'd like to work in or employers you are considering. You might get good feedback or ideas. Record these in your **Job Notebook.** Be willing to share what you know. Others will be more likely to reciprocate when they learn about something that might interest them.

✔ **Talk to potential employers:** If you stay at an RV park that looks like it has potential, introduce yourself and make an appointment to talk to the owner. If you visit an attraction you'd enjoy working for, go to the hiring official or manager. Introduce yourselves and find out about work opportunities. You may not want a job then, but you'll have an advantage if you decide to apply later.

✔ **Keep in touch:** You never know when you might be able to help each other out. In your **Job Notebook,** keep notes of people you meet, contact information and what you learned.

YOUR TURN! BEGIN YOUR JOB SEARCH

Job Search chart: You have identified the type of work you want to do or are willing to do and the location you want to work for the upcoming season. In your **Job Notebook,** make a chart of the 20 or more employers you plan to contact, along with their contact information. (See sample chart on the next page.)

- Make five columns: initial contact, sent application/résumé, interview. Leave room for notes or comments.
- In the comments, write in the date that it is due or the date completed, so you can see where in the process you are. If you need to make a phone call at a certain time, or have an application in by a certain date, highlight it or do whatever it takes so you don't forget it. You may miss an opportunity with an employer, as well as lose credibility, if you miss a deadline.
- If an employer doesn't pan out this season, cross the name out and focus on the ones still active. As you find other prospective employers, you can add them to your chart.

Employer	Initial contact	Sent applic/ résumé	Interview	Results/ comments
Tom's RV Park	Mar 4	Mar 5	April 2	Call back 4/15
Aramark	Mar 5	Mar 5	Mar 28	offer in Housekeeping

In the next chapter, we'll look at using the Internet for your job search.

Key Points

✍ **Quantity of possible employers leads to quality of job offers.**

✍ **Networking is the key to long-term success as a working Rver.**

✍ **Everyone is a potential contact, either for job information or as a connection to someone who has information.**

Notes

*"Commitment is a line you must cross. It is the
difference between dreaming and doing."
The Goals Guy at www.goalsguy.com*

"The only thing that sits its way to success is a hen."
Sign on Hwy 87, Arizona

Chapter 9
How to use the Internet to locate a job

THE INTERNET

The World Wide Web has a number of resources for working RVers. Web sites have job listings, including some sites limited to seasonal work opportunities. Employer Web sites frequently have employment information and often applications can be printed out or requested at the site. You can use the Internet for researching an area or type of work. You can also locate information that will help you in your working travels, like online campground directories. In addition to print materials and networking, the Internet is a valuable tool for locating a job.

Using your own computer

If your computer has a modem and you have a telephone hookup, you can access the Internet with your own computer. If you are staying for a month or more where you can use a telephone line, signing up for the Internet will give you plenty of time to job search.

The costs can add up, however. You will have the monthly cost the Internet Service Provider (ISP) charges. Additionally, some providers charge a setup fee. Unless you can plug into an existing telephone line, you will have to pay installation charges plus the monthly charges for your telephone. If there

> **The Internet is a valuable tool for locating a job.**

are no local numbers for your Internet provider, you will pay long distance charges as well. While the low-cost plans available through AOL, AT&T, and Earthlink work well if you are mainly doing e-mail, if you plan to use your own computer for job searches, plan to pay more like $15-25 per month for unlimited hours on the Internet.

Finding Web Access on the Road

If you don't want the expense of connecting to the Internet for a short period of time, have no way to do that, or you don't even own a computer, you can still access the Web. Grants have enabled public libraries in even very small towns to provide public Internet computers. Even better, this service is free. At public libraries, you can usually sign up for a half-hour to an hour at a time. Rules vary; some libraries allow you to continue working online if no one is waiting, others have a strict time limit.

Also check for access at colleges, local Internet providers and even coffee shops, called cyber cafes.

Many RVers are using Wi-Fi (Wireless Fidelity). This lets computer users within a few hundred feet share a high-speed Internet connection. Wi-Fi "hot spots" can often be found at truck stops, Starbucks and other coffe shops, book stores like Barnes and Noble, and at more and more RV parks. Newer laptops have built-in connections, or you can purchase a PC card for an older one.

> **Check for Internet access at libraries, colleges, and cyber cafes.**

You can sign up for free Web-based e-mail services that you can access from any computer. You'll be able to send and receive e-mail when you are online. Hotmail *(www.hotmail.com)* and Yahoo! *(www.yahoo.com)* are two popular Web-based e-mails. Go to their sites and follow instructions. You will choose a user name and password. Check your e-mail by going to the site, typing in your user name and password and go to your "in-box."

If you haven't used a computer to do an Internet search, you can read or purchase a beginners book, such as *The Internet for Dummies*, ask a librarian to get you started (if he or she is willing and not too busy), or ask most any nine or ten year old child for help! The two charts, "Computer Terms for Internet Searches" and "How to do an Internet Search" can be used to assist or remind you once you have some basics. Further information on using the Internet for job searches can be found at the Job Hunters Bible *(www.jobjuntersbible.com)* and the Riley Guide *(www.rileyguide.com)*. Both have useful links too.

COMPUTER JOB SEARCH

These are important resources and tools for your Internet job search. Take time to browse through these Web sites when you have computer time. These will also give you ideas of that are available. These Web sites will be mentioned again when they are good sources for openings for one of the job categories in **Section III** and are listed in **Resources** for easy reference.

Seasonal job leads

✔ **Coolworks:** *(www.coolworks.com)* Start your online search here. There are more than 60,000 seasonal-type jobs at this one site alone. Employers are divided into categories like national parks, ranches, RV jobs. When you click on an employer, you are often connected right to the employer's Web site. There you can usually request an application via e-mail, print one out, or, in some cases, actually complete your application online.

✔ **Workamper News:** *(www.workamper.com)* Lists featured employers, career opportunities, business and income opportunities, positions in the field of motorsport and subscription information for their print publication. Workamper Plus subscribers can post their résumés online in a searchable database, rate employers, and participate in the forums, as well as receive the Hotline (last minute jobs) via e-mail. Subscribers can also list a free situations wanted ad.

> **The Internet is useful when you are targeting a specific area.**

✔ **Additional Web sites:** Other Web sites that specialize in seasonal work are listed in **Resources.**

Locating jobs in a specific area

You may be targeting a specific area or bc looking for a particular employer. Here is how you can locate that type of information:

✔ **Employers Web sites:** To find the Web site of a specific employer in mind, do a search of the employer's name using a search engine like Google *(www.google.com)* or Yahoo *(www.yahoo.com)*. Scroll down the matches. You will likely find your employer.

COMPUTER TERMS FOR INTERNET SEARCHES

Tool bar: At the very top of the computer screen is a list of words starting with "file." Below that is the tool bar. Pictures or *icons* stand for the function of each one. If you move the mouse arrow over the icon, hold it there for a few seconds, often what it stands for will appear. The two arrows indicate forward and back. You can start a search by clicking on the "search" icon in the tool bar.

Search engine: It searches through the Web and lists all the matches it finds to the word or words you are looking for. Popular search engines include: Google *(www.google.com),* Yahoo *(www.yahoo.com),* Alta Vista *(www.altavista.com).*

Search: Look up a topic. The search engine searches the Web for matches and returns them in a list of choices called "hits." Ten are displayed at a time. When you click on one, it takes you to that address.

URL or address: This is found near the top and is the code that tells how to find it. URLs start with *http://.* Most addresses have *www,* but not all.

Scroll: Move down the screen. You can put the mouse pointer on the little black down-arrow along the right side of the screen and click. It will move the display down. Clicking on the up-arrow takes you back up. Page Down and Page Up and the arrows on the keyboard do the same thing.

Links: Usually these are words that are underlined in a different color. If you click on these, you will go to a new site. If you want to return to the original, click on the back arrow on the tool bar just above the screen.

E-zine: Electronic newsletter.

✔ **State and town Web sites:** Search for the town, like "Skagway, Alaska" for example, you will find the city visitor bureau site and the Chamber of Commerce. Tourist attractions, RV parks and major employers can help you can identify potential employers and places to stay. (For a description of how we found jobs in Alaska, see **Appendix 10**.)

✔ **Newspapers:** Many newspapers have their employment ads on the Web. If you know the name of the newspaper, search for that. (See **Resources:** Newspapers on the Web.)

Other job search sites

There are a number of online job sites where you can search for jobs and/or post your résumé. Monster.com *(www.monster.com)* and Job Options *(www.joboptions.com)* have high ratings from job seekers. All fifty states have their local job banks online too. Go to *(www.ajb.com)* and on the home page, find links to state job banks.

If you have a trade or professional skill and are seeking an assignment or project in your field, these are good sources too. There are sites which specialize in computers, technology or engineering, for example. You can also search Web sites of temporary and placement agencies for your particular field. (See Chapter 20.)

Help with résumés and interviews

Don't overlook information on obtaining jobs at job search Web sites. Many have help with résumés and interviews. In **Resources** for this chapter are listed several Web sites that will be useful. You can find sample résumés to use as templates and "do's and don'ts." See Chapter 7 about posting your résumé online.

Key points

✍ Take advantage of the Internet even if you don't own a computer. Many public libraries and colleges make online computers available to the public.

✍ Find useful information on the Internet about a town or area, or about an employer's job openings.

HOW TO DO AN INTERNET SEARCH

Start: Most libraries start with a page where you can do a "search." (If not, click on the "Search" icon or ask for help from the librarian.) Click the cursor at the line where you can type in your topic, type it, and then hit the "enter" key or click the mouse on the "search" button. The symbol in the top right corner will start moving to indicate it is searching. When the search is completed, the first ten choices will be displayed. Scroll down and pick out the most likely one. Click on the underlined title (often in blue) and it will take you to that site. You will probably find "links" to other related sites. If that choice doesn't look promising, click on "back" at the top and you will go back to your original list. If none are a match, you can either click the button for the next ten choices or refine your search. Click on the appropriate button at the end of the ten choices.

Search engine: You may also find a suggestion to use a different Search Engine. If you don't find what you need, try a different one.

The Maze: Searching the Web is like going through a giant maze. Through the use of "links" and the back button, you can explore many offshoots of your topic. Remember, the blue underlined words or phrases are links. "Back" takes you back one page or address. You can go forward, then backup and go down another path.

Go to an address: You may have a site you want to check out. If you have an address like *http://www.coolworks.com,* follow these steps: Above the screen is a place where the address for the page your computer is currently displaying, beginning with http://. Click the mouse there. Delete the current address by using the backspace key and then type in the address *exactly* as written. (You can start with *www.*) Addresses may be case-sensitive so don't use capitals unless they are in the address. Don't add any spaces. Once you've typed in the whole address exactly, hit the enter key and you should go to that address. *Hint:* if that doesn't do the trick, go back to search and type in the name of the Web site or the key words. More often than not, your site will be listed in the results.

"A window of opportunity won't open itself."
Dave Weinbaum

Chapter 10
How to interview and get results

You've found a listing for a summer job and sent in your résumé. Now you have a message requesting that you call back for an interview. Before you make that callback, review what an interview should accomplish and prepare your questions and key responses.

GOALS
Your goals in the interview are to:

✔ Find out if the job and the employer is a match.
✔ Sell yourself as the best candidate.
✔ Establish the groundwork for a good employee-employer relationship and good communication.

The interview is your chance to sell yourself and make yourself shine. If you are successful the employer will be thinking how fortunate he is that you applied. "I'd better grab that couple before someone else offers them a job. They're just what I am looking for."

You want to find out if this job is a match for you. It may meet your dreams as far as area of the country or type of work.

> **The interview is a chance to sell yourself.**

Does it meet your income goals? *Is this an employer you'd like to work for?*

If you ask the right questions, you can learn a lot about what it will be like to work there and for this individual. Besides finding out the basic information, be alert to things he mentions. "Several workers quit in mid-season last summer." This could be a red flag and certainly worth getting more information. "Oh? What happened?" could be your reply. Be fair, but read between the lines.

Keep in mind, employers have similar goals. They want you to have enough information to determine if you are interested in this position. If the job is a match, then they want to determine if you are the best person they could hire for the job. Making a mistake in hiring is very costly to their business.

PREPARING FOR THE JOB INTERVIEW

With many seasonal jobs, your interview will take place by telephone. Some companies do require an in-person interview, though perhaps not at the job site. For example, one winter we interviewed with Aramark officials from the Denali National Park location in Phoenix, Arizona. Major companies, like Princess Land Tours, will have two telephone interview sessions: one to tell you about the company and answer any questions you have. If you are still interested at the end of that interview, they will set up a second interview and ask a standard set of questions. For most other companies, the interview is likely to be less structured.

> **Making a mistake in hiring is costly to the employer's business.**

Find out about the job

If you have certain things you will not do, now is the time to make this clear. I call these "*knockout*" factors: they would knock this job out of consideration for you. If your refusal disqualifies you, so be it. It is important to clarify these things before you accept the job and drive all the way there. For you too, accepting a job that is not right for you or has unpleasant surprises is costly. The costs are not only the expense of a trip to that location, but the lost wages that you could have made elsewhere.

Have pen and paper handy when interviewed and take notes. These are the questions or categories employers should tell you about, and if they don't, you should ask about each of the following:

✔ **Duties:** what you will be expected to do. If you have a concern about having to clean restrooms and it is not mentioned, for example, you must ask for clarification. If you have a high conviction about doing or not doing something, such as cleaning restrooms or working on Sunday, and it could be a knockout factor — for you or the employer — now is the time to ask.

✔ **Pay:** Are you paid by the hour or by salary? Does part of your work time go to "pay" for your site?

◆ **Hourly:** Be aware that minimum wage varies from state to state and that not all positions come under the federal minimum wage. The minimum wage in several states is less than the federal minimum wage.

> **Get an agreement that any extra hours will earn extra pay.**

◆ **Salary:** If you are paid a salary, precisely how many hours are required and will you be paid extra or overtime pay for hours beyond that? If not, beware. Your effective hourly rate will drop.

◆ **Site plus pay:** If you are working for your site, and you work beyond that time, will you get paid? If you are working for pay and a site, clarify how many hours of work are required for the site and get an agreement that any hours beyond that amount will be paid.

◆ **Overtime:** At what point will you get paid overtime pay? Some states, Utah for example, don't require employers to pay overtime to seasonal workers unless they work well beyond 40 hours in a week. You can bet an employer will work you right up to that amount and not go over. If you are on salary, there may be no overtime pay. Note that not all salaried positions are exempted from being paid overtime for hours beyond 40 in a week. In any case, an employer can require reasonable overtime. You should be compensated for it.

✔ **Work schedule:** How many hours per week will you work? Is it the same all season? Some employers expect 6-day weeks during the busy part of their season. You may get fewer hours of work at the beginning of the season. If you are depending on a certain income, you need to find this out up front. If you and your spouse want two days off together, get that agreement from the employer during the interview. Otherwise you may find you only have one day off or you don't have the same days off. If you plan to spend days off exploring an area, different work schedules could eliminate this job from consideration.

Find out whether you and your spouse will have the same shifts. If you will be driving to the job site, you may need the same hours to share transportation.

✔ **Length of season:** Make sure you are honest with employers about when you can arrive and when you will leave. Not honoring your commitments makes it hard for other RV workers. Employers are relying on you, particularly if they also hire college kids who leave early for school. In addition, for workers staying their full contract, some employers pay a bonus based on total hours worked, while others may refund rent paid for your RV site. This money could amount to another week or two of pay. Don't blow it.

> Some employers offer a bonus for staying your full contract.

✔ **Tools:** If you will be working in maintenance or mechanics, does the employer provide the tools or do you? If you do, does your compensation reflect that? If you do use your own tools on a routine basis or to supplement the ones provided, put a colorful piece of electrical or duct tape on yours so they don't wander off.

✔ **RV site:** Will an RV site be provided? Are full hookups available and included? It would be inconvenient if the whole season you have to move your rig every week or two to dump. Is your space level? (If you are talking to a non-RVer, get specific. We've been told more than once we had a level site and it was anything but level.) Shaded or in sun? (This can be a factor if it is hot, or if you need to use your solar panels.)

✔ **Cost of RV site:** At what cost to you? It is critical to find out this information. You will need to know a dollar figure before going into negotiation in the next chapter. Find out the number of hours you need to work or the dollar amount you will be paying.

✔ **Required occupancy:** If a site is provided, can you get a written statement stating that your positions require occupancy? If you are required to live onsite, the employer can deduct the expense and you do not have to pay income tax on it. If you are not required to live onsite and an RV site is part of your compensation, you could owe income taxes on the fair market value of that site. (See Chapter 13.)

✔ **Uniforms:** Are uniforms required? If so, who provides them? Will you have to buy new items of clothing? Will you clean your own uniforms or is that provided?

✔ **Other perks:** You might get free or reduced propane and laundry privileges. Some employers offer perks such as a store discount or discounts on purchases at their property; free or discounted use of guest recreational facilities when available; tickets for free or reduced-fee area attractions; or free or low-cost meals. For the land companies associated with cruise ships, like Princess Land Tours, you could be eligible for cruises after a certain amount of hours worked.

✔ **Other concerns:** Where is the nearest grocery shopping? We usually ask if there is a Wal-Mart, since towns that large generally have supermarkets and better prices. Is there a hospital nearby? What is the availability of telephone line or cable TV? Satellite dish reception? Cellular phone reception, and is it analog or digital? Internet service? You might also want to clarify whom you will be reporting to and how many people you'll be working with. Are you covered under Worker's Compensation if you are injured?

> **Make a list of your selling points as an employee.**

Sell yourself

Besides gaining information about the job, the interview is your chance to sell yourself to the employer as the best candidate for the job. Preparation is key here too.

✔ **Review** your work history to see where you have experience or have used skills that apply in this position. Highlight them on your résumé so you remember to emphasize them.

✔ **List** your selling points as an employee. Think about traits this employer is probably looking for in his type of business. Examples might be:

♦ "If I don't have an assigned task, I look to see what needs to be done."

♦ "I have managed a business so I know how important good customer service is."

♦ "My job is to make sure each customer leaves here satisfied."

♦ "I believe in doing whatever is necessary to get the job done."

✔ **Questions:** There are standard questions many interviewers ask, particularly if this is a seasonal job dealing with the public. Think about possible answers ahead of time.

♦ What would you do if you have an unhappy customer? *(Assure the customer they are important, make the situation right if you have the authority, or get your supervisor are possible answers.)*

◆ How do you define good customer service? *(Give the customer you are helping your full attention and finish with one before you start helping another, do whatever it takes to make the customer satisfied are reasonable answers.)*

◆ How do you get along with co-workers? Or, they might describe a situation and ask you how you would handle it. *(I get along well with co-workers. If I have a problem I would talk about it with the person first and try to work it out.)*

◆ What are your weaknesses? *(Notes RV worker Phyllis: State your weaknesses in a positive way. If you can't stand a messy workplace, you could say, "I have been accused of being a neat-nik." Or, if you obsess over minutiae, you might say, "I'm a stickler for details." Phyllis once interviewed someone whose weakness was "I hate to get up early." Hearing this answer, an employer would probably think, "This person may not be on time to work.")*

✔ **Research:** Do your research on the employer and the area. Read any brochures you have received. Showing you have read the information or found out something about the company or area elevates you above candidates who have not.

Your turn!

In your **Job Notebook**, make lists in your notebook for questions you want answered and for points you can use to sell yourself.

✔ **Questions:** List your key concerns and the questions you want answered in the interview. Leave a line or two so you can jot down the answer you get from the employer.

✔ **Knockout factors:** List conditions that would eliminate this job from your consideration. Use this as a checklist during the interview.

✔ **Experience:** List your relevant experience for the position you are seeking in your notebook, or highlight it on a copy of your résumé.

✔ **Selling points:** List your selling points for the kinds of positions you are seeking. Think of the traits that make a valuable employee and list them.

✔ **Likely questions:** Prepare answers to standard questions that could apply to this job. Keep this list in front of you during your telephone interview.

Think about your responses ahead of time, but be honest. There is no "right" answer. If you would not handle a situation the way this employer would, better to find out now than after you have arrived.

Establish good communication

As you prepare for the interview, remember that a successful interview establishes good communications. You will be laying the groundwork for your future employee-employer relationship. Most problems between employer and employee occur because of poor communications and because expectations weren't clarified. Good questions about what the job entails and what the expectations are let the employer know that you are serious. It also communicates that you intend to live up to these expectations, unless you negotiate something different, and that you expect the employer to do likewise.

THE INTERVIEW

During the interview, have your résumé and list of questions and concerns, your selling points with you. Build confidence that you can do the job. As the interviewer goes over the duties of

| A successful interview establishes good communications. |

the position and his needs, let him know if you have previously done this, even if it is included on your résumé. In reviewing your work history, underscore what you have done that is similar. If he states he is looking for a certain type of person, agree and sell yourself. "Yes, I think customer service is the most important part of the job." You are conveying your interest in the job and helping the employer see that you are a good match.

Work in your positive selling points. One thing my husband, Bill, always mentions is that he believes in giving a good day's work for a day's pay. Bill is someone who likes to be busy so this is true for him.

Other interview tips:

✔ Greet the interviewer with a firm handshake, combined with a smile and direct eye contact.
✔ Be positive and energetic.
✔ Demonstrate your interest by making eye contact, leaning forward

and smiling.
- ✔ Stand or sit straight.
- ✔ Do not make negative statements about former employers or co-workers. This only makes you look bad. The employer may think you are a complainer, troublemaker, or can't get along with other people.

Telephone interviews:

✔ Use your voice to communicate your interest and enthusiasm.

> **Don't make negative statements about former employers.**

Helen Blankenship, executive director of the Plus 50 Placement Center, Inc., says "Who wants to hire a grump?" She advises, "You want to go in with a good attitude, with an upbeat attitude, with a smile on your face and a real willingness to engage in conversation. You want to act like you really want the job."

Ending the interview

At the end of the interview, the interviewer should either offer you the job or let you know where the process goes from here. He may have additional candidates to consider. Perhaps the former employee has the job if he is coming back and the employer won't know for a few days.

If you are offered a job, you should request two or three days to consider it and to discuss it with your spouse. This will give you time to consider the offer and plan your negotiations. You may have been offered a certain wage but that doesn't mean you can't ask for more. You may also have other employers you hope to hear from and this will give you time to contact them again.

Whether offered a job or not, you should make a positive statement saying that this sounds like a company you'd like to work for, and you know you would do an excellent job for them and would like the position. (Of course, say this only if it is true.) If only one of you received an offer and your acceptance is contingent on your spouse getting a position also, make sure you communicate this information to the interviewer.

End the interview with a time frame for either hearing back from the employer or a time for you to follow up.

Follow up

Follow up an interview with a thank you. Either drop a short note in the mail, or send an e-mail, thanking the employer for the opportunity to interview for the position and reiterate that you see this as a match and would like the position. Mention you are looking forward to hearing from him or working with him. This is another way to sell yourself.

Be sure to follow up as you agreed. It is also appropriate to call if an employer does not get back to you as promised. If the employer still hasn't made a decision, find out when you can check back. Take any further contacts as opportunities to sell yourself.

Key points

- The interview is for both you and the employer to find out if the job is a good match.
- The second objective for the employer is to find the best person for the job; your second objective is to sell yourself.
- The interview is your chance to establish good communication.

10 guidelines for working in RV parks

After their first job working in an RV park, Virginia and Skip and a co-worker couple came up with a list of questions/guidelines to use the next time they apply for campground jobs:

1. **Don't sell yourself short:** The campground needs someone of your caliber as badly as you need a job. Don't be afraid to tell them what you can do and what you are not willing to do! In the long run, everyone will benefit. The more adamant you are in defining both your requirements and abilities the more likely you are to find a "good fit" for both the RV park and you.

2. **Make sure you fully understand the compensation for the job:** We need full-time income. In the future we will only work for parks that pay us for every hour worked, and then we'll pay the monthly rent out of that. We figured that in exchanging 20 hours for a site, we were getting "paid" $2.88/hour for those hours. Be sure to find out the monthly rental for sites. The owners cannot value your site as an RV worker for more they value the same site for a camper. Will you get discounts on any amenities they have?

3. **Make sure you discuss all the work you will be doing:** If you need to work 40 hours a week and all of your job duties center around mowing grass, what happens if you have torrential rains for two solid weeks? Can you do other jobs to get in your 40 hours?

4. **Does the campground carry Worker's Compensation** for its employees? Requirements vary from state to state. Better to know your position before you need it.

5. **Are uniforms required?** If so, who pays for them? Will you have to go buy anything?

6. **Are the tools provided** to do the work they are asking you to do?

7. **Are you required to use your own vehicle?** In this campground, the office was over one-half mile from our site. The trips added up.

8. **Is phone, cable TV or modem hook-up important to you?** Now is the time to check out availability.

9. **What size site will you have?** Some campgrounds don't want to waste their premium sites on workers. Do you have ample room to open your front door and get in and out, or put your awning out?

10. **Ask about the distance to shopping and medical facilities:** If you are unfamiliar with the area, call the Chamber of Commerce. The more you know, the less likely you are to be disappointed.

*"A pessimist sees the difficulty in every
opportunity, an optimist sees the
opportunity in every difficulty."*
Winston Churchill

Chapter 11
How to negotiate for better compensation

Like interviewing, to get what you want, you need to be prepared going into negotiation.

PREPARATION
You have been offered a job paying $5.50 an hour plus a site. You need $6.50. Do you throw this job out? Not before you negotiate for better pay. In larger corporations, there is often a standard pay rate for each position, though individual managers may have some latitude. In smaller companies, particularly where you are talking to the owner, you can often negotiate better pay and perhaps additional perks.

> **Before you start negotiating, be prepared.**

If this offer comes during the job interview, ask for a few days to consider it and talk it over with your spouse. That will give you time to evaluate the job offer and compare it to other offers or jobs in the works.

Negotiation hints
Before you start negotiating for better compensation, consider these:

✔ **Be prepared:** Know what you want and need in terms of pay and perks. Know the going rate for this position. If you have figures from similar employers in the area, all the better.

✔ **Compute what you will be paying for your RV site:** In the interview, you should have found out what you will be paying for your RV site. It may be a dollar amount or you may be working a certain num-

ber of hours to "pay" for your site. Before you accept an offer or negotiate further, make sure you clearly understand exactly how much you
are paying. Several ways to value your RV site are explained in the
chart titled "What is a site worth?" on page 112.

As an example, if each of you will be working ten hours a week for
your site (20 hours/week) and the monthly rate for the site is $250, you
are being paid an equivalent of $2.89/hour for those hours. Figuring an
average of 4.33 weeks per month, your
computation would be as follows: Work 20

> **Know what is non-
> negotiable for you.**

hours/week x 4.33 weeks = 86.6 hours a
month for your site. $250 ÷ 86.6 = $2.89/
hour. Check additional ways to "compute"
the value of your site or your "hourly rate"
in "What is a site worth?" Is this a fair value for your time? Unless your
duties are minimal, you are working too many hours for this site. (Of
course, only you can decide this, weighing all factors.)

✔ **Know what you are worth:** If you bring added value to the job in
terms of experience, energy or job skills, you should be compensated
for that. If this employer doesn't need or isn't willing to pay for your
skills, then you have to weigh the offer in terms of the benefits to you.
For example, you really want to be in that area, so it may be worth
taking less pay. Remember there are many jobs available. If you want
higher than average pay, it is going to take you a little longer to find a
match than it is the person who is willing to take the first offer.

✔ **Know what is nonnegotiable for you:** Think about your bottom
line. What is nonnegotiable? For example, Bill and I work only for
hourly wages, not on salary. We want to be paid for the time we put
in. An attractive salary can work out to a low hourly rate when you
put in lots of hours beyond the 40-week. For someone else, cleaning
restrooms might be unacceptable. For other working RVers, a campsite with full hookups, or being near to medical facilities could be a
necessity. You probably have a bottom line as far as pay goes.

✔ **Postpone discussing actual dollar compensation until later in
the process:** While you want to find out what the usual pay is for the
position, you don't need to discuss the amount until later in the process. Operate on the assumption that this is the starting offer and
there is room to bargain. (If the amount is ridiculously low or clearly
not a match, you probably will eliminate this job in the interview.)

By postponing discussions of salary, you will be in a stronger position after the employer is sold on your skills and wants *you* to fill the position. In addition, you need time to evaluate the job offer. It is difficult to do that during discussions. If necessary, postpone discussions of pay with something like, "I'm sure we can work out a fair compensation package."

> **"There's a slight problem... money."**

THE PROCESS

We are assuming you sold yourself during the interview and underscored your ability to do the work and that you are a good worker. Before you make any additional demands, assure the employer that this sounds like just the kind of company you would like to work for and that you would do an excellent job for them. You really want this job. This puts you in a position to ask for more.

Asking for more

"There's a slight problem…money." You can use various reasons: "I really want to work here but I have been offered $6.50 an hour at another RV park. Can you do any better?" One statement Bill successfully used was "I know you are used to hiring older, retired folks, but my wife and I are still prime workers. We're not retired." (If you are retired, you can say you "aren't typical.") We got $2 an hour more than he initially offered. Even if the offer sounds fair to you, ask "Is this the best you can do?" Maybe the employer has more in his budget for your compensation.

Another approach is suggested by Jack Chapman, a career consultant specializing in salary coaching and the author of *Negotiating Your Salary: How to Make $1,000 a Minute.* When you hear the dollar offer, he advises, "You say 'Hmm,'" He adds, "Repeat the figure with a contemplative tone in your voice — like it's the start of a multinational summit meeting. Count to 30 and think. When you're done thinking — and this time the interviewer will be the one squirming in his seat — respond with the truth based on what you know you're worth in the marketplace: 'sounds great' or 'sounds fair' or 'sounds disappointing.'"*

* *(Jack Chapman quoted from Marcia Passos Duffy's "Essential tips to help you get the salary you deserve," at www. WetFeet.com Posted: 01/03/2001).*

If what you are "paying" for your RV site is not equitable in your analysis, you can use this as a bargaining point to reduce your charge for the site, increase your hourly rate, or obtain additional perks. Many park owners have not done a similar analysis. In the example above, where you worked 20 hours/week for your site at $2.89/hour, you would be better off earning your regular hourly rate for all hours worked and then pay the space rent out of your pocket.

If the salary you want isn't possible, perhaps the owner will give you free propane and laundry, meals, or some other perks. If your expenses are less, this can add a little to your paycheck indirectly. For example, a free lunch every work day can reduce your grocery bills. Maybe the employer could expand the job responsibilities or combine this job with another position, making it worth paying more.

> **Terry supplemented her salary by doing waitressing for pay plus tips.**

If you want or need to make this job work, you might find a way on the job to earn more money. Terry was able to supplement her salary by doing waitressing at the resort for pay plus tips. Meanwhile she was learning about fine dining, a skill that could pay off someday. Perhaps you could sell craft items in the store or hang a sign outside your RV advertising your service like sewing or sharpening scissors.

Keep your options open

You are trying to get the best job; the employer wants the best employee. Each of you is trying to get things lined up for the season. If you have followed the job strategy in Chapter 8, you are juggling more than one possible employer and may already have a job offer or two.

How do you keep your options open and be fair to these employers? How do you decline a job offer yet keep the door open for another season?

If you truly don't think this job is a good match, of course, gracefully bow out. "As much as I think this would be an excellent place to work, I'm afraid I need to earn more money than you can offer." Or, "This summer we've decided to work closer to our grandchildren." I recommend you keep your options open for the possibility that you might want this job another season. "I hope you will consider us again in the future."

If you are considering several employers, you need to send strong, positive messages to each even if the particular job isn't your first choice. It is much like asking a gal to marry you. If she gets any vibes she is second choice, she'll be looking for another man, especially if there is another waiting on the sidelines.

JUGGLING JOB OFFERS

If an employer offers you a job, you can, of course, request a few days to consider the offer. You and your spouse need to talk it over. Or, you can let the employer know that you are waiting to hear back from another employer whom you are also considering and should hear something within a few days. If you set a firm date to call back, most employers will respect this.

> **If she gets any vibes she is second choice, she'll be looking for another man!**

At this point, in fact, you have ammunition to call back the employer you really want to work for, tell him you have another offer but really want to work here. Will he be making his hiring decision soon? The fact that you may slip out of consideration may prompt positive action on his part. Or at least he may share with you what he is waiting for. It could be a former employee hasn't let him know if he is returning and you are his first choice if he has an opening. With this information, you can decide if you want to accept the first offer or take your chances and wait for the better position. If you stall the other employer too long, she may very well hire her second choice.

If you decide on a job you would really like to have and a hiring decision hasn't been made, be persistent without being a pest. So many employers and hiring officials have told us that when there was a candidate who kept in touch — called them, dropped them notes — they *had* to hire them. Anyone who wanted the job that badly just had to be given a chance.

You've accepted a job and you get a better offer

You have made a commitment to one employer but then get another offer. The second job pays more money or is exactly what you want to do. Congratulations! You are in an enviable position. But what do you do?

Some people feel strongly that they should honor the first commitment. You should never violate your principles. But you also have to look out for yourselves and remember this is a bidding process on both sides. If a second job offers you each a dollar more per hour, this can amount to an extra two-thousand dollars over the course of a six-month season. If you do it in a way that is fair to the employer, it can be done honorably.

First of all, begin your job search early. Then you have a good chance of lining up good offers well before start dates. It would be one thing to leave an employer in the lurch the week before he is expecting you to be there, or just not show up. It is another to give him a month or more warning. If you get the better offer within a few days of accepting, the employer probably has a number of other candidates still available.

> **Finding a job is a bidding process on both sides.**

Some employers have told me they start their job search for summer positions in November so they can get the pick of the candidates. They know some will get better offers, but they also count on the fact that many people will stop looking once they have a firm job lined up. When we told one national park we had gotten a better job offer at another park with better pay and a much longer season, he understood. He said it happens all the time. Plus we had given him plenty of notice so he could still fill those positions.

One time we told an employer we could not be there until a certain date because of a prior work commitment even though he wanted us there right away. We took our chances that he would wait. Sometimes an employer will wait in that case; other times they need someone right away and can't wait. But for us, that was the honorable action and we still got the jobs.

Turning down a job offer

If you do decide to decline a position that you have accepted, please let the employer know as soon as possible. This is a common courtesy, but one a few RV workers fail to follow. It gives all of us a bad name and may come back to haunt you. Remember, Rule #3 for job-finding success: *Keep your options open.* Another season, this may be a place you want to work.

Your turn!

✔ **Figure what perks are worth to you:** To have an idea how much a given perk is worth, look at how much you are spending on items typically offered as perks such as site, laundry and propane.

✔ **Research area equivalents:** Find out monthly rates for RV sites in the park you are interested in as well as surrounding parks. Talk to RV workers doing similar jobs and check *Workamper News* to research the going rate. Since this may be difficult to do right at the time you need it, record this information in your **Job Notebook** whenever you come across it so you have a range of what is being paid. Don't be afraid to ask for more; just ground your request in reality and what you have to offer.

✔ **Compute what you will be paying for the RV site:** If an RV site is involved, use the examples in "What is a site worth?" (See next page.) to determine what you are "paying" for the site or what you are "earning" per hour. Use area equivalents to get a ballpark figure if you don't have actual figures.

Key points

🖉 **Get prepared before going into negotiation for compensation.**

🖉 **Negotiating better compensation than what is initially offered is often possible.**

What is a site worth?

There are different ways of looking at what a site is worth in terms of compensation.

♦ What would you be paying for a site if you weren't working? If you normally boondock, then this campsite, while convenient, is actually a cost.

♦ What is the normal seasonal or long-term rate per month? The employer should not value your site at more than this amount.

♦ Fred was told by the employer that his site was valued at $700/month but regular campers paid only $300/month. Fred would be better off paying the $300/month in rent and getting the extra $400 in increased wages, or an extra $2.50/hour. ($100 week divided by 40 hours)

♦ You are working 20 hours per week for a site. You get paid $5.00 per hour for work after that. You are effectively paying $100 per week for your site ($5 x 20). Is this a fair value, both in terms of what other campers are paying and what the site is worth to you?

♦ Value it this way too. The monthly rate for your site is $200/month and you work ten hours/week in exchange for your site. You will work about 40 hours for your site in a month so 40 divided into $200 is $5.00/hour. That's not minimum wage, unless other amenities bring the value up.

♦ Consider your duties. If your duties consist of being on the premises "in case you are needed" or to "keep an eye on things," your RV site with no monetary pay may be a fair exchange.

♦ If the site is in a resort and thus valued quite high, will you actually use these extra amenities? If not, this site may be worth considerably less to you than the employer.

♦ **Note:** If you anticipate leaving for any length of time during your season (or if an emergency comes up), will you be charged rent? If so, how much? If this situation happens, you could offer to move your RV to a non-income producing space while you are gone. This information will also give you a monetary value for your site.

"We ought to be able to learn some things second-hand. There is not enough time to make all the mistakes ourselves."
Harriet Hull

Chapter 12
How to succeed on the job

In the preceding chapters, we have taken a number of steps in the job-search process to find an employment situation that meets your goals for working and an employer that is a match for you. How you handle situations on the job will, in large part, determine the sort of season you have. There are also factors out of your control.

GET OFF ON THE RIGHT FOOT
Principal factors in your success on the job are good communications and fulfilling your promises. Using these two keys, you will avoid many work-related problems. You have been doing both throughout your job search —

from your first contact in response to the ad and each subsequent contact through the interview and negotiation process. There is one more step you should take before starting your new position.

> **An employment agreement lets employers know you expect them to live up to what was negotiated.**

Employment agreement
When you accept a job, particularly if it is a small business, ask the employer if he has a written contract or agreement spelling out what was discussed. If an employer does not have something in writing, we ask, "If we send a letter confirming what we discussed, will you sign and return it to us?" We haven't been turned down. Some RVers are either uncomfortable with this or don't feel it is necessary. We feel it is a protection and lets employers know you expect them to live up to what was negotiated.

The government and larger corporations usually have employment handbooks and forms they send to new employees. In this case, it wouldn't hurt, however, to send a thank-you letter that mentions any new items your new supervisor agreed to that are out of the ordinary, such as days off together, 40-hours of work each week guaranteed, etc.

ON THE JOB

Once on the job, if problems or questions arise, discuss them right away. If things are hectic, wait until the end of the day, but address the issue as soon as practical.

Depending on the position and how closely your supervisor works with you, keep him informed of problems and accomplishments. If a customer is furious over something that happened, let your supervisor know right away so if he has to deal with the problem, he is prepared for it. When Bill is working on a building project, he keeps the foreman informed of his progress and checks to make sure that he is doing what is wanted along the way. You'll get a feel for how much to do this, but better to err on the side of too much communication than too little.

> **It is better to err on the side of too much communication rather than too little.**

Be adaptable

Take time on the job to observe how things are done before making suggestions or telling the boss "how we did it at such-and-such a company." In fact, expect that this owner or manager will do things differently than you might have done them elsewhere.

Good work habits

It goes without saying that you should be on time, do your work, and if you're not busy, look for something to do. Employers appreciate employees who are flexible. If an employer needs help in another area and an employee is willing to pitch in, that goes a long way. You may want an extra day off, or to change your schedule to accommodate an event or visiting relative. If you have pitched in where needed, your employer is going to bend over backwards to help you out if possible.

Difficult people

In any job, you can be stuck working with difficult people. It may be a co-worker, or perhaps even the boss. Some people are abrasive and even abusive. In most cases, you shouldn't take it personally. They probably treat other people much the same. This is not to say you should let it pass. Later in the day and in private, you should let this person know that this is not appropriate. If you can, state it diplomatically, "When you said '___,' I felt (distressed/uncomfortable) because I need to be treated with respect." You're more likely to get a positive response.

Some people are not even aware of how they sound to others. You will likely get much different treatment on the job if you speak up and call it to their attention.

As in your jobs or career before you hit the road, you need to set limits. You'll find a few owners or supervisors will take advantage of workers and expect them to work extra hours or on their days off. Depending on the situation, and whether or not this is a one-

> **"Start the way you mean to go"**
> *Age-old advice to daughters*

time thing, you may want to help them out. But if you sense that this could become a pattern, you must check this behavior immediately.

"Start the way you mean to go," mothers advise their daughters when getting married. If you wait on your husband hand and foot, that is what he will expect from then on. You may want to tell the owner that you are sorry but that wasn't your agreement. You have plans and are unavailable this evening or weekend.

Bill and I accepted a job at a houseboat company. At the time we interviewed, the owner wanted us to go on salary, but we declined and were hired at an hourly wage. We were also guaranteed 40 hours a week and overtime for work exceeding 40 hours. We followed up with a letter clarifying our agreement, which the owner signed and returned to us. It became clear almost immediately that we were the only hourly workers. Everyone else was working on salary and was working far in excess of 40 hours a week. Pressure was put on us to change to salary at the equivalent of our hourly rate of pay. In that case we could be required to work a "reasonable" amount of overtime at no extra pay. We declined.

Then Bill was asked to work on his day off. He said no. We left for the day to reinforce the fact that we would not tolerate the employer changing the rules. As it turned out, we left that job; there were a number of agreements the owners did not live up to and they continued to pressure us into working on salary. We at least had a written agreement the owners had signed, so they could not come back and say they never agreed to that. Know your limits and draw your lines. Otherwise, you may have a miserable season.

> **If you have a problem, try to work it out with that person first.**

Remember, if you have a problem with a supervisor or a co-worker, you should always try to work it out with that person first before going to the owner or manager.

You are only there for a short time

If you have been an owner of a business or in a supervisory or management position, it may be difficult to watch the owners of a company run their business. Some people seem to be successful in spite of themselves! Take a deep breath. You hit the road to get rid of stress. You are not there to run the business, only to do the best job you can in the position you were hired for. If the owners don't make money, there may be no business to come back to next season. Remember, it is their business. They make the decisions. Let go.

On occasion, it turns out a situation isn't ideal, but you have made a commitment. It may be too late to get an equivalent job somewhere else. Then it's time to remember that you are only here for six months, or whatever time you agreed upon. Remember that this job is a means to an end. Even if it isn't what you wanted, it is serving a purpose. This job is allowing you to live a lifestyle of freedom and choice and to explore an area. Sticking with this job may help you get a more desirable job next season. "This too shall pass."

Bill and I have had jobs with co-workers who were extremely lazy. In short, they weren't doing the job they were paid for. We have found that to be the case in a few of our government positions. Bill and I have a choice in these situations. We can make ourselves miserable by concentrating on how unfair and wrong this is. Or, we can concentrate on ourselves. We will do the best job we can, a job we can be proud of. If someone else chooses not to do a good job, it is out of our control. Bill and I have clear consciences and are always proud of the quality of work we do. We choose the second way of reacting, avoiding ulcers.

CHOOSING TO LEAVE

What do you do when you cannot work in the situation you are in? You have tried talking to the employer and it just isn't what you want or had expected. You have other options and don't need to stay in a situation you dislike. Be sure to give your two weeks' notice unless it is impossible to do so. Employers talk to one another, so for the sake of your own reputation, and that of other working RVers, follow this simple courtesy.

Unethical situations

What if you find yourself asked to do something that violates your principles? Or that violates the law? Sue worked in the accounting department for a company. Her boss did not account for petty cash properly. She discussed it with the next level of management and was not backed up. This put her in an awkward position and could have made her answerable for discrepancies. She decided to quit rather than compromise her integrity.

> **Be sure to give your two weeks' notice unless it is impossible to do so.**

You need to follow your conscience and do what is right according to your principles. It is not worth the stress it will cause. You also need to obey the law, as well as follow safety and building codes or accepted procedures, as in the case of accounting. Otherwise, you could be the "fall guy" if a problem ever arises. Do not take a chance with your work or personal reputation.

EVALUATE EACH EXPERIENCE

Analyze your situation after each job. Are there questions you should have asked? If you had known more about the actual situation, would you have accepted the job? Don't beat yourself up. Record these new questions in your **Job Notebook** for the next time.

Ask for a reference letter

When you leave a job or a volunteer experience on good terms, ask for a reference letter on company letterhead and ask your employer if you can use her as a reference for future employment. Duplicate positive letters and include them with your applications to similar employers. Many prospective employers will be satisfied with a reference letter and this will avoid having your former employer called repeatedly if you are applying to many positions.

Many employers appreciate it if you write a letter as a model. Include your duties and accomplishments and your excellent worker characteristics. Make it easy for them and you'll get a nice letter to show prospective employers down the road.

Key Points

✍ **Good communication and accurate expectations are essential for job success.**

✍ **Always do a little more than is expected of you and follow through on commitments.**

✍ **Set limits with both owners and co-workers.**

✍ **If the job goes sour, remember: this too shall pass.**

"A goal is nothing more than a dream
with a time limit."
Joe L. Griffith

Chapter 13
Legal and tax considerations

Disclaimer: This chapter is provided for informational purposes only so that you are aware of issues that may impact your finances. Nothing written here should be construed as legal or financial advice. Remember, the burden for compliance with these laws rests with you and not your tax preparer, IRS employees, or authors of any books or articles you might read. Since these issues can have considerable ramifications, if you are in doubt, see your legal and tax advisors to determine the effect on your individual situation.

There are legal and tax considerations that could affect your income and expenses.

DOMICILE AND STATE OF RESIDENCY

Domicile and residency are often confused. For people living year-round in a house, they are, for all intents and purposes, the same. They do not, however, have the same legal meaning. For an RVer, your domicile and residence will coincide, at least part of the year, but as you travel and work in other states, the two will differ.

> **As a full-time RVer, you can choose your state of domicile.**

Domicile

As a full time RVer with mobility, you have the opportunity to choose your legal domicile. This is your "home" state or where you are domiciled the majority of the time. Your domicile is the place where you intend to remain permanently. It is your true and principal establishment, to which whenever you are absent, you "intend to return." You have only one domicile. If you are domiciled in a state, you must establish this by your subjective intent as well as by actual residence.

Establishing your domicile

Some states make it easy for full-timers to get a driver's license, motor vehicle registration and tags, as well as to register to vote. RVers have reported that South Dakota, Texas and Florida have reasonable costs and are easy to work with to establish your domicile.

Just because you drive your RV to a new state, register it there, and establish an address does not mean you establish a new domicile, even if you declare it so. If you don't clearly establish one state as your domicile, more than one state may conclude they are your domicile at tax time or at the time of your death. Some states, California, New Hampshire and Ohio in particular, are very aggressive about claiming you have tax-liability even when you thought you were a casual visitor.

> **A number of actions help establish your domicile.**

In an article, "How to Change Your Domicile from New Hampshire to Florida," attorneys from the New Hampshire firm of Cleveland, Waters and Bass, P.A. list a number of actions that help establish your new domicile. *(www.cwbpa.com/domicile.htm)* As an RVer, you should consider doing as many of the following as is feasible in establishing your new domicile. This is especially true if you own property in a second state. Remember, if you are challenged, the government has the presumption of correctness and it will be up to you to prove that you are right.

✔ Remove trailers, mobile homes and boats from your old state and re-register in the new.
✔ Spend at least half the year in your new state.
✔ Do not store furniture or heirlooms in your old state.
✔ Change your driver's license to your new state. Any fishing or hunting licenses in your old state should reflect your non-resident status.
✔ File a declaration of domicile with the town clerk.
✔ Change your voting registration.
✔ File a new will in your new state.
✔ File your federal tax returns at the Service Center for your new state.
✔ File state income tax returns (if applicable).

✔ Transfer any club memberships to your new state.

✔ Change your address on your passport and any accounts to your new state.

✔ Subscribe to the local newspaper.

✔ Consider moving the remains of close deceased relatives to your new state.

✔ Make major purchases in your new state.

Impact for working RVers

Your choice of domicile will have a financial impact. Taxes, license and registration fees, and insurance rates vary by state. Working RVers often choose a no-income tax state (Alaska, Florida, Nevada, South Dakota, Texas, Washington or Wyoming) to minimize state income tax obligation. (New Hampshire and Tennessee do not tax earned income, but do tax interest and dividend income.) Besides income taxes, other taxes like sales tax (especially important when buying an RV), inheritance taxes, real estate taxes, and personal property taxes differ. Vehicle insurance and health insurance costs vary between states and sometimes even by region within the state.

> **It is worth the research to weigh all the factors in choosing your domicile.**

Research, then weigh all the factors in choosing your domicile. To get some background information, you can obtain publications from AARP with tax information by region as well as a State Personal Income Tax Comparison chart. You can also see a state income tax comparison chart at the Federation of Tax Administrators Web site or check at the individual states' Web sites. See **Resources** and **Appendix 5.**

Residency

When you are physically present in a state, that is where you are currently residing — even if only a day as you travel through. In the course of a year, you can, and probably will, reside in more than one state. You may own an RV lot or property. You could reside there part of the time, but maintain your domicile elsewhere.

States want their residents to do certain things: pay taxes, register their vehicles, and obtain a driver's license, to name a few. States will consider you a resident after a certain number of days; requirements vary by state. (Taking a job in a state may be evidence that you are a resident.) If you have spent time in a state, and you did not earn money in that state, or from a source in the state, you will not have to file an income tax return there.

INCOME TAXES

No matter where you earn income, you will be subject to federal income taxes. State tax is different. If you work in a state for part of the year, you must pay state income taxes on the income earned in that state. If you

> **No matter where you earn income, you will be subject to federal income taxes.**

work in two different states, you will pay each state income taxes on the income earned in that state (or while in that state). For example, you worked in Colorado for four months and earned $8,000. Then you worked in Arizona for four months and earned $7,000. You pay income taxes to Colorado on the $8,000 and income taxes to Arizona on the $7,000, filing non-resident or part-year resident forms in each state. (If you make under a certain amount, you may not have to pay state income taxes, however you will have to file a state tax return in order to get a refund of any money that was withheld for state income taxes.)

Your state of domicile also wants tax on your income, however you will get credit for income taxes paid to other states.

✔ In the above example, if you are domiciled in a state where you must file a tax return, you will get a credit for the income taxes paid to Arizona and Colorado, and pay taxes on any other income to your state of domicile.

✔ If your state of domicile is an income tax state and you work in a no–income tax state, your domicile will collect taxes on the amount earned in the no–income tax state. For example, if you are domiciled in Oregon and work in Wyoming, a no-income tax state, Oregon will tax your Wyoming income.

✔ If you are domiciled in a state where no filings or income tax is required, you only need to be concerned about filing in the states where you worked.

To minimize state income taxes, you should establish your domicile in one state. You then have temporary assignments in the other states and are non-resident. Otherwise, if you have income from a pension or interest and dividends, and you work six months in Utah, for example, you could have to pay income tax on six months of your pension or interest income earned while working and living in Utah.

If you do have a home base and travel to work at a temporary job lasting less than one year, you may be able to deduct travel expenses and a per diem allowance for meals. Check with your tax preparer to see if you qualify.

Each person's financial situation is a little different, tax law is complex and varies from state to state, so check with your tax preparer beforehand so you aren't surprised at tax time.

RV SITES TAXABLE?

If you receive a free RV site when you work, is the value treated as income for tax purposes? It might be considered federal income unless your employer requires that you live there. According to IRS Code Section 119, if you are required as a condition of your employment to stay at the premises, the value of the lodging which you receive qualifies as "excludable income," meaning you don't need to report it on your return. You must, however, document the value

> **Your free RV site could be "excludable income."**

of lodging you received, in case you are challenged. Keep a brochure which lists the rates, plus the manager's name, phone number and dates. Request a statement from the employer to the effect that you are required to live onsite as part of your employment conditions. The employer can also take a deduction so both parties actually benefit. Furnished meals in some cases are also excluded from taxation. Note: You may not be able to exclude this "income" for either RV site and meals when computing your income for state tax purposes.

EMPLOYEE V. INDEPENDENT CONTRACTOR

What are the differences and the financial implications of working as an employee versus working as an independent contractor?

Employees:

✔ Employer pays half the social security tax.

✔ Employer pays unemployment insurance.

✔ Employers controls how work results are achieved.

✔ Employer sets your schedule.

✔ Employer issues regular pay checks for hours worked.

✔ Employer must pay overtime according to state law.

✔ Employer must pay for Worker's Compensation to cover you in case of injury.

✔ Employer may require that you incur expenses that you may claim on your income tax return, however these are usually limited.

Independent contractors:

✔ Pay their own expenses.

✔ Can deduct many of the costs of doing business, such as travel, telephone, equipment and tools, business supplies and a home office.

✔ Set their own schedules and have little or no supervision.

✔ Are responsible for the final product and may be sued for improper performance.

✔ Pay the full social security tax (15.3%) and must pay quarterly estimated taxes.

✔ Are not covered by Worker's Compensation nor eligible for unemployment compensation.

✔ Often do work of a "professional" nature.

IRS factors

In most cases it is clear which category you fall under. In the case of sales positions, it may not be so clear since a salesperson can work either as an employee or an independent contractor. Occasionally there is abuse where employers have contracted with someone to provide services when in fact that person was actually an employee. Hiring an independent contractor saves the employer money (Payroll taxes, assessments for unemployment and Worker's Compensation coverage, etc.), but the employee will not be covered if injured on the job or unemployed. If you have any questions about a

> **An independent contractor can deduct many of the costs of doing business.**

particular job situation, you may view IRS publication 15-A at their Web site *(www.irs.gov)*, or order a copy from the IRS (800/829-3676).

DRIVER'S LICENSE AND REGISTERING YOUR VEHICLES

States require that anyone working as an employee in their state, who has a vehicle or existing driver's license, obtain a new driver's license and register their vehicles in that state within a certain number of days. If you are working temporarily there as an independent contractor or have your own business, you may be exempt. In a few states you can obtain temporary licenses and plates if you will be employed a short time. See **Appendix 6** for contact information for state agencies handling vehicle registration.

Re-registering your vehicles could be quite costly. Not only do you have registration fees that are often based on the value of your vehicle, but you will probably have to change your insurance to the new state at different rates, possibly more.

> **States require people working in their state to obtain a driver's license.**

After your job is finished, you will probably want to re-register in your domicile, an additional expense.

Most workers on the road we have talked to do not get a new license or change registration in each state; however, you are risking fines and penalties in addition to these fees if you do not switch in the time period allowed. If you choose not to re-register your vehicle, obey all traffic laws and don't get stopped. If an out-of-state license vehicle is sitting in an employer's parking lot day after day, it may be noticed. In a resort town with lots of out of state visitors, your vehicle with an out-of-state tag is less likely to be noticed. You are probably just another tourist.

You must make your own decision on this one.

The key to these factors is to do your homework ahead of time. Protect yourself and avoid costly surprises. Remember, when it comes to choosing a domicile or where to work, one size does not fit all. The best choices for may be different than ones for another RVer.

Key Points

🖎 **Your choice of domicile can impact your income.**

🖎 **States have different laws and regulations regarding income taxes, driver's licenses and vehicle registration.**

🖎 **Check the ramifications for you before taking a job.**

Section III
Job list

CHAPTER 14

Jobs at RV parks and resorts

1. Manager and assistant manager
2. Reservations clerk or guest service worker — day and night shifts
3. Gatekeeper
4. Office workers like secretary, bookkeeper or accountant
5. Maintenance worker
6. Construction — carpenter, plumber, electrician
7. Propane service technician
8. Janitor or housekeeper
9. Mechanic
10. Groundskeeper
11. Food service staff
12. Recreation or activity director
13. Craft or activity instructor
14. Golf marshal
15. Entertainer
16. Security personnel
17. Marina worker
18. Canoe rental clerk and livery driver
19. Shuttle van driver
20. Bike rental clerk, mechanic
21. Pool operations — lifeguard, pool cleaner
22. Retail stores operations — sales clerk, inventory and pricing clerks
23. Tour guide or salesperson for lots in membership parks
24. Offer services to other campers, i.e., haircuts, massages, sewing
25. Worker for contractor-offered services at RV parks and resorts - food, marina, etc.

Site-sitting jobs

26. Construction sites: mainly providing a presence
27. Construction sites: paid to provide 24-hour security
28. Storage units: management, night security, or provide vacation relief
29. House-sitter
30. House-sitter, providing also pet or plant care
31. Caretaker of ranches or other property
32. Caretaker or work in exchange for site, extra hours for money
33. Manager of a household - house couple
34. Child care provider—nanny
35. Gun club or shooting range—caretaker

Sales of Christmas trees and pumpkins

36. Christmas tree lot manager or helper
37. Pumpkin lot manager or helper

CHAPTER 15

Jobs traveling in your RV

38. Gas pipe line inspector
39. Wagon master/tail gunner for RV caravans
40. Mchanic for RV caravans
41. Deliver RVs
42. Salesperson of advertising at campgrounds- maps or directories
43. Salesperson or manufacturer's rep
44. Inspector of RV parks for directories
45. Enroller for credit card companies
46. Mystery shopper
47. Judge at dog shows
48. Circus worker
49. Booking agent for a circus
50. Groom for a circus
51. Travel with a carnival: rides, setup, welders, office, mechanics, CDL drivers.
52. NASCAR circuit help
53. Salesperson of products to businesses (open territories)
54. Product installer with changing job locations

CHAPTER 16
Jobs in RV sales and service

55. RV salesperson
56. Retail salesperson: supplies or parts department
57. Quality control inspector
58. Technician: walk-throughs with new buyers
59. Detailer
60. Mechanic
61. Service technician
62. Service writer
63. Lot attendant
64. Inside office worker: receptionist, clerk, accountant or bookkeeper, computer workers such as operator, programmer, data input

Camping World/RV supplies

65. Retail sales clerk/cashier
66. Stocker
67. Service writer
68. Mechanic
69. RV technician
70. Janitor
71. Bookkeeper
72. Parts advisor
73. Merchandiser
74. Shop attendant

Working for RV clubs and organizations

75. Paid staff for office work and club functions
76. Editorial or graphic designer
77. Webmaster or computer programmer
78. Manager and assistant manager for club RV parks
79. Activity director for club RV parks
80. RV safe driving instructor

CHAPTER 17
Seasonal jobs with the National Park Service

81. Fee collector
82. Ranger: law enforcement, interpretation, general

83. Visitor Use Assistant
84. Park guide
85. Maintenance: laborer, maintenance worker, motor vehicle operator
86. Positions in biology, archeology and other fields

Seasonal USDA Forest Service jobs
87. Forestry aid and technician
88. Aids or technicians in archaeology, biological, hydrological, lands, range, real estate and surveying
89. Fire suppression worker
90. Fire tower lookout

Seasonal BLM jobs
91. Forestry and range (fire positions) aid and technician
92. Material handler
93. Motor vehicle operator
94. Cartography aid or technician
95. Engine operator
96. Fire suppression worker
97. Horse or mule wrangler

Army Corps of Engineers
98. Park or gate attendant at COE projects (bid)
99. Hired worker for bid-winner at project

Other federal season work
100. Post office help at Christmas
101. IRS tax season worker
102. Census taker

CHAPTER 18
Working for a concessionaire in a national park
103. Hotel jobs like front desk clerk, housekeeper, back office worker
104. Restaurant jobs like cook, waiter/waitress, hostess, cashier
105. Retail store jobs like cashier, stocker
106. Warehouse workers

107. Tour or recreational activity jobs like tour guide, boat or raft operator, boat rental agent, boat instructor, golf course-related
108. Gas station jobs like cashier, mechanic, attendant
109. Medical clinic jobs like receptionist, nurse, physician's assistant
110. Campground host
111. Maintenance worker
112. Rodent and pest control worker
113. Shuttle driver
114. Helicopter pilot or worker for flight-seeing operations

Nonprofit associations
115. Clerk or cashier selling books and other items at an NPS visitor center
116. Warehouse worker
117. Bookkeeper — place orders, keep books

National forest concessionaires
118. Camphost
119. Maintenance worker
120. Manager of several campgrounds
121. Holder of concession rights to run a FS campground
122. Forest fire support worker

State parks
123. Ranger — present programs, enforce rules, give tours
124. Maintenance worker
125. Fee collector
126. Visitor center worker
127. Campground host
128. Park aide
129. Operator of a hunting check station

County and city parks
130. Maintenance worker
131. Fee collector
132. Visitor contact personnel
133. Operator of a concessionaire activity

Chapter 19
Resorts

134. Hotel and motel jobs like front desk clerk, housekeeper, child care provider, maintenance worker, waiter/waitress, chef, hostess, back office worker, security person, bellman, cashier, retail clerk, bartender
135. Activity director or recreation leader
136. Restaurant jobs like wait staff, hostess, chef or cook, busboy, bartender
137. Gas station jobs like cashier, mechanic, attendant
138. Retail jobs like cashier, salesperson, stocker or warehouse worker
139. Grocery stores like cashier, bagger, stocker
140. RV parks jobs like registration and reservation staff, cashier, maintenance, groundskeeper, store clerk
141. Adventure/recreation tours: jobs like raft guide, stable hand, tour leader, reservations staff, cashier, mechanic, maintenance worker, driver, loader or packer
142. Golf course jobs like golf pro, shop staff, groundskeeper, ranger/ starter, mechanic or helper for care of golf carts, snack bar attendant or food preparer, customer service representative
143. Marina jobs like boat rental agent, boat instructor, mechanic, fuel attendant, cashier
144. Personal services like hair dresser, nanny or childcare provider, computer programmer, handyman
145. Shows: usher, ticket sales staff
146. Flight-seeing or helicopter tour operation workers
147. Costumed character at amusement park or clown
148. Dog musher/guide, dog caretaker

Dude ranches

149. Wrangler
150. Wait staff
151. Cook
152. Housekeeper
153. Maintenance worker
154. Child care provider or worker
155. Office worker

156. Airport driver
157. Laundry worker

Bed & Breakfasts (B&Bs)

158. Housekeeper
159. Breakfast preparation like cook, wait staff
160. Guest check-in and greeting
161. Vacation relief staff or manager

Ski resorts

162. Lift ticket seller
163. Ski instructor
164. Child care provider or worker
165. Driver
166. Retail clerk
167. Food related jobs like cook, wait staff, busboy, bartender

Amusement and theme parks

168. Food service worker
169. Ride operator and mechanic
170. Game operator
171. Retail sales clerk
172. Campground worker
173. Tram driver
174. Costumed character
175. Maintenance and repair worker
176. Interpreter
177. Tour guide
178. Warehouse worker

Cruises and land tours

179. Housekeeper
180. Food preparation and wait staff, bartender
181. Lecturer or performer
182. Dance host (also ambassador or gentlemen host)
183. Recreational leader for gym, golf, dance, exercise, children's activities
184. Bus driver/guide

185. Customer service or shore representative
186. Bus maintenance and cleaning worker

Casinos
187. Blackjack dealer
188. Food preparation and wait staff
189. Bartender
190. Security

Wall Drug and similar
191. Retail clerk
192. Maintenance worker
193. Cook
194. Cafeteria worker
195. RV park-related worker
196. Usher
197. Stocking and inventory clerk
198. Demonstrator of old time crafts like blacksmithing, weaving.
199. Driver of a horse-drawn buggy or wagon.

Disney World
200. Merchandise host/hostess, cashier, roving vendor, display merchandiser
201. Attractions host/hostess, tickets host/hostess
202. Culinary: wait help, bussing, steward, cashier host/hostess, cook
203. Housekeeping: custodial, room attendant, houseman, laundry worker
204. Life guard, pool maintenance worker
205. Transportation: parking lot guides, boat pilot, tram driver
206. Custodial attendant
207. Third-shift custodial worker (heavy duty industrial cleaning)
208. Hotel-related jobs: front desk, bell services, housekeeper
209. Office, technical and reservations: front office receptionist, reservationist
210. Wardrobe: costume assistant

Working/volunteering overseas
211. Teacher overseas

212. Support worker at Antarctica
213. Short-term laborer
214. Manager for RV park in Mexico
215. Property caretaker

Chapter 20
Temporary jobs

216. Office work: clerical, accounting, computers
217. Factory or assembly work
218. Professional
219. Construction work: carpentry, plumbing, electrical, sheet rock, block work
220. Product demonstration
221. Tax season work: accounting
222. Tax season worker: clerical
223. Substitute teacher
224. Temporary medical jobs: nurse, therapist or physician
225. Fruit or vegetable picker
226. Working during a grape harvest: grape sampler, weigh master
227. Worker for wheat harvest
228. Corn detassler
229. Reservation agent in reservation center for campgrounds.
230. Flagger on highway construction projects
231. Deliver telephone books

Holiday-season work

232. UPS driver or warehouse worker for UPS
233. Christmas retail salesperson
234. Santa Claus at a mall or department store
235. Bell ringer collecting donations
236. Fireworks sales
237. Post office temporary worker
238. Post office contract worker
239. Baggage hander for cargo aircraft
240. Flower shop helper— deliver flowers or make arrangements

Contract work and temporary work for professionals

241. Computer project consultant

242. Technical writer
243. Engineer
244. Medical short-term assignment: nurse, therapist, physician
245. RN or LPN at family or children's camp
246. Teacher

Special events

247. County or state fairs
248. Sports events
249. NASCAR events in a support capacity: security, parking, cleanup, souvenirs, food service, admissions, tickets.
250. Home and garden shows
251. Shows in Quartzsite, Arizona
252. Golf tournaments
253. Events at stadiums or convention centers
254. Race tracks: horse, dog races
255. Swap meets: booth sales, parking

CHAPTER 21
Sales of RV-related products and services

256. Solar panels
257. Upholstery and carpet cleaning
258. Solar ovens
259. Laptop computers and related equipment
260. GPS devices
261. Brake assists
262. Windshield repair
263. RV repair or handyman work
264. Hair cutting, sewing, massages
265. Badges
266. Redwood signs
267. Satellite dishes and antennas
268. RV detailing
269. Pet grooming
270. Sharpening knives and scissors
271. Locksmithing

Other RV-based businesses

272. Engraving
273. Selling advertising and producing RV park maps (own business)
274. Carving
275. Artist or craftsperson: painting, beading, photography, weaving, jewelry etc.
276. Offering guided tours
277. Teaching classes in exercise, dance or crafts
278. Photographer— digital photo imaging
279. Word processing or medical transcription
280. Desktop publishing
281. Newsletter publication
282. Musician or performer
283. Giving massages

Internet-related services

284. Sales of products on the Web through eBay or other auction sites for yourself or others
285. Web site sales
286. Produce an electronic magazine (e-zine)

Consulting/professional

287. Innsitting business
288. Business consultant
289. Seminar speaker
290. Computer consultant, Web page designer
291. Freelance writer
292. Freelance photographer
293. Investor in stock market
294. Tax preparation
295. Performer at school assemblies

CHAPTER 22

National parks, forests and other federal agencies

296. Campground host
297. Environmental educator
298. Videographer or photographer
299. Construction worker

300. Grant writer
301. Visitor center attendant or naturalists
302. Law enforcement desk officer
303. Search and rescue (SAR)
304. Ranger in the back country permit office
305. Assistant on archaeological digs
306. Fire tower lookout
307. Worker on the Trash Tracker houseboat
308. Lighthouse tour guide
309. Carpenter and other tradesmen
310. Special project worker
311. Campground host at military Fam camps

State parks

312. Campground hosting, which can include a variety of tasks
313. Clerical, computer and fiscal help at headquarters
314. Maintenance projects
315. Off-season park surveillance, minor maintenance projects, weekend campground hosting and interpretive hosting
316. Fee collector
317. Staff at visitor center or naturalist
318. Tour guide or docent
319. Period-costume guide or interpreter
320. Retail salesperson in a gift shop
321. Photographer, update slide collection
322. Teacher of Off Highway Vehicle (OHV) and Personal Water Craft (PWC) safety classes
323. Golf course worker
324. Campsite construction worker
325. Archaeological assistantant or helper
326. Backcountry patrol
327. Lighthouse tour guide or caretaker

Nonprofit volunteers

328. Construction of a Habitat for Humanity Build
329. Office or computer work for a Habitat for Humanity affiliate
330. Maintenance or office work at a church camp

331. Volunteer overseas — environmental, construction, health and education projects

Exchange of services

332. Exchange work for space in an RV park
333. Work out an exchange with a private individual
334. Park at a business in exchange for night security
335. Help friends or relatives in exchange for a place to park and hook-ups.

SECTION III.
MORE THAN 300 MONEYMAKING
OPPORTUNITIES

"I flunked retirement…"
Lee Iacocca

Chapter 14
How to find jobs with a campsite

You may be parked along a stream with a view of snow-capped mountains in summer. You could be nestled among the palm trees or exploring miles of lush Sonoran desert in the winter. You could be part of the excitement of Christmas or enjoying the solitude of a remote ranch or estate. You pick the spot. A job awaits.

Fortunately, not only can you choose your desired location, you will also find employers for some types of positions prefer to hire employees who bring their houses along with them and will even provide an RV site.

JOBS AT RV PARKS AND RESORTS

1. *Manager and assistant manager*
2. *Reservations clerk or guest service worker - day and night shifts*
3. *Gatekeeper*
4. *Office workers like secretary, bookkeeper or accountant*
5. *Maintenance worker*
6. *Construction - carpenter, plumber, electrician*
7. *Propane service technician*
8. *Janitor or housekeeper*
9. *Mechanic*
10. *Groundskeeper*
11. *Food service staff*
12. *Recreation or activity director*

13. *Craft or activity instructor*
14. *Golf marshal*
15. *Entertainer*
16. *Security personnel*
17. *Marina worker*
18. *Canoe rental clerk and livery driver*
19. *Shuttle van driver*
20. *Bike rental clerk, mechanic*
21. *Pool operations - lifeguard, pool cleaner*
22. *Retail stores operations - sales clerk, inventory and pricing clerk*
23. *Tour guide or salesperson for lots in membership parks*
24. *Offer services to other campers, i.e., haircuts, massages, sewing*

RV parks and resorts hire employees during their busy season to help out. You'll find more jobs available during the summer, but don't overlook winters where the "snowbirds"are — the southwest, Texas, Florida — or parks in ski resort areas. You could work all year around.

While the owners frequently act as managers, you'll find many parks hire manager couples, assistant managers and staff to register campers, sell items in the store, provide meals in a restaurant. Maintenance staff takes care of grounds, fills propane tanks, cleans restrooms and makes repairs. Larger parks may hire activity directors as well.

> **Beautiful Lakeside Resort! Couple needed to work in store and marina. Work 15 hours for site, $ for extra hours. Many perks.**

Some of the jobs listed above are found only in the larger, resort-type RV parks. If you have skills or experience in more areas, you increase your value. You might be able to create a position combining several different jobs in a smaller RV park. A smaller park may hire someone to work part-time at a particular task, such as activity director, or to work in exchange for an RV site if the park can't afford a whole position.

Where you find these jobs

A number of RV parks and resorts advertise in *Workamper News*. You may also find advertisements in other RV publications or on RV-related Web sites and discussion groups related to working on the road.

You can also identify RV parks and resorts that are potential employers in an area using campground directories or by contacting the local Chamber of Commerce. Contact them directly. For resorts and larger parks, you may find listings in the Help Wanted section of local newspapers.

> RV workers Ron and Val: "Normally I would say 100 sites is a good measure of whether a campground would need some extra help or not. A lot depends on what amenities they have. A smaller campground with a pool and Jacuzzi, etc., probably could use the extra help but not 40 hours per week."

Compensation

The compensation for working in an RV park or resort can range from a simple exchange (with no money changing hands) to good working wages, along with an RV site.

In an exchange, you work a certain number of hours per week and in return are given a site. Hours worked may be per person or per couple. The park may or may not add an hourly wage for hours exceeding that minimum.

> **Golfers!**
> **RV resort and golf course needs you. Work for site, $$ and golf privleges.**

For paid positions, you can receive an hourly wage or monthly salary. Your RV site is generally part of your compensation. Perks — such as free or reduced-cost propane, laundry, store items, meals or other amenities — may also be included as part of your compensation. Complimentary tickets to area attractions could be part of the deal.

Compensation can vary tremendously. We have met RV workers working almost full time for just a site. Others volunteer a few hours for a site to reduce their expenses. Still others have negotiated excellent wages or salaries as well as perks and been very well compensated; for example, one couple who worked in Colorado several years ago negotiated their site, one free meal a day, propane and laundry plus $8/hour each.

So you are clear on what you are being offered and what your RV site "costs," review Chapter 10, "Find out about the Job" and Chapter 11, "What is a site worth?" (page 112) before taking a job.

As Greg Robus, editor and publisher of *Workamper News*, stated in one issue, "The employer's idea of what his or her exchange package is worth is irrelevant. It's up to each Workamper to be selective and to only accept jobs that offer a compensation package that suits their individual needs."

Finding better paying jobs

To find (or create) higher paying jobs, do your research. Know what other RV parks in the area are offering so you have an idea of what is realistic. Know your own worth. Your skills are probably worth more than a bare minimum wage, especially if you are willing to work and not just doing something to keep busy. Sell yourself and ask for more during the interview and negotiation process, especially as you accumulate experience. And look for opportunities that aren't listed in the usual publications.

✔ **Develop and your RV worker network**. See Chapter 8.

✔ **Talk to the owners** when you stay at an RV park. Conduct an informational interview. See Chapter 8.

✔ **Increase your value** by taking a training and certification program for campground managers. ARVC and National RV Park Institute offer courses and certification programs. Escapees RV Club has a training program for members desiring to work in RV park management at member parks. (See **Resources.**)

Related possibilities:

$ **Contract services:** Some RV parks and resorts contract out services like operating the restaurant, a marina, or other activities. You might be able to bid on these positions. Watch for advertisements in the previously mentioned sources, but also keep your eyes and ears open.

$ **Membership parks:** If you belong to a membership campground, there may be opportunities for paid work or for an exchange of services for your site. Talk to management.

$ **Specialized parks or camps:** Church or Scout camps may need summer maintenance and office help or caretaking during the off-season. Military RV and fam camps for families of active and retired military personnel are another possibility. Clothing-optional resorts also hire workers.

$ Offer services: Stay in an RV park for a period of time and then offer services to park residents. One fellow we worked with one summer was resident handyman during his winters in an Arizona RV park that catered to winter snowbirds. He did repairs to the inside of rigs that more elderly residents couldn't or didn't want to do. Another RVer, to raise money for unexpected truck repairs, offered to repack wheel bearings while in an RV park. Just a few jobs and he was on his way. Sewing and haircuts are services that could be offered to other residents without disruption to park activities. The management, of course, should approve these activities, and you may also need certain licensing. (See Chapter 21 for more information on operating your own business.)

$ Working specific locations: Ron & Val are exceptionally good at finding positions in RV parks and campgrounds. Ron usually works in maintenance, Val in the office or fee collection. They have been working every other year in a state park in Colorado to spend time with grandchildren. The other years, they target an area and line up positions before heading to that location. Ron and Val check with all sources. They use *Workamper News*, other job sources (Chapter 8), and network with other RVers, talking to co-workers and RVers about RV parks that are good to work for. Besides considering the salary, they weigh the perks: free site, free laundry, discounts and tickets to attractions.

$ Ski resorts: Gabby & Janice managed an RV park in Ketchum, Idaho, one winter. They are ski buffs and this job gave them the opportunity to be near Sun Valley and get discounted ski passes. Expecting to have just a few winter visitors at any given time, the owners left them in charge. More visitors kept showing up, and it turned out to be a bigger job than they expected, but they got in lots of skiing.

$ Church camps: Rich and Fran found employment at a church camp and conference center Fran had attended as a child. Pay was better than average plus they got three excellent meals each day. Fran worked in the office handling the phone and computer input as well as registration and check-in for attendees. Rich supervised a crew of four eighteen-year olds as Head Housekeeper. With free site and meals, they could bank most of their paychecks all summer.

$ Clothing-optional resorts: Al and DeAnna have worked at several clothing-optional resorts. They visited the first resort and liked it. They called a couple of years later and, after a telephone interview, ended up being the first couple hired. Says DeAnna, "Nudist and clothing-optional resorts are expensive to live in so working there is an opportunity to live the lifestyle. It's really inexpensive because you tend to do your recreational activities like swimming pool, parties, and other activities there rather than spending money out. So it was a good thing for our budget to be there." Most clubs want their employees to have experience with the lifestyle prior to working there. DeAnna advises visiting a resort before taking a job to see if you are comfortable there. Some resorts are more family oriented. They can be either privately owned or run by a board.

SITE-SITTING JOBS

26. *Construction sites: mainly providing a presence*
27. *Construction sites: paid to provide 24-hour security*
28. *Storage units: management, night security, or provide vacation relief*
29. *House-sitter*
30. *House-sitter, providing also pet or plant care*
31. *Caretaker of ranches or other property*
32. *Caretaker or work in exchange for site*
33. *Managing a household— house couple*
34. *Child care provider — nanny*
35. *Gun club or shooting range — caretaker*

Construction companies and individuals hire people to watch their property when there is no one there. We've often noticed ranches seeking this kind of help. Some jobs require simply a presence on the site for a certain number of hours per day. In other cases, you may have certain tasks to do. People seek others to help them with projects like gardening, restoring old buildings, and new construction in exchange for a site.

Often money is paid for extra hours in these cases. Nonprofit and government agencies may also seek RVers who are willing to work in exchange for their sites. Quite a variety of tasks can be involved and you can likely find one that appeals to you.

Caretaking property requires more duties than simply site-sitting, and is generally longer-term. Duties could include care of animals, garden, fencing, house repair or inside duties.

Where you find these jobs:

The Caretaker Gazette lists these types of situations in their publication. They vary in location, duties and compensation. *Workamper News* and other RV publications may also have ads of this type. Homesitters on Wheels has house-sitting and other site-sitting opportunities, though they charge a fee for materials to join, and not everyone is able to find assignments in areas they desire.

> **See the country and make money doing it!**
> **Live onsite in your own RV watching construction sites, manufacturing plants.**

Word of mouth, local classified ads, large construction companies, real estate agents, security firms, all are potential sources. Self-storage units often hire couples to manage the property and live onsite. You might see an ad in the classified section of the local newspaper, or use the Yellow Pages and contact a storage place directly.

Potential compensation:

Many housesitting arrangements and caretaking assignments are an exchange of services. You get full or partial hookups, perhaps a telephone line, in exchange for keeping an eye on the place. If you have duties beyond bringing in the mail, you can probably expect some compensation. If you work for a construction site or storage place, you should get compensation in addition to your site. All this is negotiable, of course.

Related opportunities:

$ **Housekeeping couples (and singles)** are sought in *Caretaker Gazette* and by agencies. They could have duties as cook, gardener, chauffeur, child care or housekeeping. Household managers may oversee other household and groundskeeping staff. Some positions offer lucrative compensation; $100,000 a year plus benefits is possible but these generally require a commitment of at least a year. Most employers require excellent references and previous experience or training.

Many positions like this come with housing; you would need to negotiate a spot to park your RV.

$ Gun clubs hire RVers to park onsite and keep an eye on things. *Workamper News* is one source.

$ House couple: Bill and Marna decided several years ago they wanted to work as a house couple since those positions paid almost $40,000 year. Not having any direct experience, but feeling confident in their knowledge and abilities, they asked friends to write up letters of reference and went to an agency. They were placed at an estate where they worked for one year. They were later interviewed for a position working with a celebrity.

$ Site watchers: Mike and Nancy were referred by summer job co-workers to a company that constructs microwave towers and hires RVers to watch the site. On some assignments one person was required to be onsite 24-hours a day. At others they had to be present only at night. Compensation was more when they provided 24-hour a day security. For either type of job, when workers were there, they could leave to explore the area or do their shopping. Says Nancy, "It was a pretty easy way to earn money, though on one job we got stuck out in the desert after it got very hot."

$ RV homesitters: John and Suzanne have obtained housesitting assignments through Homesitters on Wheels. Says Suzanne, "It's a nice way to supplement your retirement income." Sometimes they take their RV, sometimes the owner prefers them to stay in the house. Homesitters covers their liability insurance and bonding and refers them to assignments. The couple often care for pets, which they enjoy. Suzanne likes the fact they interview the customers before taking a job and can decline ones that don't suit them. They always get very nice comments. Many clients ask John and Suzanne to come back again and again.

SALES OF CHRISTMAS TREES AND PUMPKINS

36. *Christmas tree lot manager or helper*
37. *Pumpkin lot manager or helper*

The smell of pines, children excited about Christmas — part and parcel of selling Christmas trees. Managing a Christmas tree lot is a short but intense way to earn some cash. As the managers, you may be able to hire local workers to unload, display, water, trim, sell and load trees onto customers' cars or you could find yourselves doing all or part of these tasks. It depends on the owner and how busy the lot is. Lots usually open the day after Thanksgiving and stay open until all the trees are sold or Christmas Eve, whichever comes first.

The negatives of this job are several. Long hours and the weather can be a challenge. Many Christmas tree lots are on dirt. If it rains, you'll work extra hard at keeping your rig clean. In some cases, dealing with the owners can be a challenge. The biggest headache we had was finding and hiring reliable helpers.

Potential compensation

In the three to four weeks the lot is open, you can earn a nice chunk of money. At this writing, average compensation for managing a Christmas tree lot was around $2,500. Additionally many owners offer some sort of bonus. We earned a bonus of $1.00 or so for each tree sold; other owners give an unannounced bonus or one based on how well the managers do overall. Still other owners pay on a percentage basis. Don and Cynthia earned 18% of the after-tax sales at their lot.

Related opportunity

Pumpkin lots work in a similar way, though aren't as intense. Often a pumpkin lot reopens as a Christmas tree lot so you can work both. Compensation isn't as good because pumpkins sell for a lot less. But you might earn as much as an additional $1,000, depending on the situation.

Questions to ask

Some questions to ask if you are considering this type of work, gleaned from the experience of other RVers:

✔ **What sort of site and hookups will I have?** Are there provisions to empty your holding tanks or use a portable toilet? Do you have electricity? What volts? Is your lot paved or dirt?

✔ **How is my pay figured?** Most have a set fee for the time period. Some have a base pay and then an amount per tree sold. Others pay a percentage of sales. Make sure nothing can be subtracted for any reason. Can we earn a bonus? How is that computed?

✔ **What duties do we have?** These vary by owner. Duties may include setting up and preparing the lot, trimming trees and putting them in stands, watering, flocking trees, loading and unloading the truck, loading trees on customers' cars, etc.

✔ **What responsibilities do I have for money?** Do I have to reconcile receipts against cash or complete any forms? *(These duties can add an hour or more to an already long day)* Are tree prices firm or can I offer a discount to make a sale? (*Depending on how your compensation is figured, this could make a difference in your total income.*) How often will cash be picked up? (*Are you in a safe area if you have to keep cash overnight? Or at least in a fenced, locked yard?*)

✔ **Who will hire workers?** If I do the hiring, do I have a budget, or will this come out of or affect my compensation? If not, will there be a helper here at all times or only during certain hours? What will happen if a worker doesn't show up? Who pays them? (*The owner should take care of this, otherwise you could have a nightmare of taxes and forms to complete.*)

Where you find these jobs

Sources for jobs include *Workamper News* and word of mouth. A good way to line up a job is to stop by a Christmas tree lot or pumpkin lot in the area you might like to work the following year. Find out from this year's manager what the situation is. Get the contact name and follow up after Christmas. Most owners like to firm up their managers by September.

Check also the National Christmas Tree Association Web site for retail lots in the area you are interested. If you have targeted an area, check also with the local Chamber of Commerce. They may also be able to tell you lot locations and owners for their area.

From our experience, before taking a job selling Christmas trees, we would definitely recommend talking to someone who has previously worked for this owner. Your expectations will be more realistic and you may avoid some potential problems. In the right circumstances, we would do it again. It was fun being part of the magic of Christmas and a challenge to sell more trees and increase our bonus.

Christmas tree workers: John and Susan relate, "The first time we sold trees, we didn't know the questions to ask but we needed money so we hired on with a company in Missouri. Temperatures were as low as 20 degrees below zero, plus wind-chill factor, with frozen water for five days in a row." Electricity was only available for a few hours a day. Another disadvantage was that this was a new lot. Whereas an established lot would have clientele that would return year after year, a new lot depends on people driving by and noticing it." John and Susan were getting paid by the number of trees they sold. They only made $1,700. "Our second experience was better. There was a base of $2,500 plus an additional amount for each tree sold." They could hire employees to help out, whom the owner paid for. "We enjoyed helping people pick out their Christmas trees."

A job with a campsite is ideal for the RV worker. You will need to ask questions to make sure the position is a match. The employer has certain needs and a budget. If one situation is not right, there are plenty more in this category to investigate, so don't get discouraged.

These types of jobs can work for RV workers needing to make a living and those for whom income is not a strong consideration. If you need to make a living, you will have to look harder to find a job that pays well. All the job-finding skills you developed in **Section II** will come into play. Others have found good jobs. So can you.

Notes

"Don't say you don't have enough tine. You have exactly the same number of hours per day that were given to Helen Keller, Pasteur, Michelangelo, Mother Teresa, Leonardo da Vinci, Thomas Jefferson, and Albert Einstein."
H. Jackson Brown

Jobs 38-54

Chapter 15
How to get traveling jobs in your RV

An RV is a great way to take advantage of jobs where you move from location to location. These include jobs like checking gas pipe lines, working on RV caravans, selling advertising or other products toRV parks and signing people up for credit cards.

JOBS TRAVELING IN YOUR RV

38. *Gas pipe line inspector*
39. *Wagon master/tail gunner for RV caravans*
40. *Mechanic for RV caravans*
41. *Deliver RVs*
42. *Salesperson of advertising at campgrounds*
43. *Salesperson or manufacturer's rep*
44. *Inspector of RV parks for directories*
45. *Enroller for credit card companies*
46. *Mystery shopper*
47. *Judge at dog shows*
48. *Circus worker*
49. *Booking agent for a circus*
50. *Groom for a circus*
51. *Travel with a carnival: rides, setup, welders, office, mechanics, CDL drivers.*
52. *NASCAR circuit help*
53. *Salesperson of products to businesses (open territories)*
54. *Product installer with changing job locations*

CHECKING PIPELINES

At least one employer who contracts to check pipelines for gas leaks advertises in RV publications. Companies in this industry offer paid training and then you are assigned an area to work in. Many contracts are in metropolitan areas. You could work in one area for several months and then move to another site, depending on what contracts the company has available. In the case where the gas lines are located rural areas, you generally work in teams instead of by yourself. You receive an hourly wage and some travel expense money.

$ **Gas detection worker: Stuart** began work in San Antonio, Texas, after being trained to use gas-detection equipment. Some of the jobs were only about three weeks long. Says Stuart, "It worked out to about $400/week." Since most jobs were of short duration and they only had one car, it was difficult for his wife, **Theresa,** to get a job.

RV CARAVANS

A number of companies put together RV caravans, guiding people traveling in their own RVs to destinations like Mexico in the winter and Alaska in the summer. The caravan companies hire wagon masters to lead the trip and tail gunners to bring up the rear. Compensation depends on the size of the group and your experience. The wagon master (a single or a couple) is like the activity director and tour guide. The wagon master arrives first at each stop to verify arrangements for the RV park and any activities at the location. Being good with people, knowing the area you are traveling (most caravan companies require that you take one of their caravans as a customer first), and being able to handle the unexpected and make it look planned are all desirable traits.

> **Wagon masters and mechanics wanted.
> Lead caravans to Mexico or Alaska and travel free!**

The tail gunner brings up the rear and makes sure everyone gets safely to the day's stop. If one of the rigs has a mechanical breakdown, he stays with the rig until help arrives. Some caravans include paid mechanics as well.

Fantasy Caravans is one company that sponsors caravan trips and hires people to lead them. You must attend their training, plus have been a paying customer on at least one of their caravans. Pay is $100–$150/day and your fees for RV parks, etc. are covered.

DELIVER RVS

RVs have to be transported from the manufacturer to the dealer. Transport companies operate to do that and they in turn contract drivers who work as independent contractors. Owners of trucks capable of hauling 5th wheels and trailers are paid so much per mile from factory to dealer (one-way) to deliver the rig. Also needed are drivers to deliver motorhomes. The earning potential is more than $50K/year for the serious RV worker. A couple can increase earnings if one drives a truck pulling a rig, the other drives a motorhome. To maximize earnings, you need to line up a "back haul" on the return trip. If you can contract with an RV manufacturer directly, you can also increase your earnings.

> **Drive your own pickup.
> Deliver travel trailers and
> 5th wheels to dealers. Earn
> $1200/week and more.**
> *RV Transport*

If you don't want to work full time, transport companies also use RVers who want to make occasional deliveries, want time in between deliveries to sightsee, or prefer to deliver only occasionally. Delivering an RV, for example, could be a way to get up to Alaska in the spring to see the area.

There are a number of costs that go against that income, however. Out of this figure comes your gas, insurance, as well as wear and tear and depreciation on your own vehicle. Your earnings may pay for your truck in a year, but you will also have to buy a new one more frequently.

How to Get Paid $50,000 a Year to Travel is written about this line of work. It's a good guide to understanding the industry and getting started.

$ **Deliver RVs- long haul: Bob & Caren** delivered trailers and 5th wheels for a company. They got paid per loaded mile, meaning one way. Since they had to drive home, that meant the actual pay per mile was half that. In their case, they did not find delivering RVs very profitable once they had paid all the expenses associated with the delivery. Bob and Caren were charged for the first $1,000 worth of damage to the rig, including stone chips, that happened during the trip. If the weather was bad, they would often sit it out because of possible damage.

They could stay in the trailer or 5th wheel at night, but couldn't use the facilities.

$ Deliver RV-short haul: Bob and Andi fell into an RV delivery deal by being at the right place at the right time. The dealer from whom they had purchased three rigs was short on drivers to drive motorhomes back from an RV show. They offered, were hired and that has led to other assignments for this dealer.

Questions to ask

✔ **Driver's license:** Do you need a Commercial Drivers License (CDL)?

✔ **Pay:** Are you paid per mile or per loaded mile of travel? (Both ways, or only one-way) Can you take a side trip on the way? Are you an independent contractor or employee?

✔ **Expenses:** What expenses are you responsible for? Can you use the RV to sleep in or cook in?

✔ **Responsibilities:** What damage will you be responsible for?

✔ **Time frame:** Will you be traveling on a deadline?

Figure how much money you will really make after you pay your expenses, including wear and tear and depreciation on your tow vehicle.

SELL ADVERTISING IN RV PARKS

Several companies produce site maps for RV parks. The production of the map is financed by the sales of ads in the map to local vendors. While the couple or person is working on the map for the RV park, they have a complimentary site. The RV park gets free maps of their park and nearby area to hand out to their visitors. Management of the RV park is asked to recommend businesses for you to call on that their customers would be likely to patronize during their stay. This makes the salesperson's job easier because you have targeted businesses, a name and a referral from the park. Once you've sold all the

> **Travel the areas of your choice selling advertising. Lucrative commission. Leads and full training provided.**

spots, you send camera-ready materials to the main office. You get paid based on the dollar value of the ads you sell (and collect on).

The company may provide you with leads or names of RV parks where a former employee sold ads, or you may have to find some or all on your own. You work as an independent contractor rather than an employee. This gives you some deductions for expenses but you also pay full social security taxes at 15.3% rather than the 50% employee rate. (Obtain Publication 533 from the IRS for an explanation at *www.irs.gov.*)

You can do very well at this type of work if you are good at sales. Like any sales job, it takes a while to develop good clients and to zero in on the parks that pay off. Over time, sales people usually winnow out the low-producing parks and concentrate on a few high-producing parks. One couple worked for a company, then started their own business and now produce the maps from start to finish. Doing the site maps for just a few parks they have developed as clients they make around $40,000 a year and work only a few months.

Related opportunities

$ **Sales or manufacturer's rep:** selling things to RV parks for their use or to sell in their stores.

$ **Campground inspector** for a campground directory.

$ **Represent products t**o other types of businesses as well.

$ **Sell advertising** for a campground guides, like Wheelers Resort and Campground Guide.

$ **Advertising sales: Stuart and Theresa** worked for one of the companies that produces site maps at RV parks. After a training period at headquarters, they were given several leads in the East, parks that former representatives had done maps for. They observed that how successful they were in a park had a lot to do with the support that the park owner gave businesses in town. If the owner encouraged campers to visit them, it was a much easier sell for Stuart and Theresa. Stuart noted that successful reps have a few parks that pay off well in locations they enjoy. He also pointed out that to figure true income you must figure telephone calls, mileage and other expenses against the amount you gross. Since you are an independent contractor you have some additional deductions, but you also must pay expenses with that income.

CREDIT CARD SIGN-UPS

A number of credit cards companies subcontract other companies to sign up credit card holders. Those subcontractors in turn hire workers to go to college campuses, events like golf tournaments, or to shopping malls and airports to do the actual sign ups. Representatives offer the applicant a gift as an incentive to sign up and then are paid an amount per completed application. You can negotiate for per diem travel expenses that might cover your site at an RV park.

College campuses are popular places to sign up applicants for credit cards. Jerry and Nancy worked on a number of campuses; however, they noted that colleges were starting to limit the times credit card representatives could solicit the students. According to a March 12,1999, article in *USA Today*, 'The number of colleges prohibiting credit card marketers from setting up tables on campus has jumped from 45 in 1994 to 155."

$ **Credit card signs-ups: Jack & Lisa** worked for two companies that signed up credit card applicants. They decided from the first they would not work on college campuses. Instead they worked at festivals and golf tournaments. The hard part of the job was lifting 60-pound boxes of t-shirts and standing on their feet 10 or 11 hours a day. Other companies offer incentives like caps or sunglasses that don't weigh as much. Reports Lisa, "The first company paid promptly and gave us an honest count. The other company paid slow and cut out some of the applications if they lacked certain information (a complaint heard from reps working for several companies)."

Questions to ask

✔ **Pay:** Ask how and when you will be paid after each event. Talk to others who have worked for the company.

✔ **Requirements:** Make sure you know exactly what needs to be filled out in order to get paid. Jerry made copies of applications so he could review it with the company if they declined to pay on a particular application, an additional expense.

✔ **Supplies and facilities:** Find out if you will need to haul applications or incentives in your rig or will they be shipped to the site. Do they provide a table for you to use? Will you be outside, possibly in inclement weather?

✔ **Expenses:** Talk to other reps to find out what sort of expense money they receive. Often companies pay for reps to fly to a location and for a hotel, plus an allowance for meals. Use this to negotiate comparable RV-related expenses.

Since several RV workers have experienced difficulty in getting paid fairly and promptly by at least some credit card companies, or at least their subcontractors, I'd advise that you investigate the company and be sure to talk to actual representatives working for this employer prior to accepting a position.

MYSTERY SHOPPERS

A number of businesses contract with companies that provide "mystery shoppers" to rate their customer service. The mystery shopper goes to the store to buy a product or use the service and then rates the business on their experience. Sometimes a pre-visit phone call is required.

According to Dawn Lindsey of Genesis Group, Inc., the average shopping assignment pays $15,

> **Shoppers needed for financial institution in southern CA. Takes about 20 minutes to complete. Requires an interaction with a teller, a new account counselor and a phone call.**

but some pay $25 or $40. One job paid $190 for two-day's work. Some companies provide this service only in their own area, others like Genesis have national clients and assignments in many states. Lindsey says that a shopper can do only one assignment in a particular store and location once every six months, though they often send a shopper in one to three times a month. Notes Lindsey, "Many of our schedulers work only with shoppers who have e-mail. Assignments and reporting is all done using e-mail." Shoppers can let schedulers know their travel plans and can pick up assignments in that area

OTHER OPPORTUNITIES

$ **Judging dog shows** is one of the ways Judy helps subsidize her travel. While she only gets a small fee to judge, the clubs putting on the shows do pay expenses. Prior to hitting the road full-time she often had to fly to an assignment. Now that she is a full-time RVer, she is able to travel in her RV and enjoy the sights along the way.

$ **Sell products at shows:** Work opportunities exist selling products at various shows: RV shows, state and county fairs, home and garden shows and many more. You can sell your own products or work for another vendor. See Chapters 20 and 21, Working for Special Events and Working for Yourself for complete information.

$ **Circuses and carnivals:** Working in a circus may be your dream. Or perhaps you'd rather work on the midway of a carnival. Both move from location to location on their circuits. Most stay in one section of the United States. *Workamper News* usually has an ad for at least one circus; we've seen ads for booking agent and horse groom. Check the Internet for Web sites of circuses and carnivals. Check to see whether you'll be able to park your RV with their trucks, or if you'll have to find a nearby RV park.

$ **Motorsport tracks and circuits:** NASCAR and other motorsport circuits provide employment opportunities. You can get a job going from race to race. The tracks themselves hire workers and race teams. In addition, vendors who sell products at these events may need employees. See Chapter 21, Special Events, for working at individual tracks. Check the Motorsport page at *Workamper News'* Web site *(www.workamper.com)* for potential employers. You will need to check on an individual basis about an RV site at the event and if you will be charged.

$ **Products and services with changing job locations:** Two couples (below) who wanted to make more money and were willing to work most of the year found other opportunities. The first couple answered an ad in the help wanted section of the Phoenix paper and found a high-paying job with benefits that fit their RV lifestyle. Don't overlook "real jobs" that could lend themselves to RV travel.

$ **Installers: Dean and Judy** answered an ad in the Phoenix paper for workers to install bathtub liners in hotels. The company gets contracts to replace the liners in hotels and sends a team to do the job. Dean and Judy were the first RVers they hired. While a room for the installers came with the job, they usually brought their RV and parked it on the hotel parking lot. If they had a job in New York City or another crowded metropolitan area, they might leave their rig temporarily at a park or in storage. This full-time job had benefits and allowed for time off when needed.

$ **Field inspector: Nick's** experience site-sitting construction sites with wife Joanne, led to a job for Nick as a field inspector. In this position he traveled to construction sites making sure company standards were met. The sites ranged from California to Florida. They were in one location from a couple of weeks to several months, depending on the project. Nick's background as an electronics technician and business degree graduate, along with what he learned from site-sitting, served to make him valuable to this company.

Working at a job where you can travel from place to place in your RV combines the best of both worlds: travel and making money. You must factor in your travel expenses to judge your true income and remember that for most commission sales positions, it will take you a few years to build your client base so you have a dependable income.

Notes

*"Integrity is the single biggest character trait needed for
success. Never compromise your integrity."*
The Goals Guy at www.goalsguy.com

Chapter 16
How to get jobs within the RV industry

The RV industry itself provides opportunities for seasonal as well as full-time employment. Sales and repair of RVs, related equipment, plus working for RV clubs and organizations are a few of the ways you could earn money.

JOBS IN RV SALES AND SERVICE

55. *RV salesperson*
56. *Retail salesperson: supplies or parts department*
57. *Quality control inspector*
58. *Technician: walk-throughs with new buyers*
59. *Detailer*
60. *Mechanic*
61. *Service technician*
62. *Service writer*
63. *Lot attendant*
64. *Inside office worker: receptionist, clerk, accountant or bookkeeper, computer workers such as operator, programmer, data input clerk*

RV dealers need many types of workers to sell and service RVs. In areas that attract RVers, the dealership may hire workers to supplement their year-round staff during the busy season. In the sales area, you might find positions both selling new and used RVs as well as selling parts and writing up service orders.

Before the new buyer takes possession, the RV is inspected to make sure all systems are working properly. Then someone conducts a walk-through to demonstrate the systems to the buyer. Larger dealerships may have an individual for each of these duties, while smaller dealerships often combine these tasks with another.

> **Attention—Mechanics and Service Technicians — Seasonal or year-round positions available with large dealership in the Southwest.**

Dealers also have parts and service areas. In the service area, mechanics work on the engine, service technicians work on other systems like refrigerators, water heaters, etc. Good certified mechanics are always in demand, as are qualified service technicians.

The Recreational Vehicle Industry Association (RVIA) offers a Recreational Vehicle Service Technician course at several locations around the country for training in this field. Camping World RV Institute offers similar training. (See **Resources.)**

Where to find positions

To locate RV dealers in tourist or snowbird areas, check in the help-wanted section of the local classifieds or stop by RV dealers with a copy of your résumé and speak to the appropriate manager.

$ RV sales and service:

Page and Ardith worked in Anchorage, Alaska. Their first summer, Ardith got a job at the largest RV dealer in the city, while Page worked construction. Ardith gave walk-throughs to buyers of RVs, explaining how everything worked inside and out. When she wasn't busy with that, she might do detailing or other tasks. Salesmen would often request she perform the walk-through on her days off, paying her $25 out of their pockets for doing so. Their second summer, Page also got a job there moving RVs around the dealership, and they were also permitted to park their RV right on the dealership lot.

Sylvia and Jack have worked at Camping World and for a large RV dealer. Jack is an "Automotive Service Excellence" (ASE) certified mechanic and can also work on repairs to inside systems and structure, making him more versatile. Sylvia enjoys people. She worked as a cashier and as a quality control inspector. As inspector, she gave rigs their pre-delivery inspection, listing what needed to be fixed before delivery. She would also note the condition of rigs before they were worked on to make sure mechanics and technicians cleaned it up properly. The dealer paid for their site at an RV park, a big savings.

Charlie attended a nine-month RV Repair and Maintenance School at Mt. San Antonio College, Walnut, California. Classes covered the basics of repairing and maintaining an RV. Charlie would be able to get jobs part time with this skill and also repair his own rig. **Norma** worked for a temporary agency while he attended school. Later they both worked for a company in Glendale, Arizona, Charlie installing solar equipment on RVs and Norma working in the office.

CAMPING WORLD/RV SUPPLIES

65. *Retail sales clerk/cashier*
66. *Stocker*
67. *Service writer*
68. *Mechanic*
69. *RV technician*
70. *Janitor*
71. *Bookkeeper*
72. *Parts advisor*
73. *Merchandiser*
74. *Shop attendant*

Camping World, with more than 37 locations in 21 states, hires seasonal workers. They hire Multi Location Crew members (MLC) who can transfer on a seasonal basis from location to location. There are several options: work four to six months a year and return each year, work only nine months, or work year round with only one to two weeks between assignments. Positions include retail positions

A world of opportunity! Work for the largest retailer of aftermarket accessories for RVs. Many locations, competitive benefits.

like cashier and stocker, service writer, installer, service technician, janitor, and bookkeeper.

Apply at the nearest retail location, or obtain an employment package and mail to their headquarters.

Camping World operates the Camping World RV Institute in Bowling Green, Kentucky. It offers a nine-week Service Technician course. Camping World's own employees attend this course, but it is open to others. The course is designed to train qualified RV service technicians. Students can take the entire program or individual units.

Other large RV supply stores may also hire seasonal workers. An area like Phoenix, Arizona, which has lots of winter snowbirds, is a good candidate for openings in this area.

WORKING FOR RV CLUBS AND ORGANIZATIONS

75. *Paid staff for office work and club functions*
76. *Editorial or graphic designer*
77. *Webmaster or computer programmer*
78. *Manager and assistant manager for club RV parks*
79. *Activity director for club RV parks*
80. *RV safe driving instructor*

An organization with a sizable membership will need help. Often volunteers help with rallies, events and activities. If you find you enjoy working with a club, there might be a paid position. Most paid positions are offered to volunteers who are willing and able to do the job. For example, Pat and Dennis, members of the Escapees RV Club, worked as volunteers at the club's semiannual Escapade, a five-day educational rally. They were tapped for another club task, then were asked to be directors of the Western Escapade, making all the arrangements, getting volunteer staff and handling details.

> **Exp. manager and asst. manager couples needed. Club-affiliated RV park. Full hookup site plus salary.**

To get a paid position, become involved with an RV club or organization as a volunteer. You will probably get noticed if you work hard, but make your desires known to the manager or the person who would do the hiring. These positions are usually not advertised formally.

OTHER RV INDUSTRY MONEYMAKERS:

$ **Selling RV related products:** solar panels, auxiliary brakes. See Chapter 26.

$ **Providing services to RVers** like carpet cleaning, windshield repair. See Chapter 21.

$ **Selling maps** to RV parks or advertising in RV park directories. See Chapter 15.

$ **Writing articles or taking photographs** for RV magazines. See Chapter 21.

$ **Working as a park manager** or worker at a club or membership RV park. See Chapter 14.

$ **Teaching RV safe driving:** Instructors are hired by RV Alliance America to conduct safety courses for RVers at RV rallies.

You may be able to use skills from your former life that fit some aspect of the industry. You could also get specialized training to qualify for higher-paying jobs in the RV industry. Seasonal work opportunities exist, or you could work full-time if you are looking for a new career!

Notes

*"If you want to be happy for a year, win the lottery. If
you want to be happy for life, love what you do."*
Mary Higgins Clark in On the Street Where You Live

Jobs 81-102

Chapter 17
How to get seasonal federal jobs

SEASONAL JOBS WITH THE NATIONAL PARK SERVICE

81. *Fee collector*
82. *Ranger: law enforcement, interpretation, general*
83. *Visitor Use Assistant*
84. *Park guide*
85. *Maintenance: laborer, maintenance worker, motor vehicle operator*
86. *Positions in biology, archeology and other fields*

SEASONAL USDA FOREST SERVICE JOBS

87. *Forestry aid and technician*
88. *Aids or technicians in archaeology, biological, hydrological, lands, range, real estate and surveying*
89. *Fire suppression worker*
90. *Fire tower lookout*

SEASONAL BLM JOBS

91. *Forestry and range (fire positions) aid and technician*
92. *Material handler*
93. *Motor vehicle operator*
94. *Cartography aid or technician*
95. *Engine operator*
96. *Fire suppression worker*
97. *Horse or mule wrangler*

THE JOB PROCESS: APPLYING THROUGH *USAJOBS*

Our first job on the road was working at Grand Teton National Park. Since then we have worked at five other national parks. We have explored ghost towns and hiked colorful canyons in Death Valley. We parked our RV with a view of glaciers and the Lynn Canal in Alaska. Working in Glen Canyon, we had time to explore little visited ruins of the ancestral Pueblo people. People pay a lot of money to vacation in these places and we were being paid to be there.

Working in the beautiful outdoors and making good money — that combination is possible by working for the National Park Service (NPS) and other agencies that care for our public lands. More seasonal jobs are found with NPS than with other federal agencies, but seasonal positions can also be found with the U.S. Forest Service (USFS) and Bureau of Land Management (BLM).

USAJOBS
The U.S. Government's official site for jobs and employment information provided by the United States Office of Personnel Management.
www.usajobs.opm.gov

Seasonal work can include law enforcement, interpretation, biology, forestry (usually fire suppression), and maintenance. Some clerical, archeology, history, and specialty positions may be hired on a temporary basis, depending on the needs of the agency and the specific location.

For government positions, you will note that each job title is assigned two letters (GS or WG) and a four-digit number for the particular job series. Jobs are either General Service positions (GS) or Wage Grade positions (WG). Wage grade positions are maintenance positions, General Service positions are all the others except supervisory-type positions. The main difference is that the salary scale is different for the two types of positions, WG positions paying more per hour for the same grade level.

The government process can be confusing due to laws that Congress has passed and regulations of the U.S. Office of Personnel Management (OPM). It can seem harder to complete the application process than do the job. But don't let that discourage you. It is well worth wading through the process. If you don't get jobs the first time around, be persistent.

Many parks, as well as other agencies, have been given authority to hire their own employees. Hiring for each position includes these steps:

✔ Jobs are announced publicly.

✔ Applications or résumés must be postmarked and received on time, following all instructions. Incomplete applications, or applications received too late are not considered.

✔ Eligible applications are determined to be qualified or unqualified, that is, they meet or don't meet the basic qualifications.

✔ Qualified applications are rated on a 100-point scale.

✔ A register of the highly qualified applicants ranked with highest listed first is given to the hiring official. In the actual hiring process for seasonal workers, veterans get preferential points or consideration.

✔ The hiring official follows the Rule of Three to fill the position, which specifies how jobs must be offered.

Rule of Three
The hiring official considers the top three scores first. If the position isn't filled, the next highest score is added and the official must offer the job to one of the second three, and so on, until the position(s) is filled.

Special rules for 5- and 10- point veterans apply. If the applicant pool is ten or less, the official can consider any qualifying candidate.

In addition, some national parks fill certain seasonal positions through a nationwide process, instead of local announcements. We'll come back to that later.

Obtaining job announcements
Job announcements can be obtained from OPM's online Web site *(www.usajobs.opm.gov)* through their automated telephone system, touch screen kiosks and by contacting the individual agency location directly. Some positions are "local hire," where job announcements are posted locally and/or through local state employment job service locations. For example, the state of Washington's seasonal maintenance positions are filled through the Washington Job Service.

Jobs are announced all year long. Summer seasonal positions can be announced any time from November to the beginning of summer. Check

USAJOBS frequently. If you are interested in a particular park or location, call them in November or December to find out when they expect to announce their seasonal jobs.

Most seasonal jobs are grades 3, 4 or 5. Some are as high as grades 6 and 7. When searching through announcements, look particularly at positions with those grade levels. You will probably have to open (click on) the actual announcement to determine if this is a seasonal position. (See next page for a "partial" job announcement.)

> **USDA Forest Service Laborer positions WG 3502-02/03 (5). These are full-time (40 hrs/week) temporary positions, not to exceed 1030 hours. Salary $10.45 to $11.45 hourly.**

When you get a copy of the announcement read it very carefully. There is no set format for parks to use. Critical information may be located anywhere in the announcement. If this looks like a position you are qualified for and interested in, then you usually have two to three weeks to mail your paperwork to them. Parks can require either that the application be *postmarked* or *received* by the closing date. Check carefully. If you miss a deadline, your application won't be considered.

The application

In the meantime, prepare your application or résumé. You will make a master and send out copies. Obtain the pamphlet "Applying for a Federal Job" OF-510 from one of the 17 OPM field offices, a federal agency or online. Individual locations such as National Parks and BLM and Forest Service offices should have them, as well as offices of other federal agencies found in larger cities. Use it as a guideline for what must be included. (Job announcements may include this list.)

Although the Federal Government no longer requires a standard application form for most jobs, they do need certain information to evaluate your qualifications. A résumé with the needed information can be used and there is a Résumé Builder at USAJOBS. However, we have been advised by NPS personnel officers that the best application to use, if you can get a copy, is the SF-171 application. Though no longer in print, it includes all the required information, plus is set up to give you

PARTIAL NPS JOB ANNOUNCEMENT

MAINTENANCE WORKER   ✳ **Position**

OPEN PERIOD 09/20/2001 - 10/072001 ✳ **Submit application between these dates**

SERIES/GRADE: WG-4749-05/ ✳ **Job series and grade**

SALARY: $ 12.61 HOURLY

ANNOUNCEMENT NUMBER: ROMO-01-17

HIRING AGENCY: INTERIOR, NATIONAL PARK SERVICE

DUTY LOCATIONS: 0026 vacancies ESTES PARK, CO
          0005 vacancies GRAND LAKE, CO

REMARKS: TOTAL WORK UNDER THESE TEMPORARY POSITIONS IS EXPECTED TO LAST NOT MORE THAN 6 MONTHS (**NTE 1039 WORKING HRS IN SERVICE YEAR**) INCUMBENTS MAY ALSO BE TERMINATED AT ANY TIME PRIOR TO THE END OF THE PROJECTED SEASON. WEEKEND & HOLIDAY WORK MAY BE REQUIRED. SOME WORK IS OUTSIDE IN EXTREME TEMPS & AT ELEVATIONS UP TO 13,000 FEET. **1039 hrs indicates it is a seasonal position, lasting no more than six months.**

CONTACT: Kathy Edward   ✳ **Call for more information**
                  Rocky Mountain National Park

Applications will be accepted from: Open to all qualified persons. ✳ **Permanent positions are generally open only to current government employees. This is another indicator of a seasonal position.**

full credit for your experience and is easiest for personnel and rating panels to use.

If you cannot find a copy of the SF-171, you'll need to use the OF-612 or a résumé that includes all the required informatioin. There are software programs for your computer for the OF-612 and the federal résumé that are available. If you are serious about applying for federal government seasonal jobs, it is well worth using software if you have a computer. One company also includes help preparing the KSAs, described on the next page. (See **Resources.**)

The bulk of the information is your experience. The SF-171 provides "experience blocks" and additional pages of experience blocks can be added. Make sure if you use the OF-612 or résumé that you include month, day and year for all work experience. Do not confine yourself to paid experience. Include any volunteer, community and "life" experiences that apply to the job. For example, in getting a maintenance job, Bill included an experience block about adding onto and remodeling our house.

Completing the KSAs

KSA stands for Knowledges, Skills, and Abilities and is like an interview on paper. It is where you showcase your background and ability to do the job. You are basically telling the person rating your application where on your application to look for the relevant experience. Always submit these if required and, if in doubt, call the personnel number on the announcement. In most cases, if you do not complete the KSA, your application will not be rated beyond qualified

---

**Maintenance Worker WG 4749-05
Rocky Mountain National Park
3 positions in Estes Park
Maximum 1039 hours**

---

or non-qualified, virtually eliminating you from consideration.

In the KSA you want to give enough detail to show what you did, but not every little detail. You may be limited to one page per KSA. Hiring officials have differing opinions on how much detail to include. For example, a standard question on maintenance worker applications is "List the tools you have used, how you've used them and how you have maintained them." You may need to do this for several trades: carpentry, plumbing, electricity, painting, and perhaps others. At one park we were told to list even the most basic tools like hammers and screwdrivers. For a skilled worker, this could be a lengthy list. Another personnel officer told us to list only the more complex tools you could use which demonstrate your skill level in that trade. You'd omit the hammer and include the band saw and router.

JOB ANNOUNCEMENT KSA

Knowledges, Skills and Abilities Required: Applicants will be rated on the basis of education, training, and experience appropriate to this position as identified in the Supplemental Questionnaire (SQ). Only education, training, or experience acquired by the filing deadline will be considered. The SQ questions used to rate applications are based on the following evaluation criteria. PLEASE NOTE THAT APPLICATIONS THAT DO NOT INCLUDE THE RESPONSES TO THE SUPPLEMENTAL QUESTIONNAIRE IN ADDITION TO AN APPLICATION WILL NOT BE CONSIDERED.

Applicants will be rated on the following:
1. Ability to do the work of the position without more than normal supervision (SCREEN OUT).
2. Ability to perform work associated with the following trades: Carpentry, plumbing, painting, custodial tasks, grounds maintenance.
3. Ability to use and maintain tools and equipment required to perform maintenance and custodial tasks.
4. Ability to work safely.
5. Ability to drive safely.
6. Skill in trail maintenance and construction.
(In this announcement, a questionnaire was included for completing these KSAs. Usually you write out your answers.)

Example of a question found on a KSA:

3. KNOWLEDGE OF LIFTING, CARRYING AND LOADING PRACTICES IN PERFORMING LABORING TASKS IN A SAFE MANNER. Give examples of work you have performed that included lifting, carrying and loading cement, rocks and other heavy objects, wheelbarrow use, and describe safe practices you used to prevent personal injury.

Answer: **Glen Canyon NRA:** *Carry heavy bags of litter and debris, including items like refrigerators collected out on the lake from the boat to a vehicle,* *then put in Dumpster. Work with 2nd maintenance worker to load onto dock, lift into truck and Dumpster. Also carry cases of toilet paper, paper towels and other custodial supplies from forklift to loft where stored; inventory and rearrange custodial supplies. Move 50 gal. drums of Simple Green— tilt and roll or use refrigerator dolly. Move couches, refrigerators, beds and mattresses from one location to another. Move bags of cement from pallet to shop or to job site. Wear back brace, lift with legs. Use wheelbarrow to mix and transport concrete. Watch path, check tires prior to use.* **Grand Teton NP:** *Work on putting barrier logs in campground. Roll log close to position, then several workers lift, using legs, wearing back braces. Use wheelbarrow to mix and transport concrete, dirt, gravel when putting in several walkways and driveways. Check area for obstacles, keep load balanced and don't overload.*

The KSA takes a lot of work. A computer comes in handy. Often a KSA will be the same or similar to one you've previously answered. If you have saved them, it is a simple matter of "cutting and pasting" into the new KSA.

Tips for your application or résumé

✔ **Use active verbs:** Use active verbs to describe your work and be specific. Do not use "help" or "assist" without explaining exactly what you did. "Helping" could mean handing the hammer to your husband.

✔ **Refer to handbooks:** Personnel offices have handbooks giving position descriptions. If you are near a federal agency or employment office, ask to look at Handbook X118C for positions you are interested in.

✔ **Study announcement directions:** Read the announcement carefully and modify your application if necessary to address all the elements mentioned in the duties of the position. For General Service (GS) positions, be sure to put the percentage of time for each type of job you did. For example, the position you are applying for requires six months experience in bookkeeping. You were receptionist and book-keeper for a year, doing each job 50% of the time. If you put down 50% you will qualify with six months experience. If you do not put down a percentage, personnel MUST give you 1%. You'd only get a day or two credit.

✔ **Complete application:** Make sure the application is complete.

✔ **Be accurate:** Put your birth year, not this year's date. If you put down this year, your application will be rated unqualified. You must be at least 18 to work in a government position.

✔ **Select grade level:** Fill in the lowest grade you will accept. Some positions are for two grades, such as 4 or 5. Always write in the lowest one on the announcement. If you put a 5 but don't get a good score for that level, you will not be considered for a 4 position, even if you have a top score. Remember, you can always turn an offer down.

> **Bureau of Land Management**
> **Visitor Use Assistant**
> **Series/grade: GS 0303-03/04**
> **Six months position**

✔ **Include your original signature:** Don't sign your original application. Make a copy and sign and date it just before you mail it to make sure it has your original signature. (Sending a copy is perfectly fine and will save you from redoing the application each time.)

✔ **Claim veteran points:** Claim any veteran points you are eligible for and attach the correct forms.

✔ **Include backup documents:** Note the requirements of the position. If college is required for this particular position, attach copies of your college transcript or list of college courses. If you need additional space to list your "Other qualifications" found in Section E of the OF-612 application, you can attach additional sheets of paper.

Tips to help the rating panel give you a high score

✔ **Note employer:** List the name of the employer where you did each task. In the case of a national park, the abbreviation such as RMNP for Rocky Mountain National Park, is fine.

✔ **Application and KSA must match:** When you mention doing something in your KSA, the rater must find reference to it in your application or you get no credit. The KSA should be an expansion of what is mentioned in your application. For example:

Application: "Prepared surfaces, painted and cleaned up."

KSA: "I prepared surfaces by sanding, filling holes with spackle and making minor repairs. I painted interior and exterior surfaces using latex and enamel paint, using brush and rollers, etc."

Then what?

Double check your application to make sure you have left nothing blank. If you are using a résumé, compare it to the requirements listed in the SF-510 pamphlet. Make sure it is signed with an original signature, any other necessary forms or attachments are enclosed, and postmarked by the closing date (or mailed in time to get there by the closing date, if required.)

The process

Your application will go through the process of being determined qualified or non-qualified and then rated on a point score of 100 possible points if it was qualified. Veterans can earn an extra points for being in the military, and additional points if they were injured or disabled. These points are added to their score. Theoretically a veteran could get as many as 110 points, if he or she is a 30 percent-compensable vet.

> **Internal Reveue Service Order Entry Clerk GS 0303-03 Full-time, seasonal position. Primary work season is November through April.**

Once the hiring official has the register, she may contact you first to find out if you are still interested and available before taking the time to do reference checks. Or, you may be contacted for the first time with a job offer. It can be anywhere from 30 to 60 days or even more before an agency makes a decision.

Should you contact the supervisor who may hire you?

Some supervisors don't mind and take that as an indication of interest. Others will let you know where they are in the hiring process, but won't discuss the matter further. Still others feel any contact is improper. If you can obtain the supervisor's name, it doesn't hurt to call and at least find out when he expects to make a decision. If the supervisor seems receptive, you can express more interest and offer information, but play it by ear. After 30 days, you could contact Personnel (unless the announcement says don't do that) and find out whether or not your application was qualified and what your score was. That will give you some idea of your chances.

$ National park maintenance worker: Jim works seasonally for two national parks. Summers he works in maintenance at Glen Canyon National Recreation Area, helping the permanent maintenance workers take care of one of the uplake marina/campground areas. Winters he heads in his motorhome to Death Valley National Park where he takes care of restrooms and lookout points on a 100-mile route.

$ Forest Service workers: Jack and Sylvia worked for the U.S. Forest Service at Mt. St. Helens National Park. They were both offered jobs in maintenance. This is a national park, administered by the U.S. Forest Service.

NATIONAL APPLICATIONS

Several agencies that hire numerous seasonal personnel use a national application process to fill some of these seasonal positions.

National applications for NPS ranger-type positions

NPS uses a national application process to fill some seasonal positions. Not every park uses this process, but included are park rangers (general, interpretation and law enforcement), biological technician, park guide, and visitor use assistant. (At some point, all parks may be required to use this process though at the present time it is optional.) Announcements are still posted on the USAJOBS Web site but they refer you to a different Web site: *(www.sep.nps.gov)*. You apply online. You'll complete a questionnaire with short answers and you have space to post your résumé. You can enter data or update it at any time. All the applications for that park are rated according to the weighted criteria that the park submits; in other words, certain

> **Park Ranger (General and Interpretation) GS 0025-05/07 These will be filled year-round as needed. Go to *www.sep.nps.gov* for current vacancies and to apply online.**

answers may count for one position and not another, depending on the requirements of the particular position. The park receives a register of qualified applicants, ranked on a scale of 100.

You can either look for these positions at *(www.sep.nps.gov)* or through USAJOBS. If you do not have access to a computer, you can call toll-free 877/554-4550 to receive a hard copy application package.

Keep an eye on the USAJOBS announcements to see when the park you are interested in applying for is taking applications. You can also contact that park directly to find out the dates you can apply. Check both Web sites at least once a week so you don't miss the chance to apply to the park where you'd like to work.

National applications for BLM and USFS

Finding seasonal work for the Bureau of Land Management (BLM) and the USDA National Forest Service (USFS) is similar. Sort for those agencies at USAJOBS to find job announcements.

The BLM also has a similar site for nationwide seasonal and temporary positions. They could include aid and/or technician positions in cartography, engine operator, fire suppression, forestry and range (fire positions), horse wrangler, material handling, and motor vehicle operation. See *(www.nc.blm.gov/jobs)*. You can apply online.

The USDA National Forest Service (USFS) lists nationwide seasonal positions at the bottom of their search for jobs on USAJOBS. They refer you to their Web site. *(www.fs.fed.us/fsjobs)* Positions included at this time are archaeology, biological, forestry, hydrological, lands, range, real estate and surveying aids or technicians. Another heading takes you to fire suppression positions including dispatchers and fire tower lookouts. See Chapter 18 for information on working for Forest Service concessionaires.

The U.S. Forest Service hires low-income workers 55-years of age and older for a work experience and job training program, Senior Community Service Employment Program (SCSEP). Wages are at least minimum wage. Training is available in research, clerical, archaeology, maintenance, computers, forestry, and information, as well as other fields. Contact Personnel in individual Forests.

Watching fire towers

Most positions for manning fire towers are through the U.S. Forest Service. Positions are both paid and volunteer. If looking for paid positions, look at USAJOBS site under Forest Service (Department of Agriculture) for forestry technician positions. Check also the "Fire Hire" section of the USFS Web site. You can also contact Personnel at individual forests who will usually put you on a mailing list to receive their job packets. In some cases they may only have one paid position at a particular fire tower, but the spouse could work as a volunteer. Contact the forest you are interested in directly for volunteer positions.

> **Forestry Technician**
> **GS 0462-05 Man fire tower.**
> **Spot, report fires, and direct**
> **firefighters to location.**

$ **Fire tower lookout: John** mans Mount Cooledge Fire Lookout summers at Custer State Park in South Dakota. Every 15 minutes, from 7:30 a.m. to 8:00 p.m., he makes a 360-degree sweep with binoculars, looking for fires. If there are lightening storms, he stays up past their shift in case there is a hit, plus searches carefully the next morning. Smokes can appear immediately, or delay for several days. John has had lightening hit the tower when he was in it. "A tremendous flash and then the crash. Not so good for the eardrums. We can stand on a wooden stool with glass insulators if we want."

If John spots smoke, he uses an Osborne Fire Finder to locate the azimuth direction line of the fire and then guesses the distance out. He tries to locate it to the quarter section of a quarter section. Once the fire is located, he contacts the agency responsible and uses his radio to direct the crew to the scene. During the fire, crews use the tower to relay communications, coordinate helicopter or tanker air drops, order meals and other communications. When nothing is going on, he acts as the communication for Custer State Park (where the tower is located), answering visitor calls, helping staff and directing 911 emergency traffic.

GETTING THAT FIRST JOB

Breaking into a federal agency can be challenging. Once you have some experience and have supervisors within the agency, getting other positions becomes easier. We are assuming, of course, that you did a good job. If your experience does not lend itself to the position you want, you might want to consider volunteering for the agency. This way you get agency experience, which is as valuable and counts as much as paid experience, and you'll have contacts and references.

$ **SCA volunteer: Tammy** was a Student Conservation Association (SCA) volunteer at Glen Canyon National Recreation Area. She received a small stipend and her housing while working as a SCA and did basically the same job as the other interpretative rangers. The following summer, Tammy was hired as a paid ranger at Glen Canyon.

You might also apply for the entry-level positions, even if you would prefer a higher position. If your goal is interpretative ranger, for example, you might apply first as a Visitor Use Assistant. You may be collecting fees or strictly working an information desk, but it is a stepping stone to the position you want. Likewise in maintenance, the lower grade positions or laborer positions can give you an entry to jobs requiring more skill.

Once you have a job or two under your belt, you will find that the agency is like a fraternity. Invariably as you move to a new location, you will find that you and the other workers know some of the same people. Often a hiring official will see a supervisor or reference that she personally worked with and give that person a call first. If you have done a good job, this reference will go a long way.

BENEFITS OF FEDERAL SEASONAL WORK

In addition to higher wages, there are other benefits to working for the federal government. You receive four hours of sick leave biweekly, which can be carried from one seasonal position to the next, and four hours of annual leave. Annual leave for seasonal workers is paid as a lump sum payment about a month after your last day. There are paid holidays and a Sunday differential. The government must pay overtime for any days over eight hours (unless you are on a nine- or ten-hour per day schedule) or for hours over 40 in a week. If your position requires wearing a uniform, you will receive a uniform allowance to help pay for it.

In maintenance, you do not drive your own vehicle or use your own tools. Those are provided. Interpretative rangers may have to drive their own vehicles to a job site, but if they have a job-related assignment, they are usually provided a government vehicle to drive.

If you successfully complete your season and have worked under six months (1040 hours), you will likely get "rehire" status. This means that next year, if you want to come back and the position is still there, you can be rehired without having to re-compete. In other words, you do not have to go through the whole application process again; you'll complete a short rehire form. Since there is no guarantee you will be rehired, to be on the safe side, you may want to send in another application anyway. (That way you must be considered.)

ARMY CORPS OF ENGINEERS
98. Park or gate attendant at COE projects (bid)
99. Hired worker for bid-winner at project

The Army Corps of Engineers (COE) obtains park and gate attendants through a bid system to perform much of the day-to-day operations at its more than 460 water resource projects and more than 4,000 parks. When a contract comes up for bid, you must write or call for a bid package, which contains the scope of the job and prior successful bids. The package is comprehensive, detailing what the job entails, hours, what you must provide and what the agency will provide. If the successful bid is not included, you can call the contact number for that information. If you are the lowest qualified bidder and win the contract, you work as an independent contractor, not an employee. Contracts vary tremendously so you need to read them quite carefully. The successful bidder usually has the option to renew without competition for a second and third year, at the government's option.

Each year, *Workamper News*, in its September/October issue, lists projects that will solicit bids as well as those seeking volunteers. The annual issue also explains how the bidding system works in more detail, as well as things to consider before placing a bid. They recommend you visit the park manager at the project(s) you would like to work.

Things to consider:
✔ **Number of days and hours coverage:** Some contracts require 6-7 days of coverage.
✔ **Tasks:** Some contracts mix maintenance and gatekeeper work.
✔ **Shared or solo:** Will you be sharing duties with another couple?
✔ **RV Site:** Does the contract come with a full hookup site?

✔ **Previous bids:** Check the previous bids for what the hourly rate actually was. To underbid or match that bid, will you be working at less than minimum wage?

✔ **Taxes:** As an independent contractor, you must pay estimated taxes and full social security tax.

✔ **Visit first:** If at all possible, visit the site first so you can better assess what the position requires.

Since 1998, Department of Defense regulations require contractors to register with the Central Contractor Registration and obtain SIC, CAGE Code and DUNS numbers. These numbers are explained and can be obtained over the Internet. Instructions are included in the bid package.

$ Gate attendants:

Dave and Linda successfully bid on a Corps of Engineer contract at Lake Shelbyville, Illinois. The request for bids was listed in *Workamper News*. As gate attendants, they were required to be bonded. They bid the jobs at around $6.00/hour each but know people who have gotten more and some who have gotten less. Their particular position did not require any maintenance, nor enforcing any of the rules, which they prefer. Says Dave, "We worked in a nice, spacious fee booth that's equipped with air conditioning, computer, TV, phone and radio communications with the rangers."

Richard and Juli bid successfully for gate attendant positions at The Greers Ferry Lake Project in Arkansas and worked there for two summers. He would rate his experience an "8" on a scale of 1 to 10. Advises Richard, "Read the scope of work very carefully in order that you fully understand what you are agreeing to do. Contract requirements, as well as successful bid prices, can and do vary dramatically between and even within districts." He strongly recommends visiting the parks you are considering bidding for, on a weekend during the busy season. Amenities can vary considerably even within a project area.

OTHER FEDERAL SEASONAL WORK

100. Post office help at Christmas
101. IRS tax season workers
102. Census takers

Other federal agencies may also have temporary work. The Post Office hires additional workers at Christmas. The Internal Revenue Service (IRS) hires more workers to process tax returns in some locations. At Census time, thousands of workers are hired to prepare for and administer the census.

VOLUNTEERS

Most federal agency sites are searching for volunteers. Usually a certain amount of hours per week is required for your free site. At some locations, particularly if amenities are limited, you might get a stipend in addition to your site. For more information, see Chapter 22.

When you work in a national park or forest for a government agency, you are paid well and work in a beautiful or interesting location. More effort is required in the application process than for other seasonal jobs, something not every RV worker is willing to do. For us the payoffs are worth the extra effort.

Notes

"Attention is like a searchlight; when its beam is spread over a vast area, its power to focus becomes weak, but focused on one thing at a time, it becomes powerful. Great men [and women] are men [and women] of concentration. They put their whole mind on one thing at a time."
Paramahansa Yogananda

Jobs 103-133

Chapter 18
How to get jobs working in the outdoors

For many RVers, getting to spend time in the beautiful, less crowded areas of our country is high on their list of RVing goals. In addition to seasonal opportunities with the federal government, there are many other ways to work in the outdoors. Main employers are concessionaires and state and local agencies. Second only to working in RV parks, this type of employment is most likely to have RV sites available for their workers. If not included, sites are usually at a very low cost compared to staying in a regular RV park.

WORKING FOR A NATIONAL PARK CONCESSIONAIRE

103. *Hotel jobs like front desk clerk, housekeeper, back office*
104. *Restaurant jobs like cook, waiter/waitress, hostess, cashier*
105. *Retail store jobs like cashier, stocker*
106. *Warehouse jobs*
107. *Tour or recreational activity jobs like tour guide, boat or raft operator, boat rental agent, boat instructor, golf course-related worker*
108. *Gas station jobs like cashier, mechanic, attendant*
109. *Medical clinic jobs like receptionist, nurse, physician's assistant.*
110. *Campground host*
111. *Maintenance worker*
112. *Rodent and pest control worker*
113. *Shuttle driver*
114. *Helicopter pilot or worker for flight-seeing operations*

WHAT IS A CONCESSIONAIRE?

Concessionaires are private companies that have been granted the right by a government agency to provide visitor services on government land. Many larger national parks have concessionaires. The Forest Service has turned over many of its campgrounds in many forests to concessionaires. And state and local agencies may also have private industry provide visitor services at their parks.

National parks

In large parks such as Yellowstone, concessionaires provide visitor services like hotels, stores, gas stations, and recreation within its boundaries. Private companies bid on the rights to offer services and in return are regulated by the National Park Service and pay a percentage of their profits to the government. These concessionaires hire many more people than the government agency. Some concessionaires like Aramark and Xanterra Parks and Resorts operate in more than one national park, making it possible for employees to transfer easily to another location.

Concessionaires generally begin hiring for summer work in January and February. A number of concessionaires are listed on the Coolworks seasonal work Web site. You can find out the types of jobs available and often download or complete an application. Contact information is listed there too. Several concessionaires advertise in *Workamper News*.

> **Earn a free houseboat vacation! Work at beautiful Lake Powell.**

If you don't have access to a computer, you can contact the national park where you'd like to work and ask them for contact information for the concessionaires in their park. Call or write for an employment package.

Mind-boggling job possibilities!

To give you an idea of job possibilities, think of all the jobs associated with hotels and retail operations like gift shops, grocery stores, gas stations. Then remember that in some parks you can raft down a river, rent a boat and go fishing, or ride horseback. In recreation areas, the emphasis is on water activities. At Glen Canyon National Recreation Area on Lake Powell, for instance, houseboat rentals are popular. Seasonal workers are hired to clean, maintain, and rent out houseboats, instruct customers, and sell fuel. Jet skis and motorboats are also rented. At the

Grand Tetons as well as Lake Powell, tour boats offer scenic boat rides. At Death Valley, there is a golf course. All these activities require workers.

Advantages and disadvantages

Concessionaires generally do not pay top wages but instead offer a number of benefits to employees. These might include:

✔ **Low-cost housing,** dormitory or RV site.

✔ **A low-cost meal plan** is often available. At Death Valley, at this writing, employees get two free meals a day, paying just for dinner.

✔ **Employee discounts** may be given on purchases. Often use of recreational facilities is permitted either at no charge or for minimal cost when available. Employees who work the entire season at Lake Powell get a one-week houseboat vacation, paying only for fuel and insurance. Boats can be rented during the season when available for the cost of fuel and insurance. At other locations, raft trips, horseback riding and other activities would work the same.

✔ **Spend time** in a place that tourists spend big dollars to visit is the *real* benefit that most concessionaires tout.

Wages are the big drawback. Most pay around minimum wage, though skilled jobs like mechanics could pay higher. Supply and demand affects wages. I've seen housekeeping pay up to $8.00 in some locations because they had a difficult time getting enough workers.

> **Golf in beautiful Death Valley!**
> **Furnace Creek Resort now**
> **hiring for winter positions.**

Ask questions

Be sure to check when and how you will earn overtime pay. Certain seasonal businesses do not fall under the Fair Labor Standards Act, and therefore regulation is up to the state. Arizona is a state that does not have a minimum wage or overtime law. Certain Arizona employers may not have to pay any overtime. Some states don't require seasonal employers to pay overtime until an employee has worked more than 48 or even 52 hours. You can bet they will work you right up to that limit.

As with every employer, it is important to clarify conditions of employment, your site, what you pay for (utilities or other) and how much, days off, etc. At Lake Powell, they changed the meal plan so a nonworking spouse could not eat in the dining room. During the busy season you might be expected to work six-day weeks at Hamilton Stores in Yellowstone. Is that acceptable? Will you and your spouse have same days off? The time to negotiate is *before* you accept the job, not after you arrive and find conditions not to your liking.

Tour boat: Chuck worked on the tour boat going to Rainbow Bridge for Aramark at Lake Powell, Utah. He usually worked four long days with three days off. Each morning, he cleaned the windows, then cleaned and vacuumed the inside. Next he picked up the lunches. The tour lasted most of the day. They would gas up and then, if enough people had signed up, get ready for the evening tour. "If we had an evening tour, we turned right around again. The crew did get a free box lunch, and if we went out again at night, we'd get another box lunch for dinner! It cut down on the food bills. If we went out at night it could be a 14-hour day." One captain let him pilot the boat occasionally.

Concessionaire employees: Jim and Barb have worked for several national park concessionaires doing a variety of jobs. These have included gas station attendant, housekeeping, gift shop sales, houseboat instructor and boat rental agent, reservationist, bookkeeper, tour guide and bus driver, and front desk clerks. Some of these positions have been more enjoyable than others, often depending on the quality of management. They note, "Sometimes even the good places will have a bad season if there is a lot of turnover in key concession and park management staff." They also advise not taking a supervisory position before working as an entry-level employee. This gives you a chance to look at how the company works and the problems faced by first-level supervisors.

Boat instructors: Bob and Michelle also worked at Lake Powell for Aramark. They corresponded with their manager and were offered a position via e-mail. The perks were a real attraction. They were able to raft down the Colorado south of the dam at no cost. They joined the Fishing Club and could rent a speedboat for the day for a total of $20, including a full tank of gas. (With 40 gallon tank and gas at $2.40/gallon, this was a great deal.) The employer set up trips for employees to neighboring parks such as the Grand Canyon and Bryce Canyon. At the end of the season, they were eligible for a houseboat rental for a week for the cost of insurance and fuel. Aramark's cafeteria offered discount meals cards, purchased with pre-tax dollars, another savings.

Mixed reviews

Experiences working for concessionaires are mixed. If the company has trouble filling positions or has high turnover, you may be asked or even expected to work more hours than you want. If you were not interviewed by your supervisor at the time of hiring, you should insist on talking to him or her since the supervisor may have different ideas on how to run the department than what you thought had been agreed upon. On the bright side, in many cases employees of concessionaires come back year after year and their co-workers are their summer families.

In working here, as elsewhere, you need to know your limits, make sure you and your employer are clear on them and then stick to them. Be realistic. Concessionaires are in business to make a profit and most cut costs to the bone. Then sometimes

> **Work in Sequoia Nat'l Park!**
> **Cheerful, outgoing couples**
> **with RV needed, April-Oct.**

you need to remember why you are working here — to be in a beautiful place and earn enough money so you can live this great life on the road. As Jim and Barb say, "Remember, it ain't a career, and your home is on wheels!"

NONPROFIT ASSOCIATIONS

115. Clerk or cashier selling books and other items at an NPS visitor center
116. Warehouse worker
117. Bookkeeper/orders

In most national park visitor centers and national forest offices, books and other educational items are offered for sale in the visitor center or a separate store by a nonprofit association. Congress established these to support education, research, and other programs for the benefit of the Park or agency. They often publish books and literature for visitors, using the profits to support programs in the Park. For example, since its inception in 1932, the Grand Canyon Association has provided the Park with over $15 million in aid.

Most associations hire seasonal help. They usually pay more than entry-level concessionaire jobs. Contact the national park or forest to get contact information for its nonprofit association and apply to them directly. They may have an arrangement with the agency or concessionaire for an RV site or other housing.

> **Work at the Grand Canyon!**
> **Sell educational items at**
> **visitor centers.**
> **Must have own RV.**

$ **Nonprofit association managers and sellers: Jim and Alida** have worked two summers for the Grand Canyon Association. Answering an ad in *Workamper News,* they sold books and other items at one of the five locations in the Park. Their second season they were promoted to managers of the store at the north rim. "We share space with the Park Service so we help answer visitor questions and assist Rangers in administering the Junior Ranger program to young visitors ages four to fourteen. We have enjoyed this part of the job too." They are asked all sorts of questions about lodging, hiking trails, scenic drives and about other parks and attractions in the greater Four Corners region. As managers their duties have expanded to include inventory, the daily remit of funds, and ordering, among others. An RV site is included, as well as free membership in the Association, which entitles them to discounts on books and merchandise here and in many other national parks. They are also eligible for a sales and end-of-season bonus.

NATIONAL FOREST CONCESSIONAIRES

118.   *Camphost*
119.   *Maintenance worker*
120.   *Manager of several campgrounds*
121.   *Holder of concession rights to run a FS campground*
122.   *Forest fire support worker*

The U.S. Forest Service has contracted the running of many of their campgrounds to private individuals or companies. These concessionaires in turn hire personnel to manage and maintain their campgrounds. A concessionaire might have one campground, several, or campgrounds in more than one national forest.

If you work for one of these contractors, you will have a site (not all have hookups) and certain duties in return for a salary or hourly wage. The company may provide uniforms and tools, but in many cases you provide your own vehicle and tools. The concessionaire will provide supplies like toilet paper if your duties entail stocking and/or cleaning restrooms.

Concessionaires advertise for employees in *Workamper News*. I have seen at least one concessionaire in Quartzsite, Arizona, recruiting for employees during the big shows in January and February. You can also contact a U.S. Forest where you'd like to work to find out if they have a concessionaire running their campgrounds.

Experiences of RVers working for forest service concessionaires have ranged from "wonderful" to "the pits." Again, it is important to clarify just what will be expected of you and what the company will provide. As an employee, you may have to draw some lines so you are not taken advantage of. Since you will likely be parked right in a campground, visitors think you are available 24 hours a day. You might feel that if you don't do something, it won't get done. However, you could end up spending a number of hours at no pay.

$ Paid campground hosts:

Laurel and Dave worked as campground hosts in the Stanislaus National Forest in California. The woman who hired them was the concessionaire for two campgrounds. Laurel collected the fees, making three rounds during the day, and another just after sundown. When the campground filled, she hung up the "Campground Full" sign. In between, she raked out campsites, cleaned fire pits, stocked the pit toilets with toilet paper, and kept it litter-free. The hardest was reminding people about the rules, particularly that dogs must be on leash. Says Laurel, "I would have to remind people more than once, especially if it was a tiny dog that everyone thought was cute and, of course, would never bite anyone." Once a week she cleaned the pit toilets. Dave's primary job was picking up the garbage from the Dumpsters twice a week (in a real garbage truck), and taking it to the landfill. He also maintained the water pumps, ran the backhoe, and did odd jobs as they occurred. Between them they earned $1,500/month plus propane and a site with sewer and water but no power. They worked 8–10 hours/day and had two days off a week.

Ellie and Weldon worked for the concessionaire as campground hosts at Odell Lake in Oregon. Their campground had twenty-two campsites, a five-slip boat dock with ramp, a fish cleaning station and eight pit toilets. Each day they opened the pay envelopes at the self-pay station, then later went to each site, collecting from anyone who had not paid. They also cleaned the restrooms and the fish station. The day after a camper vacated a site, they cleaned out the firepit. Weekends were busier. They were on duty by 5:00 a.m. to control the parking of boat trailers and turning people back when the lot was full. Twice a week they picked up trash around the sites, picnic areas, and parking lots as well as the boat dock area and along the roads.

They were issued a golf cart, buckets and litter sticks and had plenty of cleaning supplies, toilet paper, paper towels, etc. Says Ellie, "Our supervisors were great, bringing our supplies each week when they picked up our accounting sheets."

They were paid $500 a month and received a full-hookup site and propane. Since there were only two full-hookup sites in the district, it was on a first-come, first-served basis. The other campground hosts had to use the public toilets or drive to the RV dump in town every couple of weeks.

"It was a good experience, totally stress-free and fun," recounts Ellie.

$ **Helicopter tour pilot: Terry** flew helicopters in Vietnam and had his helicopter pilot's license. He had also gotten his commercial rating, which is necessary to transport passengers. Ultimately he wanted to fly for one of the companies that contracts with the Forest Service to fight forest fires. To get some current flying hours, he worked for one of the helicopter tour companies at the Grand Canyon. A Web site *(www.justhelicopters.com)* lists jobs for helicopter pilots and mechanics. In talking to a company with a listing, he heard about this job. Pay was very good and Terry was paid for his shift whether he flew customers or not. **Heidi** worked for a stable that rented horses. She was able to ride, which she enjoys, and earned tips from riders she took out.

Other Forest Service concessionaires

The Forest Service also contracts other tasks such as firefighting support services. These companies provide water trucks, mobile laundry units, shower trailers and other miscellaneous items and services. Pay for fire camp work usually starts at about $100 a day with more for workers having advanced skills like a Commercial Drivers License (CDL). You need to be flexible and available on short notice. How much you work depends on how busy the fire season is that summer. Contact either a regional or local Forest Service office to find out contact information for the contractor.

Companies also contract with the Forest Service to supply commissaries at the base camp for fires. Firefighters can buy items like toothpaste. One enterprising fellow printed 50 t-shirts of the fire and set up a stand outside the firefighters' base camp. He was sold out in a matter of hours.

Become a U.S. Forest Service Concessionaire

If you are interested in bidding on campgrounds yourself, ask to be put on the mailing list for requests for bids so you are notified the next time campgrounds come up for bid.

> **Fire support workers needed for fire season.**

Intermountain Region USDA Forest Service: *"Concessionaires are selected from competitive solicitations that are offered from time to time. Most concessionaires operate under a special use permit from the Forest Service for one to five year periods. To obtain such solicitations (commonly called a prospectus) when they are offered, one needs to get in direct contact with the specific National Forest in which one is interested."*

STATE PARKS

123. Ranger- present programs, enforce rules, give tours
124. Maintenance worker
125. Fee collector
126. Visitor center worker
127. Campground host
128. Park aide
129. Operator of a hunting check station

Don't confine your search for an outdoor job to the federal level. State parks also hire seasonal workers. These positions could be in fee collection, maintenance, and visitor contact positions like a visitor center or interpretive activities.

> **Washington State Parks hiring Park Aides. 3-5 month temporary positions.**

Pay at state parks may be less than at federal parks but is usually above minimum wage. Contact a state or district office, or a state park directly for more information. You may also find information at a local job service. (See **Appendix 4** for state park contact information or check government pages of local phone books.)

$ State park workers:

Ron & Val have worked several summers at Cherry Creek State Park in Colorado. Ron worked in maintenance and Val worked most recently supervising fee collection. Working here let them spend time off with their grandchildren. Since they want to see other parts of the country, they usually work here alternate summers. They do such a good job, they can come back anytime they want.

John & Ginger have worked at Custer State Park in South Dakota several summers and also at Anza Borrego State Park in California. At Custer State Park, John manned one of the fire tower lookouts, sweeping the skies regularly for sign of fire or lightening strikes. When there were fires, John worked at the communications center, helping staff, visitors and directing emergency traffic. Ginger worked at one of the entrance stations as a crew leader. Housing is provided at $3/day for RV site or other housing, if available, and the park provides a pass good to all area attractions like Crazy Horse Memorial and Black Hill Playhouse stage productions.

Nick and Joanne also worked at Custer State Park one summer. Joanne worked at the entrance stations and Nick worked with another man heading up the seasonal campground attendant staff. The highlight for Joanne was helping out with the annual buffalo roundup. She got to play cowgirl, driving buffalo into the chutes for their inoculations. Whoopee!

COUNTY AND CITY PARKS

130. Maintenance worker
131. Fee collector
132. Visitor contact personnel
133. Operator of a concessionaire activity

Local agencies at the county or city level are also potential employers. Sharon & Ron ran a concessionaire operation for a county park in San Diego County.

$ **County park concessionaire: Ron and Sharon** worked at Lake Miramar in San Diego, California for the concessionaire. They worked four days a week, with three days off to explore area attractions. They had a variety of duties: sell bait and tackle, sell lake permits, operate the snack shop, rent boats. They ran it like it was their own business, doing the ordering, completing paperwork, and making the deposits. For their rig, they were provided a shaded, fenced enclosure, close to the stand.

GATEWAY TOWNS

Many businesses locate just outside national parks in gateway towns, providing tourist services and activities. Rocky Mountain National Park in Colorado, for example, provides no housing and very limited food services within the park. Visitors obtain these at Estes Park and Grand Lake. See Chapter 19 for job ideas in these towns.

When Bill got a job at Rocky Mountain National Park I needed to find a job. We arrived the first of June and nearly every business had a Help Wanted sign in the window. If you wanted to work in retail, you could have had a position that day! I worked first for Safeway and then gave tours at the Stanley Hotel.

This category of jobs is huge and usually comes with either a free or low-cost RV site. Many job sites are in beautiful places where you can enjoy outdoor activities like hiking, boating and fishing. While pay tends to be lower, you may have a skill that is worth more (or in demand due to short supply) or be willing to take on management responsibilities.

Notes

"It's only work if you'd rather be doing something else."
Flagstaff Tea Party newspaper

Jobs 134-215

Chapter 19
How to get jobs at resorts and travel destinations

Where tourists go, there are jobs! Resorts, amusement parks, and tourist destinations hire workers during busy seasons for their operations. Whatever your skill or desired type of work, you can likely find a position. It's fun being behind the scenes and paid to work at a place where vacationers spend big bucks to be there. Often you can take advantage of perks or local discounts.

RESORTS

134. *Hotel and motel jobs like front desk clerk, housekeeper, child care provider, maintenance, waiter/waitress, chef, hostess, back office worker, security person, bellman, cashier, retail clerk, bartender*
135. *Activity director or recreation leader*
136. *Restaurant jobs like wait staff, hostess, chef or cook, busboy, bartender*
137. *Gas station jobs like cashier, mechanic, attendant*
138. *Retail jobs like cashier, salesperson, stocker or warehouse worker*
139. *Grocery stores jobs like cashier, bagger, stocker*
140. *RV parks jobs like registration and reservation staff, cashier, maintenance, groundskeeper, store clerk*
141. *Adventure/recreation tours: jobs like raft guide, stable hand, tour leader, reservations staff, cashier, mechanic, maintenance worker, driver, loader or packer*

142.   *Golf course jobs like golf pro, shop staff, groundskeeper, ranger/starter, mechanic or helper for care of golf carts, snack bar attendant or food preparer, customer service representative*
143.   *Marina jobs like boat rental agent, boat instructor, mechanic, fuel attendant, cashier*
144.   *Personal services like hair dresser, nanny or childcare provider, computer programmer, handyman*
145.   *Shows: usher, ticket sales staff*
146.   *Flight-seeing or helicopter tour operation worker*
147.   *Costumed character at amusement park or clown*
148.   *Dog musher/guide, dog caretaker*

Towns that attract a heavy tourist population during a season often need workers to supplement the year-round work force. You may or may not be provided housing by the employer; it depends on the type of work and how scarce housing is. In some towns, like Jackson Hole, Wyoming, and Skagway, Alaska, housing is in such short supply, or so expensive, that some employers must provide a place for employees to live if they want to have enough workers. Resort towns are similar to concessionaires in a national park (Chapter 18), only on a larger scale; think of all the services that are required — hotels, shops, gasoline, restaurants, and activities — to name a few.

> **Resort in Cody, WY Send photo of self and RV. Bonus for working full season.**

If a resort area interests you, call, write or e-mail the local tourist information center for a trip planner or brochure. Call or write the Chamber of Commerce or check its Web site for a listing of members who are then potential employers.

Housing

It is important early in the application process to find out about housing or RV sites. You may be on your own. If that is the case, ask the employer if he has contacts in town or is able to get you a discounted site. The earlier you make arrangements, the better your chance of lining up something. Obtain a list of RV and mobile home parks from the Chamber of Commerce or visitor information center.

You might also be able to find an RV spot if the employer has none available. Here's what some working RVers have done:

✔ **Employer:** One couple, working for a bed and breakfast in Moose, Wyoming, helped put in hookups next to the garage so they could park onsite.

✔ **Mobile home park:** Another working RVer couple in Ft. Meyers, Florida, found a low-cost site close to work in an older mobile home park. Resort RV parks were charging up to $800/month.

✔ **Friend or relative:** If you have a friend or relative in the area, you might be able to work out something with them. Be polite guests and pay your expenses.

✔ **Campground host:** Still another couple camp-hosted at a small nearby park, working ten hours/week on their own schedule, leaving time for jobs in town.

✔ **Membership park:** A couple, working at Disney World, worked out an arrangement at their membership park to work in exchange for their site.

✔ **Elks Lodges:** Members of Elks Lodges can park their RVs at a reasonable rate, at lodges all across the United States.

✔ **Talk to locals:** Get to know the locals and ask around. If there is a park that already has a campground host but is a good prospect, express your interest and keep in touch. We did just that in Alaska and half-way through the summer took over the position at a National Park Service campground with a stipend.

$ **Tourist town: Jay and Sandy** were headed west when they stopped in Tombstone, Arizona, for a few days. They loved it. Says Jay, "You can watch Wyatt Earp and the boys shoot it out three times a day. You can have a drink in an authentic and haunted saloon and sit and talk to anyone from a tourist from Ohio to a Hell's Angel from Liechtenstein. We were going to stay three days and it turned into months, perhaps the most fun we've ever had." Sandy quickly got a retail job and negotiated higher pay and benefits too. Jay happened to mention at the local corral that he was from Montana. They assumed he knew a lot about horses (he knew a little) and after an informal chat with the boss, he was hired on by the Tombstone Stage Lines. He got people to ride the stage, giving them a history lesson. Soon he was driving the stage too. Reminisces Jay, "One of the men I met had the distinction of being the only man in the U.S. convicted of a DUI on horseback. It made the national news!"

To escape the summer heat, Jay and Sandy found jobs on *Coolworks.com* as Jeep tour drivers up in the Grand Canyon area. They negotiated a free RV space, an increasing pay scale, and received tips. They worked here for two seasons. "Good money, good people, but Tusayan is a small town that hosts five million people a year. Not the best living conditions but we were able to save money."

DUDE RANCHES

149. *Wrangler*
150. *Wait staff*
151. *Cook*
152. *Housekeeper*
153. *Maintenance worker*
154. *Child care provider or worker*
155. *Office worker*
156. *Airport driver*
157. *Laundry worker*

People who want a western experience on a ranch can visit a dude ranch. According to The Dude Rancher's Association, their 100-plus member ranches hire seasonal employees for positions such as wranglers, cooks, wait staff, housekeepers, maintenance workers, child care providers, and office workers. Northern ranches do their hiring for summer positions from November to April. Southern ranches do their hiring for winter positions from August to October.

> **Dude Ranch**
> **One couple from May-Sept.**
> **Positions in housekeeping,**
> **cooking, maintenance.**

Jobs on dude ranches typically involve hard work, long hours and participation in evening guest activities such as line dancing, hayrides and staff talent shows. They also require good people-skills and an ability to live and work well with others. Employee housing is provided, but you would need to check on an individual basis whether they would have a space for and would permit an RV parked on the premises.

$ **Dude ranch workers: Rich and Fran** found a summer job at a family-owned dude ranch in Colorado. They saw a brochure about the ranch, looked it up on the Internet, and then contacted the owners directly. Rich worked as head of maintenance doing everything from painting to feeding the pigs. Fran worked in the office handling the phone and registration, as well as marketing and writing ad copy. They were asked to stay through a Colorado winter and work the following summer, so were given a two-room cabin to stay in for the winter. They also got three meals a day and a good salary and their RV site for summer. Notes Fran, "Most dude ranches house employees in cabins. Our employer put in an RV site, and after having a positive experience with RV workers, has added two more RV sites for employees."

BED & BREAKFASTS (B&BS)

158. *Housekeeper*
159. *Breakfast preparation like cook , wait staff*
160. *Guest check-in and greeting*
161. *Vacation relief staff ormanager*

B&Bs may hire help during their busy seasons. Duties could range from food preparation, housekeeping, checking in guests to any and all of the above.

Owners may hire people to run the B&B on a temporary or full-time basis. Some people make a living as innkeepers, taking over for owners when they want to get away for a while. You can take classes and obtain a free "aspiring Innkeepers" kit through the Professional Association of Innkeepers International (PAII). As a member, you can be listed at their site as available for short term or substitute assignments. (See **Resources.)**

$ **Bed and breakfast workers: John and Kay** spent two summers working at a B&B near Grand Teton National Park. They assisted the owner in all aspects of running it. They were able to park their RV right by the garage after John put in the connections. They had actually applied to an ad in *Workamper News* to work at a nearby RV park. The park owner passed their résumé on to the B&B owner and they were hired.

SKI RESORTS

162.   *Lift ticket seller*
163.   *Ski instructor*
164.   *Child care provider or worker*
165.   *Driver*
166.   *Retail clerk*
167.   *Food related jobs like cook, wait staff, busboy, bartender*

Don't rule out ski resorts. They too provide plenty of jobs if you don't mind the cold. For ski buffs, these jobs could get you a free season lift ticket or at least a discounted one. Janice and Gabby have worked in a number of winter resorts so they could ski. See their story in **Appendix 10.**

$ **Ski shuttle drivers: Joe and Terry** worked for two winters in the Aspen/Vail area for Colorado Mountain Express. They drove ten-passenger vans between Aspen and the Denver airport after a one-week training period. They worked four-day weeks, usually 10-15 hours/day. The job averaged $10/hour plus tips, which could be quite good. The second season they averaged between $12-14 hour with tips. Says Terry, "The job had minimal supervision, which appealed to us." Loading luggage on the van was hard work, but they enjoyed playing tour guide and answering visitor questions. They received uniforms, discounted seasonal ski pass and a 10% bonus for staying the whole season. They found their job at a job fair held by Hamilton Stores, their summer employers, in Yellowstone National Park.

AMUSEMENT AND THEME PARKS

168.   *Food service worker*
169.   *Ride operator and mechanic*
170.   *Game operator*
171.   *Retail sales clerk*
172.   *Campground worker*
173.   *Tram driver*
174.   *Costumed character*
175.   *Maintenance and repair worker*
176.   *Interpreter*
177.   *Tour guide*
178.   *Warehouse worker*

Like resort areas, amusement parks hire lots of seasonal workers. They may also contract out services and that person or company then hires employees. *Workamper News* has ads for some amusement parks or else contact the park you are interested in directly. The park may not have an RV site, so clarify that first. If you have to pay resort prices for a site in town and commute to the park, you may not reach your money goals. On the other hand, if this is something you have always wanted to do and it is worth the cost to you, go for it!

> **Get in the fast lane with our cool summer jobs!**
> **Job Fair**
> *Legoland, CA*
> **Where work is play!**

$ **Amusement park workers: Ray and Pat** worked at Adventureland in Iowa, after responding to an ad in *Workamper News*. They both started out in food service. When an opening occurred in maintenance in the campground, Ray transferred there. The RV park provided for employees for a fee was one of the nicest they have stayed in while working, with large blacktop sites, trees and some sites with telephone hookups. A heated pool and clubhouse were available. They enjoyed their jobs and found Iowa an interesting state to explore.

CRUISES AND LAND TOURS
179. *Housekeeper*
180. *Food preparation and wait staff, bartender*
181. *Lecturer or performer*
182. *Dance host (also ambassador or gentlemen host)*
183. *Recreational leader for gym, golf, dance, exercise, children's activities*
184. *Bus driver/guide*
185. *Customer service or shore representative*
186. *Bus maintenance and cleaning worker*

Cruises transport hordes of visitors to Alaska in the summer and to warmer destinations in the winter. They hire many workers, particularly in housekeeping and food service. From talking to those who have tried it, cruise work is not the glamour job portrayed on the *Love Boat*. Unless you are part of the professional staff, you are not allowed to be on deck during off-duty times. One cruise line we contacted told us they did not allow husband-wife teams to work on the same ship. A nice benefit, however, is that seasonal cruise employees are eligible for free cruises after a certain number of hours worked.

If you do have an area of expertise and could provide educational talks, you could offer to exchange your services for passage. One of my former supervisors who works for the National Park Service does this each year.

> **Work for the leader in the Alaska cruise industry! More than 1500 summer seasonal workers needed.**

Single men are in demand as dance partners on cruise ships and at least nine cruise ship lines seek them out for employment. Another RVer is a golf pro and found that cruise lines hire golf pros on their Caribbean cruises. One line has an artist-in-resident on board their cruises. If you have something to offer and you enjoy cruises, check it out.

A better way to earn a cruise might be to work for a cruise line's land-based operations. Both Princess Land Tours and Gray Lines of Alaska offer free cruises after working approximately two summer seasons.

In Alaska during the summer, Princess Cruises and Holland America/ Gray Lines operate hotels and provide many tours for their passengers at each port. Seasonal workers are hired to greet the ships and load passengers on their buses. Bus drivers transport cruise passengers to their local tours or between Anchorage and Skagway by bus to continue their tour package. Both companies hire hotel staff and have a domed train running between Anchorage and Fairbanks via Denali National Park. Training and testing to get your Commercial Drivers License (CDL) is provided for bus driver trainees before starting work. Some work locations do have RV sites for employees for a fee.

 Cruise line land tours: Bill, my husband, briefly worked part-time for both Princess Land Tours and Gray Line in Skagway, Alaska, before finding a full-time job he liked. At Princess he greeted passengers getting off Princess cruise ships and directed them to the proper bus for their tour. He and the other customer service reps collected paperwork from the drivers used for paying tour vendors. Bill enjoyed working with the mostly college-age kids and talking to visitors. Had the position been full-time, he might have stayed on the whole summer. "Princess bus drivers made excellent tips," observed Bill. His very brief stint with Gray Line was prepping buses for the day's tours.

CASINOS
187. *Blackjack dealer*
188. *Food preparation and wait staff*
189. *Bartender*
190. *Security*

Every once in a while, bells clang and the one arm bandit pays off. Or someone hits big at black jack. To be part of that excitement may be on your wish list. In the long run, you'll probably end up with more money working as a dealer than being on the other side of the table.

In gambling towns like Las Vegas and Laughlin, nearby community colleges offer courses in becoming a dealer. Most courses last 4–6 weeks and cost from $300–500. Weldon, who completed a dealer's course in Bullhead City, across the river from Laughlin, Nevada, explains what happens:

The only casinos in Laughlin that would take break-in (new) dealers were Circus, Circus, Edgewater and Riverside. When your instructor feels you are ready, you go to casinos and "audition," or try out. They will either hire you or tell you that your game needs more practice. When you are hired you go on the Extra Board, which means that you work at their whim, maybe only one day a week or every two weeks as needed. At certain times of the year they need more Extra Board than others. The time on the Extra Board can be anywhere from three months to a year. Once you get off the Extra Board, you will probably be working five days a week and will know what your days off are, though they'll vary from week to week.

You are observed constantly and rules are very stringent. Explains Weldon, "You can't be self-conscious because you have floor people watching the dealer, you have pit bosses watching the floor people, you've got the "eye in the sky" watching the floor people and the pit bosses and the dealers, you've got floor surveillance that is watching everyone, so it's very security-conscious."

Pay is minimum wage plus tips. At some casinos you are eligible for health insurance after three months.

To earn more, you need to learn more games. First are usually the "circus games." These include Pai Gow, Let it Ride, War, Caribbean Poker, and Baccarat. To learn Roulette you can go back to school or learn on your breaks and after hours. Weldon learned on his breaks. After a while, they pulled off the regular Roulette dealer and gave Weldon a try.

Weldon also notes that going to other states from Nevada is easier than the other way around. In Nevada you "toss cards," or deal hand-held games and also deal from a four to six-deck shoe. In most other states dealers use only the shoe. Weldon remembers first learning to toss cards: "You hold the cards in your left hand, then flick a card with your finger to get it to spin. I had cards going through the Venetian blinds, underneath the table, everywhere."

Advises Weldon, "If you want to deal and travel around the country, go to Nevada, learn to do the hand-held games as well as the shoe. Get that Nevada gaming card, because with that you can get in anywhere."

Casinos also hire workers as change people, cashiers, in food service, security and housekeeping.

A FEW RESORTS THAT HIRE RV WORKERS

Wall Drug and similar
191. *Retail clerk*
192. *Maintenance worker*
193. *Cook*
194. *Cafeteria worker*
195. *RV park-related worker*
196. *Usher*
197. *Stocking and inventory clerk*
198. *Demonstrator of old time crafts like blacksmithing, weaving.*
199. *Driver of a horse-drawn buggy or wagon.*

Drive west on I-90 through South Dakota and see sign after sign announcing Wall Drug. In the 1930's the owners put signs out on the highway advertising free ice water, which brought in the customers. Now on peak summer days, Wall Drug can have 15,000 to 20,000 visitors a day and is a tourist destination in its own right. They hire a number of RVers and students to work in the cafeteria, retail sales and maintenance. Pay is a little above

> **Portray a character of the historic gold rush!**
> **Work in the beautiful Black Hills of South Dakota.**

minimum wage, overtime is paid after 40 hours. In addition Wall Drugs provides uniforms, gives an employee discount and has low-cost RV parking in their trailer park. Half of the trailer park fee is returned if you stay the whole season. Other similar resorts also hire workers but may have a different focus or theme such as history. RVers with the ability to do old-time crafts like blacksmithing or weaving may find work dressed in period costumes.

Disney World

200. *Merchandise host/hostess, cashier, roving vendor, display merchandiser*
201. *Attractions host/hostess, tickets host/hostess*
202. *Culinary: wait help, bussing, steward, cashier, host/hostess, cook*
203. *Housekeeping: custodial, room attendant, houseman, laundry worker*
204. *Life guard, pool maintenance worker*
205. *Transportation: parking lot guide, boat pilot, tram driver*
206. *Custodial attendant*
207. *Third-shift custodial (heavy duty industrial cleaning)*
208. *Hotel-related jobs: front desk, bell services, housekeeper*
209. *Office, technical and reservations: front office receptionist, reservationist*
210. *Wardrobe: costume assistant*

Disney World recruits full-time RVers. They appreciate their work ethic and offer full-time, part-time and seasonal positions at The Magic Kingdom, EPCOT, Disney MGM, Disney's Animal Kingdom, plus their resort hotels and the three water parks. The water parks tend to hire more seasonal workers in the summer. Disney's Wide World of Sports also employs workers.

Employees are known as "Cast Members," and their uniforms, which are provided, are "Costumes."

$ Disney workers:

Bill and Jean worked at Disney World for three and one-half months one winter. They stayed at a membership park nearby, and Jean worked about 17 hours a week there for free rent. At Disney World they each worked from 24 to 45 hours a week, but after the first of January, hours were cut. Before that you could work as many hours a week as you wanted. Jean notes, "Disney is very flexible; some RVers worked only three weeks." One perk they enjoyed was seeing the dress rehearsal of the Christmas shows and parade, complete with snow and no one else around. They also watched the Spectro Magic parade from the balcony of the Castle and met Tinkerbell. Jean worked in Costumes, taking care of Cinderella and the girls. As a result she got autographed shirts for family who visited.

Paul and Stephanie worked for Disney MGM for two winters. Explains Stephanie, "The first winter we worked in crowd control for the Indiana Jones show. We would greet the guests, answer questions, get them into the theater, pack the theater (fit as many guests in as possible), and then get them out of the theater and prepare the theater for the next show. We also worked on some special assignments like crowd control when the Disney Christmas Parade was filmed for TV.

"The second year the Indiana Jones show was shut down for rehab so we worked some holiday specials, "Honey I Shrunk the Kids" and "Hunchback of Notre Dame." Paul also worked the Indiana Jones Street Show and Star Tours. The diversity the second year made our jobs even more enjoyable.

"It is wonderful to be able to meet people from all over the world and help them have a magical time. The perks at Disney are wonderful, which brings a lot of RVers to Disney. What some RVers forget, however, is that this is a real business and you are taking on a real job when you work for Disney."

Working for the Mouse —Stephanie Bernhagen © 2001

Disney World in Florida employs between 51,000 and 57,000 people.
Disney offers several categories of employment:

food and beverage	culinary
custodial	merchandising
attractions	transportation
housekeeping	office, technical, reservations
life guard	

Employees are called "cast members" and uniforms are called "costumes." This goes hand in hand with cast members being "on stage" when they are in the park. When "on stage," Disney has set guidelines cast members must follow.

There are three levels of employment—full-time, part-time and seasonal. Full-time positions include paid benefits. Part-time positions, referred to as Casual Regular (CR), do not pay benefits. CR's must be available two days a week and must not exceed 24-hours a week for more than six months of the year.

Seasonal positions, referred to as Casual Temporary (CT), are employed during peak tourist season. These positions may last from a few days to a few months. CRs and CTs receive overtime when they exceed eight hours in a shift.

A benefit to being a cast member is the ability to enter Magic Kingdom, Epcot, Disney MGM and Animal Kingdom with your ID. For cast members who work six months of the year or less (CTs), you must work 300 hours for two consecutive years to receive a limited-use Main Gate Pass, which allows you to take a limited number of guests into the parks a limited number of times per year. CRs receive Main Gate Passes after 90 days and may keep their IDs and gate passes all year.

Cast members who are hired before the end of October normally receive a Christmas package that includes discounts in stores and restaurants on Disney property, plus guess passes. Throughout the year other specials for cast members are offered.

The hiring process starts with an interview with a Casting Representative. Once hired, you attend a class called Traditions, which provides background on the Disney Corporation. Next you attend a training day for the park or resort area where you will work. Finally you are trained in your specific area.

Jay and Sandy also worked at Disney World in outdoor foods, opening up Animal Kingdom. "How often do you get to be an Opening Crew Member in a new theme park for Disney?" enthuses Jay. "We signed on and had a blast! We worked with kids young enough to be our own, laughed everyday we went to work, shared the magic, played for free all over Disney and met others older than ourselves who had found this great place to work in the winter months."

Dan and Sue also had fun. Quips Sue, "They paid me to stand around and talk to strangers! It was perfect." Sue's job entailed standing outside with one of the characters, such as Winnie the Pooh, Tigger, Woody or Buzz Lightyear, and making sure the guests got autographs and photos. Her job included "holding the Disney line," saying things like, "Piglet is not here today because he and Eyore are off looking for Eyore's tail." Dan, having previous experience with boats, trained for and then piloted 600-passenger ferry between the Transportation Center and the Magic Kingdom.

Skip and Virginia enjoyed working at Disney World, but they did learn that you have to be insistent on where you want to work. Food and Beverages were short-handed so their recruiter steered them to that department. They would have preferred Attractions. Foods involved standing (not leaning) for your entire 6- or 8-hour shift, though Virginia eventually was able to work as cashier where she was able to sit. She said they would choose Custodial if they came back because you work more independently and have more opportunities to talk to guests and make their visits more enjoyable. She recommends that if you don't like your position the first week, go back to Casting and ask to be reassigned.

Branson, Missouri

Silver Dollar City in Branson, Missouri, as well as other employers in Branson, make it attractive for RV workers. If you like country western shows, here's your opportunity to see your fill for almost nothing. Shows cost from $19–$40 so this is quite a value. Many establishments give generous discounts to full-time and seasonal employees in town.

Working at Silver City: CC likes to go to Branson around Christmastime for the Veteran's program and to see the Christmas lights. Before he began working during his visits, he would stay 7-11 days and see three shows a day. Working, he can stay six-seven weeks for the usual price of one and one-half weeks. At that time of year, there are also free or discounted programs for veterans, which cuts his expenses.

Silver Dollar City is a family destination and a big seasonal and short-term employer. It has a live play, and multiple live entertainers that put on shows throughout the day. It also has crafter demonstrations and several restaurants as well as an RV park.

During one visit CC applied at both the largest theater and largest employer and got job offers from both. Each provided free or standby passes to 99% of the shows and attractions and a 10-50% discount at most restaurants. The wages were at $6.50 and $7.00/hour, which about covered his meal expenses, while his badge and pay stub saved him $40-$75 per day in show fees. CC only worked about 15 hours a week, leaving plenty of time to see the shows.

WORKING/VOLUNTEERING OVERSEAS

211. *Teacher overseas*
212. *Support worker at Antarctica*
213. *Short-term laborer*
214. *Manager for RV park in Mexico*
215. *Property caretaker*

Many countries have laws restricting foreign workers, so earning money to support yourself overseas is difficult unless you have a particular skill that is in demand. An RV couple who are psychologists were able to work in New Zealand and other countries because their position couldn't be filled by psychologists within those countries.

Teaching overseas is possible with a college degree. You do not have to have teaching credentials for most positions. Agencies of the federal government also hire teachers for overseas locations and for other positions. See the USAJOBS Web site at *(www.usajobs.opm.gov)*.

> **Teach English in Japan!**
> **BA/BS degree required.**
> **Japanese language ability**
> **not required.**

For a real adventure, consider working in Antarctica! Ratheon Polar Services is the primary support contractor for the National Science Foundation's U.S. Antarctic program and hires approximately 800 employees to work in various jobs. Most jobs are from four to six months during the *austral* (southern) summer season, from October to February. Check their Web site for positions needed.

You may also be able to pick up laborer jobs in other countries like harvesting crops, waitressing, bartending or other similar positions.

Caretaker Gazette has overseas exchanges and caretaking positions listed. Occasionally you'll see an ad for Mexico.

> **Couple wanted to manage 30-space luxury RV park in Cabo San Lucas, Mexico. Full-time. House with utilities plus salary.**

Volunteering in another country can be a way to see it. Although you may be charged a fee and be expected to pay for your travel expenses, the cost is usually lower than a tour or vacation to the same country. In many overseas volunteer positions, you can stay with a local family and get a whole different experience. See Chapter 22 for ideas and resources.

$ **Overseas teachers: Bill and Marna** left their motorhome on the mainland and took teaching jobs in Japan for a year. They taught conversational English in a junior college in Hiroshima. They were furnished a house and car and only worked 14 hours a week. They had plenty of time to explore the area and visit hot springs. Bill climbed Mt. Fuji. Since they were already in Asia, after their assignments ended Bill visited China and Marna traveled to Indonesia.

Resorts and travel destinations are good places to look for jobs. There is a high demand for seasonal workers. Many jobs are closer to minimum wage but that isn't always the case. There's a reason people like to go to these places and they pay lots of money to do so. You'll get paid for being there.

Chapter 20
How to find temporary jobs
and work at special events

Temporary jobs can be found through a number of sources. Agencies specializing in placing temporary workers are an excellent source for these jobs. Holiday season work can be found through agencies and local classified ads.

TEMPORARY JOBS

216. *Office work: clerical, accounting, computers*
217. *Factory or assembly work*
218. *Professional*
219. *Construction work: carpentry, plumbing, electrical, sheet rock, block work*
220. *Product demonstration*
221. *Tax season work: accounting*
222. *Tax season work: clerical*
223. *Substitute teacher*
224. *Temporary medical jobs: nurse, therapist or physician*
225. *Fruit or vegetable picker*
226. *Work during a grape harvest: grape sampler, weigh master*
227. *Worker for wheat harvest*
228. *Corn detassler*
229. *Agent at reservation center for campgrounds.*
230. *Flagger for highway construction projects*
231. *Deliver telephone books*

HOLIDAY-SEASON WORK

232. *UPS driver or warehouse worker for UPS*
233. *Christmas retail salesperson*
234. *Santa Claus at mall or department store*
235. *Bell ringer collecting donations*
236. *Fireworks sales*
237. *Post office temporary worker*
238. *Post office contract worker*
239. *Baggage handler for cargo aircraft*
240. *Flower shop helper—deliveries or make arrangements*

Temporary agencies

Temporary agencies provide other employment opportunities. According to the American Staffing Association (ASA), more than 2.9 million people per day are employed by staffing companies and 90% of companies use temporary help services. Employers, not you, pay the fee to the agency.

If you have a trade or professional skill, the wages earned can be much better than many temporary or seasonal jobs. The average assigned worker earns more than $10 per hour according to ASA. A quick stint with an agency might add a bit of traveling cash to your pockets.

> **Costumed characters**
> **$8/hour**
> **Fun, Fun, Fun!!!**
> Manpower

Usually you find temporary or staffing agencies in mid-sized to larger towns. There are specialty agencies that place only accounting or financial type workers, others place strictly day labor. Nurses have their own agencies and physicians can work as a "locum tenen," getting placed at hospitals and practices around the country.

There are agencies with branches in cities throughout the U.S. and world like Manpower or Adecco. If you register and work regularly through these agencies, you may be able to get health insurance and other benefits. You won't need to re-register or take tests when you move to a new location. Your records are available by computer or can be transferred.

How to locate agencies

If you are planning to stay in a location for a while and want to find a temporary agency, you can look in the employment section of the classified ads and in the yellow pages. The American Staffing Association Web site allows you to search for member agencies in each state. Many have their own Web sites. You can also search the Web sites of more well known agencies like Manpower, Adecco, and Ameritemps for locations in your area. You can even make contact ahead of time. Larger newspapers are often found on the Web. Yellow Page directories are listed on the home page of most search engines. Before traveling check ahead to find out possibilities.

Unless you have previously registered with another branch of that agency, you will need to go to the office with your résumé, references, and copies of any professional or trade licenses. You may need to take a test. Most agencies that place secretarial help require a typing or word processing test to determine words per minute.

How it works

✔ **Landing assignments:** You will need a telephone number where you can be reached. A cell phone or telephone hookup where you are staying is more convenient, and a pager even better. A voice mail number can work, however, you should plan to call in at the times they might call to see if you have an assignment. Most agencies line up their temps the afternoon before the assignment, but they may also have last-minute cancellations or requests, so if you are eager for work, an early morning call as well is a good idea. The agency will give the job to the first person they can contact so keep that in mind.

✔ **Hourly pay:** You can also specify a minimum amount you are willing to work for. You don't want to price yourself out of the local job market, but you also want to cover your costs.

✔ **When paid:** Since you are employed by the agency, not the employer you work for, you will be paid by the agency, usually once a week.

✔ **Your choice:** You can also decide whether you want a specific assignment. Perhaps the location isn't convenient or they want too long a commitment. If you have a doctor's appointment scheduled, for example, you can let the agency know you won't be available that day. Keep in mind that if you turn down or are unavailable for too many assignments, you are less likely to be the worker who gets the call.

✔ **Free training:** Since 90% of staffing companies provide free training, check into acquiring new skills to make you more valuable.

✔ **Reference letters:** You can ask for reference letters from both the agency and employers at job sites.

The nice thing about temp work is that you can set parameters. If they are realistic and you are a good worker, you'll get plenty of assignments. If they are too high or you aren't getting good evaluations from employers, you won't get many calls.

What you can earn

Many companies today are turning to the temporary market to find employees as a cost-saving measure. They pay a little more to an agency, but save on benefits and paperwork. They can build up their work force when needed and don't have to worry about paying unemployment when the work force drops. Plus, the agency does the screening for them and if one worker isn't what they are looking for, they can request another.

> **IMMEDIATE OPENINGS**
> **Housekeeping, production,**
> **assembly, shipping & receiving**
> tops® Staffing

What you earn will depend on the position and the job market. Check the help wanted ads and talk to the agency counselor to find out the going rate for your type of work. The agency will give you an idea if your desired earnings are realistic.

If there is more than one staffing or temporary agency in the area, check to see if any offer benefits such as health insurance, vacation or sick leave and what the requirements are.

$ **Temporary workers:**

Wally is a trained electrician. **Patsy** saw an ad on the Web site Monster.com *(www.monster.com)* for a special project. One hundred electricians plus numerous helpers were being hired for a six-month project. Helpers were being paid $12/hour. Says Patsy, "Don't overlook this resource."

Skip and Virginia worked at temporary agencies while parked at their son's home. They only took jobs paying at least $8/hour. Advises Virginia, "There's nothing that says you can't sign up with more than one agency at once." Their first agency was not a match; the other was great to work for. Skip signed up for "light industrial," and Virginia for clerical. Both were given some basic tests. After Skip's first assignment at a warehouse, Virginia added light industrial work to her job availability — more exercise than sitting at a desk. She ended up working first for an interior design company filling in for the receptionist (boring), then for a company that managed seven parking garages and later for a small manufacturing company. One advantage of this type of work, they could decline an assignment on days they had medical appointments scheduled.

$ **Tax season worker: Bea** has been working for H&R Block during tax season for eleven years, six while full-timing. H&R Block has an initial training for tax preparers, taking place over three months. She also took other pre-work training required of first year preparers. Each year thereafter, about 40 hours of training is required, learning about changes and more advanced tax law. Tax preparers earn a commission on each tax return they prepare and she figures she is now averages around $29/hour. Bea has transferred twice to a different location after a telephone interview.

While in Kissimmee, Florida, husband **Ken** ended up working for a rental equipment repair place. He found that position by calling places in the Yellow Pages after a promised job at Camping World fell through. They had gotten an RV spot near Camping World, so did have to get a second car.

Related sources

Locate temporary job openings through local classified ads and employment publications in larger cities; search Internet job sites using the terms "seasonal" or "temporary."

You may be able to register and use the State Job Service, particularly if you apply for unemployment.(See state government pages in the telephone book.)

Things to consider

There are a couple of drawbacks to temporary work that may affect you.

✔ **No RV site:** The agency will not provide an RV site. You may have other options besides a costly RV park. If you are lucky enough to have relatives or friends with room in their driveway, like Skip and Virginia, this is a low-cost option. You will want to pay them for any expenses incurred such as electricity or telephone calls. If you don't have this option, check with mobile home parks. They often have a lower monthly or long-term rate than RV parks and can accommodate an RV or two. You might also be able to combine a temporary job with a site-sitting or house-sitting assignment. While I worked for an accounting firm during tax season, Bill volunteered for the Forest Service for our site.

✔ **Transportation:** If both you and your travel partner are working, transportation to job sites may be a challenge. If you have to purchase a second vehicle or pay for bus fares, this will lower your wages.

✔ **Attire:** Some types of work require professional attire or at least not jeans. You don't have to be a fashion plate, just neat and clean. When I worked during tax season as a secretary at an accounting firm one winter, I told the gal I was working for that my wardrobe was limited because of my RV lifestyle. I went to a local thrift store and purchased a couple of skirts plus a nice blazer, all for under $10. When finished, I donated them back to the thrift store, since I didn't have room to carry them.

Other seasonal temporary work

Other industries hire workers for their busy season. Some ideas:

$ **UPS:** United Parcel Service hires drivers and other workers during the Christmas season. Check at their Web site or locally in employment guides or help wanted ads in larger towns. UPS hires about 95,000 seasonal workers nationwide.

$ **Airport:** Ramp agents and other additional help for loading and unloading cargo aircraft may be needed during the holiday season. Check local employment guides or help wanted ads.

$ **Retail sales:** Christmas-help in retail stores is always needed. You might also find a gig as a Santa Claus.

$ **Charities:** Paid bell ringers for Salvation Army and other charities collect money at Christmas.

$ **Postal work:** A test is required but this is another source of work during the holiday rush.

$ **Post office contract work:** Post offices often contract out hauling mail from one post office to another. The contractor might need holiday or vacation relief help. Check with the Postmaster to find out the name of the contractor.

$ **Tax season:** Accounting firms hire tax preparers and clerical help for approximately three months.

$ **Public and private schools:** If you have a college degree, you might be eligible to substitute in public or private schools. Pay varies by school district.

$ **Fruit or vegetable picking:** Usually strenuous work, but it doesn't last long. Apple picking involves less bending and stooping than most harvesting jobs. You can usually find at least one employer in *Workamper News* recruiting workers.

$ **Fruit processing:** Work in a processing plant in Florida. Jobs include the Juice Room, retail, order-taking by phone, shipping and warehouse, food service.

> **Substitute teachers needed. $125 per day Hawthorne School District**

$ **Wheat harvest:** Follow the harvest in several plains states. A Commercial Driver's License is helpful.

$ **Corn fields:** Earn $1,400 to $2,200 in three weeks detasseling corn in the Midwest.

$ **Campground reservations:** Work in a call center for camping reservations like Reserve America.

$ **Flagging** for highway road construction projects. You need to take a short training course. The Laborers' International Union of North America includes these workers. If no union hall is located in your area, check with the road construction company to find out who does the hiring or provides flaggers.

$ **Delivery of telephone books:** Use own vehicle to deliver locally. Check local papers or call phone book company to find out who delivers.

$ **Selling fireworks:** Sales of fireworks in roadside stands.

$ **Delivery of flowers:** Before holidays like Mother's Day and Valentine's Day, flower shops often need extra help.

$ **Temporary fruit processors: Ken and Jan** worked for Sun Harvest in south Florida. Ken worked in the Juice Room, keeping an eye on the machinery that squeezes and bottles the juice. Jan took orders by telephone and typed them up. Says Jan, "Patience and tact is a must." Besides working in the mail order department, Jan worked at other times in retail or serving ice cream cones.

$ **Apple picker: April** worked picking apples one fall in Washington state. This company only hires retired RVers and even has an RV park with full hookups for them. April described the work as strenuous and not for anyone with a bad back. However the owners included time in the schedule to take tours and explore the area. Pay depended on the variety and quantity picked. April found the listing in *Workamper News.*

$ **Winery workers: Charlie** worked two seasons for Beringer Wine Estates as a grape sampler during the fall harvest. His job was to drive to designated grape vineyards and pull off a sampling of grapes so the lab could determine if they were ready for harvest. The first season **Norma** got a position through Manpower Temporary Agency in Sonoma. The second season she was hired on as a weigh master for Beringer. Using a computer program, trucks were weighed both full and empty to figure tonnage delivered. In 1999/2000, Charlie was paid $12/hour, while Norma earned $11 and had lots of overtime. The season is approximately three months long. They were able to park their RV at a family member's house.

$ **Sell fireworks: CC** saw an ad in the *El Paso Times* newspaper for selling fireworks for Fourth of July. Working about two and one-half weeks, you could earn between $3000 and $4000 dollars. Since it is illegal to sell fireworks within the city limits, stands ring the city. The stands are adjacent to a power pole for light and for electricity for your RV. The seller gets 20-30% of total sales.

CONTRACT WORK AND TEMPORARY WORK FOR PROFESSIONALS

241. *Computer project consultant*
242. *Technical writer*
243. *Engineer*
244. *Medical short-term assignment: nurse, therapist, physician*
245. *RN or LPN at family or children's camp*
246. *Teacher*

Contract work

If you have specialized computer skills, Web design skills, copyediting or technical writing skills, or other "high-tech" skills, there is whole market out there for your services. You may be able to do all or part in your own RV, in which case you will need to be where you can get a telephone line. You may travel to the company or provide your services via the Internet. You will also work as an independent contractor, rather than an employee. It does mean you will need to pay full social security tax. And if you get your jobs through agents, they will collect part of your fee as their cut. (See discussion of employee vs independent contractor in Chapter 13.)

$ **Computer consultant: Byron** is a traveling computer consultant. He has taught himself several computer programs which he uses to help clients either onsite or from his RV. He specializes in Crystal Reports development, MS Access development, and Interactive Voice Response development. Most of the time Byron finds his jobs through one of hundreds of consulting companies. Byron sets his fee, normally at least $60/hour, and the consulting company adds their fee on top of that. He needs a computer, the development software (tax deductible as a business expense), and telephone contact if he is performing the work in his RV. Onsite, he uses the company's equipment. Says Byron, "It's truly fun to be able to go, at a moment's notice, anywhere in the country, to get the best-paying opportunities which wouldn't be available to those with more traditional lifestyles."

$ **Contract consultant: John** has associate degrees in Journalism and Broadcast Electronics and finds short-term work as "technical editor," "technical writer," and "technical illustrator." He earns from $20 per hour in communities with a moderate cost-of-living and $45 to $100 per hour in major cities with high costs of living. He mainly uses Monster.com for finding assignments since it is one of the few online job search sites that does not limit your search to one city or state. If he wants to work in a particular area, he locates an agency there and sends his resume. *C.E Publications Directory of Contract Service Firms* is a good resource, as is the *U.S. Register of Technical Service Firms* available from National Technical Employment Services. Agencies like Manpower, Aerotek/Maxim Group and CDI have offices nationwide and assignments for contract consultants. In any case, the employers pay the fee. One advantage of being an RVer is that if you travel more than 50 miles from your domicile you are often eligible for per diem pay and deductions, and no lease hassles if your job ends early. Some employers also reimburse travel expenses to get there. Says John, "There are literally millions of high-tech consultants worldwide, working in a multi-billion dollar industry."

Training

If you don't already have these computer or technical skills, you can acquire them as Byron did. You can take an online computer course if you will have Internet access while the course runs. Some courses are also self-paced where you can work at your own speed and take the final exam whenever you are ready.

For those interested in copyediting, *The Well-Fed Writer*, by Peter Bowerman, offers guidance in getting started. (See **Resources**, Ch 21.)

Temporary work for professionals

Professionals like accountants, nurses and physicians can find agencies that specialize in their discipline. During tax season, many accounting firms hire extra tax help: tax preparers and clerical and data-entry workers.

Travel nurses and physicians take short-term assignments. For nurses, according to wannabee RVer Maryanne, "Critical care, such as cardiac ICU or surgery, or ER or neonatal ICU are the most in demand, because there is currently a shortage of nurses in those areas in particular."

$ **Registered nurse: Mary** is an RN and accepts assignments through an agency in Salt Lake City. **Tony** picks up one or more jobs where Mary's assignments are. While in Page, Arizona at Lake Powell, Tony put together a series of ways to earn money. He did grant writing, tutored a woman on computer software, sold advertising, did substitute teaching, taught at the community college, and guided float rafts from Glen Canyon Dam to Lee's Ferry. Mary receives a housing allowance when she takes a temporary assignment and this pays for their RV site.

$ **Nurse without a Purse: Dave,** who calls himself the *Nurse without a Purse,* has worked as a nurse at a number of children's camps, sometimes staying in his RV. He also took a year off to work on a wagon train that went from Pennsylvania to Florida and back. Dave says the nonprofit camps pay the best and have better food. He rates the Girl Scout camp food the best, although he had to help with the dishes.

SPECIAL EVENTS

247. *County or state fairs*
248. *Sports events*
249. *NASCAR events in a support capacity: security, parking, cleanup, souvenirs, food service, admissions, tickets.*
250. *Home and garden shows*
251. *Shows in Quartzsite, Arizona*
252. *Golf tournaments*
253. *Events at stadiums or convention centers*
254. *Race tracks: horse, dog races*
255. *Swap meets: booth sales, parking*

Home and garden shows, county and state fairs, RV shows, festivals, dog shows, golf tournaments are all possibilities for picking up some short term work. Often exhibitors hire local help onsite for these events. Some will advertise in the local newspaper, but most hire a few days before the event right onsite. The most effective way is to stop at booths and ask if they are hiring. You will probably get minimum wage unless you have a special skill. If you work in sales, you might work on commission or a combination hourly wage plus commission.

A number of RVers have found that selling products at fairs and other shows is lucrative. You can work for someone else on commission or sell your own product. You are often able to park your RV where you sell though you may pay almost as much as a regular campground for it. See **Resources,** Chapter 20, for information on locating shows and products to sell.

> **Ushers, ticket-takers & Guards**
> **$8-$16/hr Del Mar Fair**
> **$6.25-$8.50 Padres Baseball**
> Elite Show Services

If you are interested in selling at shows for an employer, one good way to find an employer is to spend some time at fairs and shows. See what products seem to be selling well. Talk to workers in the booths when they aren't busy and find out more about the industry and their product. Ask other vendors about the reputation of perspective employers. Some employers are difficult to work for and have a bad reputation.

In working the show circuit, you usually start out doing the less lucrative shows. As you get experience, you'll find opportunities to move into more lucrative shows. Since employers nearly always have someone working the better shows, it can be a matter of waiting for turnover.

Also use your network to find other RV workers who are making money this way. You can learn a lot about the questions to ask and situations to avoid. Some considerations to get you started:

✔ **Driving distances and costs:** What area of the country will my shows be in? Consider that it will cost you each time you drive from show to show. A route that minimizes driving distances is preferred.

✔ **Delivering product to shows:** Will I need to carry product or will you ship it? One RV couple found they had to buy a van to carry all their product; another was able to work out getting shipments to the site.

✔ **Booth set-up:** Who is responsible for setting up the booth and getting it there? Will I need to carry that in my rig from show to show? Consider the space it will take up, plus the weight, which adds premature wear and tear to your rig.

✔ **Compensation:** How will I be paid? If another worker also shares the booth or a related booth, will we be splitting the commissions or each keep what we earn. Consider the abilities of this other salesperson. Will you come out with less if commissions are split?

✔ **RV site:** Will I be able to park on site and will there be any charge? If there is charge, who will pay for it?

✔ **My needs:** Does the show schedule meet my needs — for income, time off, and travel locations?

Related

$ **NASCAR races** also provide temporary employment. *Workamper News* advertises event employment in their publication. You might also be able to follow the circuit, working at each event

$ **Quartzsite, Arizona** is the scene of one of the world's largest flea markets. Over one million RVers spend some time here in winter. Quartzsite has acres of shows and flea markets in January and February. Some vendors hire help. Besides working in sales for a vendor, RV workers have gotten jobs at restaurants and installing solar panels.

$ **Credit card applications.** See Chapter 15.

> **New Hampshire Intern'l Speedway. Positions in security, parking at several major events.**

$ **Quartzsite, Arizona: Terry and Joe** were in Quartzsite, Arizona. Another RVer was looking for a couple to sell their product at RV shows. Terry and Joe were looking for a different way to make money and decided to give it a try. "The product was good and the owner excellent to work for. However, we realized selling was not for us. It worked out well because we earned some money and had a chance to try it out without traveling out of our way." Another time they were boondocked in New Mexico and noticed a road project in progress. They talked to the supervisor and were hired for two weeks.

$ **NASCAR race workers: Ron and Val** picked up four-day jobs at the NASCAR Winston Cup Race at Talladega after working first at the Formula I Grand Prix at Indy and enjoying it thoroughly. Both events were listed in *Workamper News*. With tight security, they were instructed to check everyone coming through for proper tickets or credentials. Days were long, usually from 7 a.m. to 6 or 8 p.m., but they were in "spitting distance of the track." Says Val, "We got to see everything going on." They were paid $6.75 an hour plus given a free dry-camping space. Dale Earnhardt, Jr., Ricky Rudd, Dale Jarrett and other drivers got a kick out of the lady at the south tunnel entrance who insisted on checking out their credentials because she didn't recognize a one of them! Officials were so delighted to get such good workers, they practically begged them to come back and work the race in the spring.

Temporary positions can be well-paying jobs. You decide when you want to work and for how much. You can turn down assignments that aren't a match. Temporary jobs and at special events can be a way to pick up some quick cash. Rarely does an RV site come with a temporary job, but you may find you make more money even after paying for your site. A temporary agency may have specialized training you can use to improve your job skills and marketability while you gain experience in a new field.

Chapter 21
How to operate your own business on the road

Approximately 70 percent of U.S. businesses are run by self-employed entrepreneurs. Operating your own business on the road may give you the income and flexibility that you want. Many working RVers are doing just that. The new technology available to RVers — computers and cell phones — makes having a business on the road more feasible.

The type of business you run is limited only by your imagination and willingness to make it happen. Several areas seem to lend themselves to working for yourself.

SALES OF RV-RELATED PRODUCTS AND SERVICES

256. *Solar panels*
257. *Upholstery and carpet cleaning*
258. *Solar ovens*
259. *Laptop computers and related equipment*
260. *GPS devices*
261. *Brake assists*
262. *Windshield repair*
263. *RV repair or handyman work*
264. *Hair cutting, sewing, massages*
265. *Badges*
266. *Redwood signs*
267. *Satellite dishes and antennas*
268. *RV detailing*

269.   *Pet grooming*
270.   *Sharpening knives and scissors*
271.   *Locksmithing*

The list of products and services above are ones that RVers might need or want. Your business could cater strictly to other RVers. You could use these ideas to pick up some extra money, or work harder and make a living from them. Often RV entrepreneurs combine several ways to bring in money on the road.

Finding customers

One of the best ways to find customers is to park where other RVers are located. RV parks and campgrounds are good spots, or in boondocking areas where RVers congregate at certain times of the year like Quartzsite, Arizona in January and February. A sign on your vehicle may bring inquiries. If you are outside working on your business, for example making signs, other campers may ask you about your business. Use every opportunity to let people know about the product or service you provide. Carry your business cards with you at all times.

> **Make money repairing windshields. Unlimited potential.**

If you are parked in an RV park, check with management about their rules for conducting your business in their park. There may be local licenses or permits required. The park owner could be liable if you do not follow these local regulations and incur liability if someone is injured on their property. You may be able to negotiate an agreement with the owners. For example, one dog groomer pays 50 percent of her fee to the RV park. She makes money while the park offers a service to their guests.

Attending RV rallies or educational events brings you in contact with potential customers. You could have a booth or you may be able to find customers without one (if allowed). Offering a seminar is a way to create interest in your product or service.

 Carpet cleaning and windshield repair: Gene has found he prefers to work for himself rather than for an employer. He and **Kathy** have gone back to an area they know well and fixed up houses and then sold them. They have also cleaned RV carpets and upholstery. Now Gene repairs chips in windshields. They find customers by parking in strategic places and by attending some rallies. Gene also assists people in getting started in the windshield repair business. In addition, they sell Christmas trees in Texas and Kathy works for her former employer in the town where they lived before hitting the road.

$ **Solar power: Tom and Nancy** have been committed for years to solar energy and alternative technologies. They left northeast Pennsylvania where the sun rarely shined and traveled in Mexico for two years, promoting solar solutions. Infected with the traveling spirit, they wanted to find a way to help support their dreamed-about nomadic lifestyle. After trying a couple of other businesses, Tom came back to his earlier fascination: solar. It required a lot of initial research but Tom has been successfully marketing solar ovens and solar electric systems. Nancy has also picked up extra cash with her sewing business, doing sewing repairs for RVers.

OTHER RV-BASED BUSINESSES

272. *Engraving*
273. *Selling advertising and producing RV park maps (own business)*
274. *Carving*
275. *Artist or craftsperson: painting, beading, photography, weaving, jewelry etc.*
276. *Guiding tours*
277. *Teaching classes in exercise, dance or crafts*
278. *Digital photo imaging*
279. *Word processing or medical transcription*
280. *Desktop publishing*
281. *Newsletter publication*
282. *Musician or performer*
283. *Giving massages*

Other businesses are not aimed particularly at RVers, but can be done on the road because location doesn't matter, bulky supplies or equipment are not needed, or you may travel from one location to another to conduct your business.

Selling at RV and other shows and fairs

Products of a more general nature can be sold at RV shows as well as Home and Garden Shows, state and county fairs or flea markets. You can pick your "circuit" and hit the shows in a particular area you like to travel or where your product does well. RVers we know sell clothes, redwood signs, digital photos transferred onto shirts and cups, cleaning products, and more. Several RVers make and sell badges and pins at RV and other shows.

> **Finally, a screen printing business anyone can afford! Package includes equipment, accessories & training.**

Members of clubs like to have distinctive name tags, and all the equipment fits nicely into a small trailer.

A number of publications and Web sites are available to locate shows that dovetail with your product and provide sources of saleable products.

$ **Sales at shows: Wally and Patsy** have sold electric barbeques, a wood cleaning product, clothes and a needle threader at fairs, home and RV shows.

After an initial two years on the road, Patsy and Wally decided their dream was to stay on the road for as long as possible, be debt free and have money to do the fun things they enjoy. At first they sold products for other owners on a percentage basis. Then they decided to work for themselves. Now, says Wally, "we sell what needs to be sold." Patsy and Wally have looked at many ways to earn money. Sales has the best income potential, Patsy observed, and has enabled them to reach their goals.

$ **Redwood signs and digital photo imaging: Tom and Nancy** made and sold redwood signs traveling a show circuit in Michigan in the summer, as well as other shows in their travels. After several years they sold the sign business and began a digital photography business. They travel to many of the same shows, taking photos and then putting them on t-shirts, mugs, mouse pads and other items they stock.

They do their work and transport their equipment in a small trailer they tow behind their motorhome.

INTERNET-RELATED SERVICES

284. *Sales of products on the Web through eBay or other auction sites for yourself or others*
285. *Web site sales*
286. *Produce an electronic magazine (e-zine)*

Internet

RVers maintain Web sites and sell products like books and newsletters. They make money through affiliate programs where you earn money each time someone at your site clicks on a link and goes to the affiliate site. In some cases, merely going to the new site earns money, in other cases you earn a portion of any resulting sales.

> **Have your own online mall! Only $39 a month. Ready-to-use professionally designed Web site.**

Participating in Internet auctions has developed into a moneymaker. RVers sell products on eBay, the biggest Internet auction site, or act as agents for other sellers. Web design is another service that RVers can provide.

$ **Auctions on eBay: Ernie and Nancy** sell items on eBay while traveling in their RV. According to Ernie, "Requirements are a computer, digital camera or scanner, and e-mail accessibility." They use library computers or take their laptop into a truck stop when a telephone hookup is not available in the campground where they are staying. In order to start selling, you first set up an account with eBay. Small fees are charged. Then you post the item. Auctions run from three to ten days. Then you notify the highest bidder who sends check or money order to you. "We've had people send checks for as much as $1,400 in care of General Delivery!" reports Ernie. Since carrying inventory is cumbersome in an RV, they are branching out by selling items for antique stores for a commission.

$ Web sales: Bryce and Lisa's two-year travel dream to see the U.S. by RV started to fizzle short when they ran out of money. They were having too much fun to settle down so they needed to find a way to earn money on the road. For awhile, they worked for American Guide Service (AGS), a company that makes maps and guides for RV parks and resorts.

When Bryce discovered the Web, that opened up a whole new world and additional ways to make money. Bryce and Lisa have their own Web site at *(www.webworker.com)* with all sorts of free information on creating and using your own Web site to have a home-based business, and making money from affiliate programs. This has branched out into several other businesses, such as eBay sales and e-books.

$ Web site design and a travel Web site: Carl and Rhonda left high tech computer jobs when they were in their mid-thirties. Now they are using these skills to earn money while traveling. Carl is writing a book on Web hosting for beginners and reviews technical manuscripts for publishers. Rhonda designs Web sites and also does nature/rock animal painting. They have a popular travel Web site, *(www.southpoint.com)* that includes a campground directory by state, as well as a directory listing campgrounds with instant phone hookups at the site.

$ Web sales: Stan was a computer programmer and started a side computer business five years before hitting the road. Now he and **Connie** travel and earn money from several different computer ventures. These include selling shareware programs through his Web site *(www.CottonwoodSW.com)*, and selling screensavers at *(http://AwesomeScreens.com)*. Recently Stan developed a low-cost campground reservation system which he plans to market through other RVers acting as commissioned sales agents. (The agents would make most of their money through consulting fees.) In addition he has a couple of other sites where he makes some money through advertising. Links to all his ventures are at *(http://StanAndConnie.com)*.

Stan shares these methods he has used for increasing sales:

✔ **Offer free trial versions** of his shareware good for 30 days as an incentive to buy.

✔ **Use press releases** to get free media coverage in computer magazines.

✔   **Advertise on other Internet sites.** This is usually a free listing on other shareware Web sites.

✔   **Run a Web site** to sell your programs.

One of the most difficult aspects of running an Internet-related business on the road is connectivity. Stan prefers to check his e-mail once a day and has a lot of Web surfing to do to keep up with competition and new technology as well as marketing. He usually stays at campgrounds with instant phone hookups, or stays long enough to justify getting his own phone hooked up. Modem-friendly campgrounds or truck stops with modem hookups work for overnight stays. You will get so much e-mail if you are in business that using your cellular phone for Internet is not adequate.

Taking orders and customer service are also difficult on the road. Buyers like to purchase immediately. You can contract with companies to provide this service so you do not have to have a credit card merchant account. He handles customer service with a voice-mail messaging service that gives him a toll-free number, along with a message box, Fax box, and e-mail notification of incoming calls. He can also forward the call to another phone when he has one available.

One further note, Stan advises that to succeed in this business you need computer knowledge, Internet savvy, and basic business skills. This may not be enough to make a living out of it right away. It usually takes time to build up business (and develop your products), though there are overnight success stories too. Says Stan, "Most successful programs are the culmination of a few years of constant improvements and consistent marketing efforts. And most started out as a part-time side business."

CONSULTING/PROFESSIONAL

287. Innsitting business
288. Business consultant
289. Seminar speaker
290. Computer consultant, Web page designer
291. Freelance writer
292. Freelance photographer
293. Investor in stock market
294. Tax preparation
295. Performer at school assemblies

Vacation relief or short-term management

A business providing vacation-relief for businesses like bed and breakfasts, motels and other businesses is feasible. To be viable, you would need to have experience in this area or have made contacts.

> **Jackson Hewitt Tax Service Franchise opportunities available. Small start-up fee, state-of-the-art tax software.**

Some businesses hire consultants to turn them around. One couple with a background in apartment management went to apartment complexes around the county and got them back on track. They got rid of undesirable tenants and cleaned the apartments up in order to provide positive cash flow. Each job took six months to a year and paid very well. They had an excellent track record in this field prior to hitting the road, however.

$ **Innsitters: Bill and Marna** always had enjoyed staying in bed and breakfasts. They started their own business providing vacation relief or "innsitting" to B&B owners. As they traveled, they would stop and meet owners and leave their business card. Owners contacted them later when they needed short-term relief. "What was great about being innsitters was that we were able to stay in lovely places, meeting interesting people and choose when we wanted to work," notes Marna.

Seminar speakers

Giving seminars for corporations in various locations is another way RVers make money. Usually this type of business is an outgrowth of work done before hitting the road. A client base has already been developed.

$ **Corporate trainer, motivational speaker, and nature photographer: Kay and Tom** knew they wanted to hit the road as soon as their kids were out of college in 1998. Kay began developing a business doing corporate training and motivational speaking in 1991. Her background was in corporate consulting and project management, so her business evolved out of that experience. She has broadened her topics since then and now has three separate businesses, each with a different focus. Says Kay, "My work is a forum for teaching, uplifting and inspiring." Getting into this business takes expertise and networking. And she recommends joining the National Speakers Association. Tom takes nature photographs. The RV lifestyle is perfect for visiting beautiful scenery so Tom can build his portfolio.

$ **Publishers and consultants: Annette and Larry** have two family businesses involving publishing and consulting. Annette says, "The key is planning. It took us five years of development to feel confident that we could make the same amount of money 'on the road' as before." They usually stay in one location one to two months, taking advantage of monthly rates at RV parks. Overall it costs about the same as their traditional life. Though they still work pretty much full-time, the real advantage comes with their breaks. "We walk outside into a wonderland of nature whether we're in the mountains, prairies, deserts or coastlines. It's wonderful to be able to live in a vacation setting. We take days off during the week when the parks are quiet and go biking, hiking or exploring," she says.

Freelance writers and photographers, craftspeople

Writing — particularly about the RV lifestyle or travel — seems made for RVers. Your house on wheels takes you to explore new areas to write about them. Other writers have incorporated a facet of their lives into their writing. To name a few:

✔ Stephanie Bernhagen and her husband Paul, hit the road when Stephanie was 36. She became intrigued with the RV lifestyle and the freedom, and she wanted to share it with others. Her book, *Take Back Your Life! Travel Full-Time in an RV,* is an outgrowth of that. She also founded *RVHometown.com*, which I co-host with her, and together we co-edit the RV Lifestyle e-zine.

✔ Betty Prange, photographer and writer, has sold many articles to travel and RV magazines.

✔ Alice Zyetz also had a dream to write. Her book, *You Shoulda Listened to Your Mother,* was written on the road. Many articles have also been written and published.

Other RVers pick up money through arts or crafts they do on the road:

✔ Donna Ellis is an avid beader. As she has traveled she has improved her craft and now has necklaces, anklets and bracelets placed in several shops around the country.

> **Wanted: Freelance Writers Seeking nonfiction articles for *Composting News* — The latest news in composting and scrap wood management.**

✔An RVing weaver travels in a van with a small loom. She sends her work back to a co-op in Massachusetts to be sold. Another RVing woman makes framed scenes of fabric she has overpainted and dyed, and quilted wall hangings. She sells her work through several galleries in California and Arizona.

Investing in the Stock Market

RVers also make money in the stock market. That is their job — to study the stock market and invest in it to make money. Right before we went on the road, we attended an Escapade, an educational RV rally put on by the Escapee RV Club, which includes five days of educational seminars. A couple was making their living by their investments. They were quite disciplined about tracking stocks before they bought and did their homework. Most of us would be better off consulting a licensed, practicing professional. I would urge caution with the volatility of the stock market. Day-trading is particularly risky; many investors have taken big losses. Especially during bear markets, investing in the stock market may not be the best way to make money unless you have real expertise and can withstand loses.

GETTING STARTED WITH YOUR OWN BUSINESS

First you need to determine whether or not you have the right personality and the desire to operate your own business. It helps if you are a self-starter, self-motivated and a risk-taker. Long hours may be necessary to begin making money and you should be well-organized and comfortable making decisions.

Do some market research. Publications, the government, trade associations, and checking your competition can provide information about your market.

Is there a demand for your product or service?

✔ Do you know how to reach your potential customers?

✔ Do you have a network of contacts to help you get started?

✔ Would you be better off considering a franchise opportunity, and if so, do you have the necessary capital?

Becoming a consultant in the field you worked in prior to hitting the road might be a viable option. In rough economic times, businesses often turn to consultants rather than hire more employees.

Two big factors in starting your own business are commitment and enough money to keep you going until income reaches the level you need. Most small businesses fail because they did not have enough capital in reserve. Fortunately there are business opportunities where minimum inventory are required.

If you haven't yet hit the road, you might develop current or related skills into a self-supporting business like Kay and Tom, and Annette and Larry did. They each started several years in advance of their planned leaving date. If you have lead time, gradually building up your business before you need to rely on the income makes sense.

Many writers, artists and photographers begin their craft as a hobby, developing it into a paying business over time. Some have no desire or need to make a

> **Sell products for some one else while learning the business.**

living from their profession, but find the extra money a nice reward for their labors.

If you are already living in your RV and are interested in selling a product, you could start like Patsy and Wally; sell products for someone else while learning the business and finding which products do well.

If you are committed to earning a living as your own boss, you can do it. You'll be investing time and hard work and possibly some capital, but the payoffs will be great. Sharlene Minshell, RV author, was widowed suddenly. She and her husband had been planning to go on the road. She decided to go anyway and write, something her kids and husband had encouraged her to do for years. She worked hard, persevered and has now written several books about her adventures traveling as a solo plus numerous other articles and columns. Knowing you need to make something work is a big motivator.

Tax, insurance, and legal considerations

As a business owner or independent contractor, you will pay both the full Social Security and Medicare taxes, totaling 15.3% of your gross income. And you must send in quarterly estimated tax payments or be penalized. You will be paying for any benefits, such as retirement and health insurance, yourself.

Owning your own business or working as an independent contractor could give you additional deductions for expenses on your income tax returns. People who use their homes for business purposes can generally deduct a percentage of expenses and depreciation. Use of vehicles for business purposes can also be deducted. It will be more difficult meeting requirements for similar deductions on your RV. You will need to talk to your tax preparer to see which, if any, expenses and depreciation can be deducted in your case, and what records you need to keep to do so.

> **You must send in quarterly estimated income tax payments.**

Another consideration is that using your RV and vehicles for business purposes will probably increase your insurance rates. Not letting your agent know of their business use could jeopardize your coverage should an accident occur. You may need higher liability coverage as well. Or you may need to purchase a separate liability policy to sell at fairs and shows, for example.

To conduct business in a state could require licenses or permits, or a resale tax number. For example, beauticians must obtain a license in each state that they want to do business in.

Business form

There are three main types of businesses: single proprietorship, partnership and corporation. Each has advantages and disadvantages. If your net income is more than $35,000 you may want to consider an S Corp or even a C corporation. Being incorporated limits your liability and you may have lower income taxes. You (or the corporation) will pay for your health insurance and you can also set up a medical savings account to pay for any deductibles, using pre-tax dollars. You will be able to save more pre-tax dollars for retirement in tax-deferred saving plans. The Small Business Administration is an excellent source of information for starting a business and choosing which form is best for you. (See **Resources.**) As always, check with a qualified accountant to analyze your personal situation.

Owning your own RV business works for many RVers. While you give up the security of steady income, you are not limited in what you can make either. You may be able to make the money you need in a shorter period of time, leaving more time for travel and play. You are also free to set your own schedule and you answer only to yourself. An RV business is not for everyone, but it just might be for you.

Notes

"The problem is never how to get new, innovative
thoughts into your mind, but how to get old ones out."
Dee Hock, Founder, VISA

Jobs 296-335

Chapter 22
How to help the budget by volunteering

Volunteering is an excellent way to reduce your expenses on the road. Money saved is money in your pocket. Volunteers have the satisfaction of contributing to a worthwhile cause, helping others or helping the environment. If you volunteer in exchange for your RV site or other privileges, you will have a lot more freedom than in a 40-hour, nine to five job. You will probably have a lot more say in when you work and what you are willing to do. Often you can volunteer for a short period of time rather than a whole season.

Savings
Volunteering with a federal or state agency usually includes a place for your RV. If your expenses are higher than normal, or your income is slumping due to economic times, eliminating your campground expense saves a chunk of money. You may also save by:

✔ **Gas expense:** Driving your toad instead of your motorhome should save you money on gas. You might get better gas mileage with your pickup when not towing your RV. You can also save wear and tear on your vehicles when you aren't putting as many towing miles on them.

✔ **Recreation and entertainment:** Without having to pay admission fees, you'll have plenty to do. Often you get training or experiences that regular visitors don't get. Or, you might be invited by area attractions to visit at no charge so you can let visitors know about them. While employees for the federal government are prohibited from accepting these invitations; volunteers are not.

Exchange - commercial v. agency or nonprofit

Normally when an RV site is involved, you are doing an exchange for services that you provide. You work a certain number of hours per week in exchange for your RV site. The number of hours required varies tremendously. Agencies and commercial employers that offer this arrangement set their own time requirements.

If you are volunteering for a nonprofit or a government agency like the National Park Service, then it is similar to a charitable contribution in that you are giving your time instead of money to assist the agency in their work. You are working for a good cause and not expecting "payment." You may be able to take some charitable deductions on your federal income tax return and have a place to park your RV while you provide this service.

> **Work 20 hrs/wk in exchange for site with full hookups. Sam's RV Resort**

When it comes to volunteering or an exchange of service for a commercial RV park, private individual or enterprise, then you need to look at your time differently. Make sure you are working a fair amount in exchange for your site and not getting taken advantage of. Reread "What is a site worth?" in Chapter 11 (page 112) and determine if you are "paying" a fair amount. Here is an extreme example of a listing for a commercial exchange:

RV worker Phyllis saw a posting at a Web site by an RV park in New Mexico offering an RV site in exchange for 48 hours of work per week (two 12-hour days each for a couple). The sites rent for $110 a month plus electricity. During the winter the park is filled. Let's say your electricity brought the value up to $150/month. You are working at least 192 hours/month. If you figured the equivalent hourly rate, it would be about $.78 per hour. Need I say more!

If this were an agency or nonprofit, the difference between $.78/hour and a fair wage would be the contribution you are willing to give. For a commercial operation, I believe the employer is taking advantage of you. Bottom line, however, only you can decide if you have made a trade you are happy with. Go into it with your eyes open. And remember, if employers who are in business to make a profit can get people to work for

$2/hour, why should they pay more? Indirectly, you hurt RV workers who need to earn decent money to live.

You'll find plenty of options for volunteering. In **Resources** are additional Web sites and contacts.

NATIONAL PARKS, FORESTS AND OTHER FEDERAL AGENCIES

296. Campground host
297. Environmental educator
298. Videographer or photographer
299. Construction worker
300. Grant writer
301. Visitor center attendant or naturalists
302. Law enforcement desk officer
303. Search and rescue (SAR)
304. Ranger in the back country permit office
305. Assistant on archaeological digs
306. Fire tower lookout
307. Worker on the Trash Tracker houseboat
308. Lighthouse tour guide
309. Carpenter and other tradesmen
310. Special project worker
311. Campground host at military Fam camps

Government agencies like National Park Service, USDA Forest Service, National Wildlife Refuges, Bureau of Land Management and U.S. Army Corps of Engineers rely heavily on volunteers and not just campground hosts. Agencies can use volunteer help in maintenance, the office, in fact, almost any area you can think of. If you have a skill, you can probably find a volunteer match. Not all locations have RV sites for volunteers; however, if a site is available, you will have a minimum number of hours to work each week.

Several publications and Web sites listed in the **Resources** section list opportunities in many different locations. "Get Outside," published by the American Hiking Society (AHS), not only lists the agency and location but the skills the agency is seeking. Those skills are indexed so you can look up "photography" or "maintenance," for example, and see where there are openings. You can purchase this resource at the AHS Web site.

Another option is to contact agencies directly or check the agency Web site. Stopping by the agency you are interested in is an excellent way to be selected, especially if volunteer spots are competitive. You can meet and talk to the selecting official, which improves your chances greatly.

The National Park Service calls their volunteers VIPs for Volunteers in Parks. They have a print brochure so named, available from most any NPS unit. The excellent map of the park system is a handy reference whether you volunteer or not, and contains an application and contact information for the coordinator of each unit. You can also contact any unit directly about volunteering.

> **Photograph recreation activities and forest scenes. Expenses negotiable. Boise National Forest**

Some regions of the Forest Service are putting out small booklets similar to "Get Outside" for forests in their region. A volunteer can do most any job other than law enforcement. Write or call the volunteer coordinator where you want to volunteer. You will need to complete Form 301, Volunteer Application. Pick up a brochure at any Forest Service office or ranger station, or contact a regional office.

$ **VIPs: Bob and Sylvia** have volunteered at three National Parks and one National Wildlife Refuge. Acadia National Park was their first "job" and they have been back three times. Sylvia worked for Interpretation in the Visitor Center and Bob worked in maintenance on some interesting and rewarding projects. Sylvia also offered a weekly Historical Art Walk in the park. In exchange for their full hookup RV site, Bob worked 32 hours/week and Sylvia from 20-25. As perks, the concessionaire offered them free admission to their activities on a space-available basis.

At Grand Teton National Park, Sylvia worked in the Back Country Permits Office while Bob hiked or drove into the back country, testing the water supply. In Everglades National Park one winter, they were caretakers at Hidden Lake Environmental Camp, assisting with canoeing lessons to 5th graders. Bob and Sylvia also volunteered for St. Marks Lighthouse National Wildlife Refuge south of Tallahassee. They planted 10,000 trees with a local elementary school, built bluebird boxes, among other things.

Sylvia and Bob agree, "These experiences have not only been rewarding but have helped out with the budget. We consider the RV site 'free,' and have lots to see and do without driving the RV, saving on gas. We have made lasting friendships with other volunteers as well as many wonderful rangers."

$ Camphosts and community volunteers: Tom and Nancy volunteered in Prescott National Forest close to Nancy's mother while she adjusted to a new living situation in nearby Prescott, Arizona. Their duties as camp hosts entailed answering visitor questions, checking permits and a daily walk of the trails and loops of the campground to pick up litter. Since they set their own schedule, they had plenty of time to visit regularly with Nancy's mother during the week.

Tom also signed up as an "elder-mentor" with Big Brothers/Big Sisters and worked on a site development committee for the local Natural History Center by conducting research, surveys and whatever needed doing. Remarks Tom, "We've had a very blessed life on the road and feel it is important to share wherever we can. We get to feel good about whatever we do, but the benefits go beyond ourselves. It takes many caring communities to build a world we can all be proud to live in."

$ National parks and military Fam camp volunteers: Jim and Barb have volunteered four different seasons at Casa Grande Ruins National Monument in Arizona. They answered visitor questions and occasionally gave a short tour. They also did some special projects. This national monument has only five hookup sites for volunteers so positions were competitive. They kept in touch and note, "Timing and staying in contact with the Volunteer Coordinator seems to be the key to getting a position." One winter Jim and Barb also volunteered as camphosts at a military Famcamp. These are camps for military and retired-military families.

Unusual jobs with public agencies

$ **Passport in Time** is a volunteer archaeology and historic preservation program of the USDA Forest Service (USFS). You work with professional archaeologists and historians on projects including archaeological excavation, rock art restoration, survey, archival research, historic structure restoration, gathering oral histories, or writing interpretive brochures. A publication and Web site list projects for the year.

$ **Fire lookout towers** might suit you. Spot fires, greet hikers or other visitors. Most are operated by public agencies. (**Resources,** Ch 17.)

$ **Lighthouses** are another unusual place to help out. The National Park Service maintains a listing of historic lighthouses. You can find out more about individual lighthouses at this site. (**Resources,** Ch 22.)

$ **Houseboat working vacation:** At Glen Canyon National Recreation Area on Lake Powell you can sign up for a week's houseboat trip on the Trash Tracker picking up litter and debris along the lake shores. It's a fun way to see the lake and its canyons. (**Resources,** Ch 22.)

$ **Leave no trace volunteers: Steve and Pam** have volunteered in national forests in Arizona and Virginia. They worked on the trails, educating hikers to "leave no trace." Additionally, they completed projects, inventoried facilities and gave talks to groups. For these duties, they received their RV site plus stipend, mileage and other perks. What makes them especially desirable volunteers is that Steve adds magic illusions to each of the seven principles of "leave no trace," followed up by discussions for each. This makes learning fun and helps insure their audience remembers these important principles when camping and hiking in the forest.

Pam and Steve say, "We enjoy the flexible schedules, working at our own pace, working together as a couple and enjoying the out-of-doors plus getting the inside track on great places to visit."

$ **Lighthouse tours: Ralph and Mary Lou** spent a month two different summers at a lighthouse on South Manitou Island in Sleeping Dunes National Lakeshore in Michigan. Each day they gave five to seven tours of the lighthouse to visitors who ferried over in the morning and returned to the mainland in the afternoon. They gave 103 lighthouse tours to 1021 people in 22 days. With 117-step stairway, they climbed up 12,051 steps in that time! Ralph and Mary Lou brought all their food for eight days and lived in a historic village home, returning to their RV in the park campground on the mainland for their four days off. The park provided ferry transportation, island housing and a campsite.

State parks may need volunteers in:

312. *Campground hosting, which can include a variety of tasks*
313. *Clerical, computer and fiscal help at headquarters*
314. *Maintenance projects*
315. *Off-season park surveillance, minor maintenance projects, weekend campground hosting and interpretive hosting*
316. *Fee collector*
317. *Staff at visitor center or working as a naturalist*
318. *Tour guide or docent*
319. *Period-costume guide or interpreter*
320. *Retail salesperson in a gift shop*
321. *Photographer, update slide collection*
322. *Teaching Off Highway Vehicle (OHV) and Personal Water Craft (PWC) safety classes*
323. *Golf course worker*
324. *Campsite construction worker*
325. *Archaeological assistant or helper*
326. *Patrolling the backcountry*
327. *Manning a lighthouse*

STATE PARKS

State parks also recruit volunteers. Campground host positions along the California coast, for example, are highly coveted. Betty and her husband, Lin, updated the park's slide collection at Patrick's Point State Park in California and gave evening programs on taking better photographs. Contact any state parks you are interested in working at as well as the volunteer coordinator or volunteer office at the state or regional level. See **Appendix 4** for contact information.

$ **State park volunteers: Bob and Caren** found their position giving tours of the North Head Lighthouse at Ft. Canby State Park in Oregon throught the National Listing For Lighthouse Employment (NLLE) subscription data base. (Now defunct.)

GETTING A POSITION WITH A PUBLIC AGENCY

After you identify the location where you want to work, contact the volunteer coordinator there to find out their needs and procedures. Check the resources for this chapter to find contact information and applications. Many are listed on the Internet. Or, contact the coordinator by phone or mail. Begin lining up volunteer opportunities as early as autumn for summer positions. Some are quite competitive and have only a limited number of slots.

You will want to ask plenty of questions, just as if you were working there. Clear expectations on both parts will make for a much better working experience.

- ✔ **What are my duties?** Be sure to clarify what you will or will not do. If you do not want to clean restrooms, let the volunteer coordinator know. If there is a task you really want to do, perhaps take photographs for the park's slide collection, or hike in the backcountry, get a commitment that a certain portion of your time will be allotted for that task.
- ✔ **How many hours will I work for my site?** Can those hours be split between a couple or a family? Will I have set hours or is the schedule flexible?
- ✔ **What sort of time commitment must I make** in terms of weeks or months?
- ✔ **Will I be provided training** or have opportunities to explore the area?
- ✔ **Will I be provided with uniforms?** If not, must I purchase certain clothing?
- ✔ **Will I have an RV site?** Level? In trees or the open? Full hookups? Cable or satellite TV reception?
- ✔ **Can I accept free tickets** from local attractions or outfitters?
- ✔ **Am I covered by Worker's Compensation** or other insurance if I am injured on the job?
- ✔ **Will you provide a vehicle or tools** for me to use if necessary, or must I provide my own?
- ✔ **Can my visitors camp** or park their RVs on my site at no charge?
- ✔ **How far is it to shopping or medical care?** If it is a great distance, do you have a refrigerator where I can store groceries in between trips to town?
- ✔ **Will washers and dryers be available to use?** Any charge?
- ✔ **Will the IRS consider my site as income?**

Even if you don't have something lined up, if you get to a park or forest that you really like and you'd like to stay awhile, talk to the volunteer coordinator, or speak to the heads of the various departments that might need volunteers to see if they have any short-term projects you can do.

$ Drive-in volunteers:

Tom had parked the 14-day limit at one of the beach campgrounds in Glen Canyon but wanted to stay longer to drive more of the 4-wheel drive roads in the area. He approached the district ranger about staying and was allowed to stay on in return for camphosting duties.

John, a maintenance volunteer at the Grand Tetons, had some visitors in the middle of the season. They were enjoying the area and wanted to stay longer. His visitor, Mike, was able to work with John for a few weeks in exchange for his site.

Family volunteering

Volunteering as a family is on the rise so RVing families have plenty of opportunities to contribute their services as a family. Hope Sykes, writer and columnist, has felt for years that having a mobile lifestyle offers the best of both worlds: travel and community service. RVers can be ideal volunteers since they can pick up at a moment's notice and travel to areas of the country where the need is highest without putting a stress on already strained community resources when housing might be in short supply. Her column, The RVing Volunteer, offers resources and tips for the mobile volunteer; she shares some of these here:

RV volunteer: Hope Sykes

Volunteering as a family is an ideal way to help those in need. Traveling RV families can now extend their "neighborhoods" and go where help is needed most and have familiar housing and cooking facilities onboard.

To get the most out of your family experience, I recommend you start with these five simple steps:

Step 1: Develop an awareness of what problems or issues that you would like to involve your family's efforts in.

To be most effective, you'll want to find out what issues your family is passionate about. Did a newspaper story catch someone's attention? Did you spot a homeless person during one of your travels? Did you see litter scattered about in an otherwise beautiful state park?

Step 2: Develop a set of questions to help tackle the project.
Examples would be:

✔ Where would we like to volunteer?

✔ How much time do we want to devote to the project? A day? A few hours? A week? Longer?

✔ What skills do we each have that would work for this situation? Remember that even young children can pick up litter, sort items by color, or pass out information.

✔ Are there any new skills that we would like to learn?

✔ In addition to giving of our time and talents, what would we like to learn from this experience?

Step 3: Research the volunteer topic so that you will be better informed and can educate others.
Examples would include things like the number of homeless in America or to discover how much food is wasted in the U.S. per year.

Identifying the problem can help you research the topic more easily through the Internet or will assist a librarian in your search. Don't forget to check area phone books under "Social Service Organizations" to see if an organization already exists in your area where you can get both information and an outlet for volunteer activities.

Now's a good time to see how you can integrate these activities into home schooling lessons or even résumés. If you or some of your family members want some college credit on the road, check with an area university and see if some of you can receive credit for your participation.

Step 4: Put your family's ideas and planning into action.
Family volunteering is on the rise; however, RVing volunteers are still uncommon in many communities. You'll want to have a list of questions prepared to determine if the facility will be able to accommodate you.

Here are some of the questions that you should ask:

✔ Are all ages able to participate?

✔ Are children allowed to work independently or are the parents required to accompany them?

✔ We have very young children. What sort of arrangements are available should we need a sitter?

✔ Will we be allowed to park at the volunteer site?

✔ Is the RV site included as part of the position? What hook-ups are available? Are they included?

✔ What is the maximum length of rig that the campsite can accommodate? Can I park my truck or van nearby?

✔ If our entire family volunteers and a campsite is included as part of the benefits, can the work be divided up so that each person's time will count collectively to the requirement?

✔ Are pets allowed? What are the rules?

✔ What is the minimum and maximum time that we will be allowed to volunteer?

Once you accept a volunteer position, make sure to arrange your schedules so that you can trade off volunteer work and other activities if you have young children. Children often aren't interested in intense volunteer activity for the entire day so break up the time by other enjoyable sessions. Make sure that you have planned your activities so that the entire family can end on a happy note rather than feeling rushed, cranky, or exhausted.

Step 5: Make sure that you decide on how you want to record your efforts.
Picture taking and journal writing can be fun and educational. Web sites can often be set up for free or at low cost and allow others to follow your progress.

Documentation is also a great way to discover how much impact you've really had on the world. How many homeless did you feed in one day at the soup kitchen? How many aluminum cans equal one pound? How many pounds of cans did you collect?

If the activity was really fun and productive, recording your efforts will then give you a template for what to look for in another adventure:

✔ What did you like best about the experience?

✔ What made it so successful and rewarding?

✔ How could the experience be improved?

✔ Who at the facility made an impact?

Volunteering as a family, you'll find, is a great way to have quality family time. See you there!"

Working vacations

Recently working vacations have become popular. You pay a fee and then work on a project of some sort. You'll find a variety of humanitarian, environmental and archaeological projects both in the United States and overseas. In most cases you would leave your RV and travel to the site to complete the project. Some projects might be able to accommodate RV parking or permit you to stay in it. Volunteers on Lake Powell's Trash Tracker can leave their RVs on a parking lot while out on a houseboat picking up trash.

A number of organizations are listed in **Resources** that specialize in working vacations both in the U.S. and in other parts of the world.

NONPROFIT VOLUNTEERS

328. *Construction of a Habitat for Humanity Build*
329. *Office or computer work for a Habitat for Humanity affiliate*
330. *Maintenance or office work at a church camp*
331. *Volunteering overseas - environmental, construction, health and education projects*

Habitat for Humanity

Habitat for Humanity's goal is to provide affordable housing for those who are in need. Recipients of housing must contribute a certain number of hours. Jimmy Carter is perhaps the best known worker for this organization. Habitat has offices in many towns across the U.S. They also have international builds. Their RV-Care-A-Vanners is just for mobile volunteers. You may or may not get an RV site when you volunteer (depending on the build), but you have the satisfaction of helping with a very worthwhile project that gives dignity to recipients.

Habitat for Humanity builders: Bob and Sylvia haven't worked with Jimmy Carter but find great satisfaction in helping this organization. The RV arm of Habitat for Humanity, RV-Care-a-Vanners, usually consisting of 10 to 12 rigs, meets at a build site a spends approximately two weeks working as a team. Some groups build a home from the foundation up, while others arrive at a site consisting of partially completed homes. In this case, they may work on tasks like roofing, siding, landscaping, and interior finish. "My husband Bob and I have done roofing, insulation, vinyl siding, electrical and plumbing, as well as the odds and ends of the job. Many times we have the opportunity to meet the homeowner as they work to complete their 300 to 500 hours of 'sweat equity' prior to moving in," explains Sylvia. The RVers generally stay in a local public or private campground at reduced-fees. Lunches are often provided by local sponsors and the group socializes after work and visits local attractions." Adds Sylvia, "Each new home offers us a new challenge and many rewards."

American Red Cross Disaster Services: Debbie and Les have enjoyed the RV lifestyle for the past eleven years and have looked for ways to "give back." They have found volunteering for the American Red Cross (ARC) to work well with the RV lifestyle. They decided the best way to help out was to become part of the Disaster Services Human Resources system. They took classes that prepared them to be sent to other states, at Red Cross' expense, to work for a minimum of 3 weeks. The same classes — Introduction to Disaster Services, First Aid and CPR, Mass Care, and Shelter Operations — can be useful locally if they find themselves caught up in a nearby disaster. Once on an assignment away from home, lodging is covered as are food and incidentals up to a set amount.

In September 2001, Debbie received a call from her home chapter to go to New York City because of the World Trade Center attack. (Les was lacking a couple of classes so didn't accept this assignment.) Explains Debbie, "Upon reaching ARC Headquarters in Brooklyn, I attended an orientation session, was checked out by health services nurses, and received an assignment to support a mobile kitchen set up about a mile from 'Ground Zero.' I also was given the name of a hotel, one of several offering rooms to Red Cross workers. My assignment was logistics person for the mobile kitchen, acting as a liaison between the ARC and numerous service providers, including companies providing lights, Dumpsters, ice and portable toilets. In addition, I responded to dead batteries, excess food to be donated to local missions, and sudden shortages of food and supplies. Running a household and a business was excellent preparation for this type of job, which required persistence and attention to details. Other volunteers at the kitchen prepared the food, loaded it into vehicles, drove it to several feeding sites, or manned the radio."

Debbie notes, "Whatever your skills or interests, the Red Cross can put them to use. After attending the "Introduction To Disaster" class, you can choose several areas to pursue further. Classes are available at no charge and do not require local residence, so whenever we are in an area for a while we check the schedules at the local chapter office. There are about 50,000 members of the Disaster Services Human Resources System in the ARC, and it is a privilege to be a part of the Red Cross family. The feeling of camaraderie that happens when people from all over come together for a common purpose is unforgettable."

Volunteering overseas

Besides Habitat, a number of agencies recruit volunteers for either short or long term commitments at overseas locations. Volunteering overseas can be a way to travel at reduced cost. You may be helping Third World communities, working on environmental projects, or in archaeology, a couple of the many possibilities. Most projects have fees associated with them, but usually cost less than taking a tour. For some trips, the agency sets up excursions for volunteers or arranges home-stays so you get to know the locals and the area. You may see areas the average tourist never visits.

EXCHANGE OF SERVICES

332. *Exchange work for space in an RV park*
333. *Work out an exchange with a private individual*
334. *Park at a business in exchange for night security*
335. *Help friends or relatives in exchange for a place to park and hookups.*

There are many opportunities for exchanging services for an RV site and other perks. You'll find listings of employers and individuals looking for people willing to make such an exchange in both *Workamper News* and *Caretaker Gazette*.

You can also create your own opportunities for exchange of services. If you like an RV park, talk to the owner about doing a project or helping out in exchange for a free or reduced rate site. By meeting locals and asking around, you might find someone who needs a housesitter or a business that will let you park in return for keeping an eye on things at night.

$ **Work for friends: Charlie and Norma** stopped at friends while traveling through the Northwest. They stayed a month, helping with a landscaping project. Their friends gave them full hookups, plus a small amount of cash.

$ **Folksingers: Chuck and Alice** usually volunteer their services to lead or participate in singalongs in RV parks, senior centers, plus schools in Mexico, as they travel. They were at a county fair in Maine and went to the office to offer their services in exchange for an RV site on the fair grounds. As it happened, the entertainment director had just had a strolling musician cancel at the last minute. He offered them $250 to perform that afternoon!

If you are in a position to volunteer, you'll find rewards to the community and your pocketbook. You'll also have the satisfaction of knowing you are helping others and making a difference.

Notes

*"It will be a great day when our schools have all
the money they need and the Air Force has to
hold a bake sale to buy a new bomber.'
Seen at www.coolsig.com*

SECTION IV. RV LIFESTYLE CONSIDERATIONS

Chapter 23
How to manage RV expenses

Each time you reduce your expenses, you need less income. Expenses go hand in hand with what you need to earn. RVers have some unique expenses. Living the RV lifestyle can be inexpensive compared to living in a house but some expenses are greater, vehicle insurance and repairs, for example. It is easy to eat out more. Health insurance, which we will consider here, will probably not be provided by your employer.

CAMPGROUND FEES

Any night you don't have to pay campground fees saves money. Campgrounds with only a few amenities can charge upwards of $25 a night and I've seen state parks with no hookups charge $15-20 a night. That can play havoc with a budget.

> **Each time you reduce your expenses, you need less income.**

Owners of some RV parks or membership parks are open to an exchange of labor for a free or reduced site. If you will be staying at a park for at least a week, you can approach the owner or manager with an offer to work for free or reduced rent. In state or federal parks, you may be able to volunteer your time in exchange for a site. Usually the park requires a set number of hours to work for your site and may also have a minimum time period, such as a month. Depending on your skills, that commitment could vary, especially if you have a special project in mind. It never hurts to ask.

While you are working, a free or low-cost site might be included. When you aren't working, there are places where it is free to park, though those areas are diminishing. The past few years have seen a real push to limit areas where RVers can park free even overnight, as well as instituting fees where none were charged before. You may have to be more creative!

RV site: weighing the costs v. pay

You might find you earn more working for an employer who does not have or provide an RV site, even after paying for a site in another location. (See *What is a site worth?* Ch. 11). Also figure costs of transportation if you drive any distance. How will you handle transportation if you have different work schedules? If one starts early and the other works late, it could be quite inconvenient. A bicycle or small motorcycle could be the solution, as could public transportation or carpooling.

Boondocking

Boondocking is the term for camping without hookups. RVers typically use the term when that area or spot has no fee. State and federal parks do have campgrounds with no hookups and usually charge a fee. This is usually referred to as dry camping.

Much of Bureau of Land Management (BLM) and Forest Service land is open to boondocking, with restrictions. Usually there is a time limit, typically 14 days. At that point you might have to move 20 miles or so to a new location. In popular areas, there may be a yearly limit or a shorter time period allowed. Boondocking may be restricted to a limited distance from the road or to areas previously disturbed, and even prohibited in certain areas. With the Fee Demonstration Act, many former boondocking areas are now fee areas and that trend will probably continue.

> **"Boondocking" means camping without hookups.**

To locate boondocking areas or "dispersed camping" areas within BLM and Forest Service lands, check with the local office of the agency. U.S. Army Corps of Engineer projects may also have dispersed camping. Locals may know of good spots. Many RVers are willing to share their knowledge about spots if you ask. If they seem reluctant it could be because they have seen many spots disappear as RVers took advantage of these areas by staying too long, bringing in more RVs than the area could handle, and destroying vegetation or leaving trash.

If you do find an area where you can boondock, please use simple courtesy so this area is preserved for future boondockers:

✔ **Use existing cleared areas to park.** Do not cut or damage vegetation.

✔ **Dispose of your black and gray water** in proper sewage dumps and not on the ground.

✔ **Leave the area cleaner than you found it** and pack your trash out to a dumpster.

✔ **Limit the time you stay there** and keep the area neat and tidy. What can frighten locals is that squatters are setting up in the area. This happened at a nice beach near Eureka, California. Considerable tax dollars are paying welfare benefits and money for relocation of the squatters.

✔ **Let businesses in town know you are an RVer** and you are shopping here because you are camped near town. RV parks often lead the fight against boondocking in their area because they see it as competition. We like to let businesses know we would not be there if we had to stay in an RV park but do spend money at other businesses in town.

RVers often equip their rigs to make them more self-contained and to be able to boondock for longer periods of time. Solar panels recharge batteries and allow you to run all or most of your appliances without shore power or fear of running your batteries down.

> **Leave an area cleaner than you found it.**

Generators are part of the package for many motorhomes, or at least an option. While noisy, they do provide power if there are several cloudy days and your panels don't recharge your batteries. Small generators such as the Honda 1000X work well to supplement solar panels and are much quieter than standard generators. If you run your generator, please respect other RVers in the vicinity. Don't aim your generator towards them. Turn your generator off by 10 p.m. at the latest and don't start it again before 7 a.m. If you're meeting other RVers and plan to run your generator, try to park away from those who don't run theirs. The noise, even from small generators, can be annoying. When parked near others, try to limit generator time to a minimum.

Catalytic or ceramic heaters also make boondocking easier. These heaters are much more efficient than the propane heaters RVs come with. Be sure to have a qualified person install your heater and follow all safety precautions.

One limit on boondocking is the capacity of your gray and black water tanks. In some places, emptying your gray water (dish water, shower water, etc.) is legal. In most it is not. Dumping your black water on the ground is never legal. Two items could help you extend your stay. If you are near a sewer outlet but not hooked up to sewage, a macerator could be useful. Rather than drive your rig to a dump, the macerator pump grinds up the solids in your black water tank so they will run out through a garden hose. We used this weekly as campground hosts in Alaska. No dump was available at our rig, but there was a small sewage outlet about 50 feet away. We have also used our macerator pump to empty our tanks at my sister's house.

> **Dumping your black water on the ground is never legal.**

Other RVers carry Blue Boys® or similar tanks. These are blue plastic tanks on wheels. You drain your holding tanks into the container (sizes vary) and then transport the Blue Boy® to the RV dump, enabling you to stay in your boondock site for a longer period of time.

Before assuming it is permissible to dump your gray water on the ground, check with the agency, town or owner to make sure you are not violating any laws. Otherwise, a hefty fine could result. Keep in mind that gray water has a strong odor. Dump daily and choose a time when you won't disturb your neighbors.

Long term visitor areas (LTVAs)

BLM has created seven LTVAs in the deserts of Arizona and California. On most BLM land, camping in one spot is restricted to 14 days and then you must move at least 20 miles to a new spot. To camp in a LTVA, you purchase a permit, either by the week or for the entire season, and you may park at any of the sites for as long as you want from mid-September through mid-April. BLM provides some services in central locations like water, trash Dumpsters and RV dump stations in exchange for the fee. You can move from one LTVA to another with the same permit. At the time of this writing, the season pass was $140, a bargain in any book.

Desert Ecology: A reminder by Chuck Wright

Many of us are concerned about losing the right to park on national forest, the Bureau of Land Management (BLM) and other "free" lands. We must be mindful of the impact our parking has on these areas, especially in the desert.

Escapees chapter and BOF (Birds of Feather) group gatherings are becoming larger, and many are held in the desert. We must not lose sight of how easily this delicate environment can be damaged. Even the smallest plants have a role in anchoring the soil, and they have a hard time establishing themselves once driven on or simply stepped on.

We all have a responsibility to do as little damage as possible to these lands. Some of us are new to the desert and are not aware of this. I'm afraid others of us forget when we get together, to treat the desert with the respect it deserves. I, too, have been guilty.

A number of us have been parking in winter in Arizona near Ajo on BLM land. Our presence was largely ignored. Our numbers grew as several Escapees groups held gatherings in the area. Damage was done to the desert. Now there is a ranger there to enforce the 14-day limit. Will it be posted "No Camping" next?

We mean well. Most of us try not to disturb the environment. We usually don't leave trash; in fact, many of us pick up trash after others have left the area. We usually don't build firepits or burn desert wood. We do drive over or trample plants occasionally.

We are required to park off the desert roads and tracks, but we should confine this parking to previously disturbed areas. Then we must restrict our driving to existing roads, or it seems certain we'll lost the right to use these areas. For the sake of all of us, please be careful. Every plant and animal in the desert has the right to coexist.

Of course, this is not only true of the desert. It's just that the desert is particularly vulnerable. If we fail to heed these concerns — do our part and also speak up if we see someone being abusive — I fear we will lose the rest of the wonderful places we like to park. We're likely to have to host our gatherings in less attractive places.

So please, folks, don't damage our deserts, do treat them responsibly. Let's share in the stewardship of the land so we may be able to continue to use it.

© Chuck Wright. Previously published in Escapees Magazine.

Free overnight parking

Many RVers save money when traveling from one location to another by camping overnight at rest areas, truck stops or large parking lots. While some states prohibit overnight parking in rest areas or limit the number of hours you can stay, generally that is not enforced unless a vehicle is there for more than one night. You are likely to have an 18-wheeler parked nearby with engine running all night plus lights shining outside your rig, but the price is right. Some rest stops do have separate areas for RVs, such as the ones along I-70 in Kansas, but they aren't the norm.

> **Follow "boondocking etiquette" when parked overnight on Wal-Mart parking lots.**

Truck stops generally will accommodate RVs; however they are noisy. If possible, look for a spot away from where trucks seem to be parking. As a courtesy, ask permission from the owners and spend some money there. Buy gas or eat a meal and most owners will be happy to give permission to park overnight.

You have probably noticed a number of RVs parked in Wal-Mart parking lots. Wal-Mart is usually RV-friendly, though some towns are pushing to revoke this privilege. Again, while shopping in Wal-Mart, request permission from the manager. Park your rig out of the way and do not use extra parking spaces. Do not put out your awning or set up your chairs. One night should be your limit, otherwise it is camping and gives RV park owners just cause to complain. If you see an RVer abusing this privilege, leave a copy of Boondocking Etiquette (found at the Escapees Web site, *www.escapees.com*) tucked in their door, or under their windshield wiper. The letter reminds RVers that we could lose this privilege if we don't follow common-sense guidelines.

Other parking

✔ **Driveways or in front of houses of friends and relatives:** Don't overstay your welcome and contribute a fair dollar amount for water and electricity used. (Some towns have ordinances against parking RVs on city streets.)

✔ **RV club friends:** Some RVers have a house or RV lot with room for visitors and invite others to stay a night or two if their travels take them to the area. The Escapees RV Club, for example, publishes names and addresses of members who invite visitors to stop by.

✔ **Work out an exchange of services:** In *Home is Where You Park It* Kay Peterson relates how they were able to find places to exchange services and obtain a site while Joe was working. A business might like someone parked on the premises to keep an eye on things. A home or farm owner may want a housesitter to bring in the mail, feed pets and water plants in exchange for water, electricity and a place to park.

FOOD

Your food expenses will probably be similar to what they were prior to hitting the road. Eating out can knock your budget for a loop, yet eating regional foods adds enjoyment to traveling. Terry and Connie eat out for lunch rather than dinner, or eat later in the afternoon at lunch prices, keeping these expenditures down. Casinos, too, often have moderate prices to pull in customers. A late lunch buffet can easily be the main meal of the day at a lower

> **Towns with more than one supermarket usually have better prices.**

cost than dinnertime. Check local newspapers for coupons. Usually a mid-week issue features restaurants.

Towns with more than one supermarket usually have better prices than a small town with one grocery store. Stock up.

Janice Lasko developed a generic form on the computer for her grocery list to use in any store, no matter what the layout. Having a list keeps the grocery bill down, and I can attest to the difference the list makes in finding items quickly. (See **Appendix 7**.)

FUEL AND VEHICLE COSTS

Driving techniques can affect fuel use. A heavy foot on hills consumes more fuel and lowers the life of your engine.

Working for part of the year will reduce your gasoline or diesel consumption, since you will not be traveling to new locations as frequently. Your truck probably won't be used as much and may get better mileage when not towing. If you have an RV site where you work, you'll save commuting costs, or you might be close enough to walk or ride a bicycle.

Catalytic or ceramic heaters are much more efficient than RV furnaces. They must be installed correctly and safety precautions taken, but you will use much less propane and there is no draw on your battery. When we are working and have an RV site, if utilities are included, we plug in a small electric heater and use that as our main source of heat.

HEALTH INSURANCE

Can you afford health insurance? Can you afford not to have health insurance? This is probably the most difficult issue full-time RVers have to face, unless they are lucky enough to have continued coverage included with their retirement package. Due to the expense, some RVers go without. Others must choose such a high deductible, that they are effectively covered only for catastrophic illness or accident.

The real challenge, if you are not eligible for Medicare, is finding coverage that is adequate and doesn't break your budget. Rates will vary by state, and can be a factor in choosing a domicile. Order AARP Publication D-17022, "Health Insurance. Options for Midlife Adults: Finding and Keeping Coverage" for a start.

Some ideas:

✔ **Employers:** A few seasonal and temporary employers do offer health insurance, though it may be reserved for employees who work all or most of the year. National temporary agencies often have policies and a couple of national park concessionaires likewise offer limited health insurance to employees.

✔ **COBRA:** If you are just hitting the road, you may be eligible to convert your health insurance policy under your employer to COBRA. You can keep your group coverage by paying the full premium (by law, no more than 102% of the cost of group coverage) for 18, 29 or 36 months, depending on your situation. (Note: Smaller businesses do not have to continue health insurance coverage through COBRA.)

✔ **Low income:** If your income is low enough, you might qualify for Medicaid, a Federal/state program. Each state has different eligibility and benefits. Check the Georgetown University Institute for Health Care Research and Policy Web site.

✔ **Veterans:** If you served in the Armed Forces, you might be eligible for health care through the Veterans Administration (VA).

✔ **Join an association for a group rate:** Civic organizations might have a group rate. Business or trade organizations may also offer insurance to members. *Word of warning:* Make sure it is actually a group rate and not just a carrier with a low premium but poor coverage. Check also to see if the insurance company is regulated by your state, otherwise the company could increase premiums or drop coverage at any time. RVer Shaneen learned the hard way; after dealing with breast cancer, her company raised her premiums to more than $1,800 a month.

✔ **Open enrollment:** Some states require HMOs to have a limited open enrollment time. During that time, any pre-existing conditions cannot be considered. The Georgetown Web site has links to all state insurance departments. This could work for you if you spend part of the year in that state and will be able to visit HMO facilities.

✔ **High deductible:** Policies usually offer a variety of deductibles. For many RVers policies with high deductibles are the only option. Under some policies, you may have full coverage for one physical examination or routine tests like mammograms and pap smears each year. You are covered if something catastrophic occurs, but may have to shell out a lot before you reach that point. One broker we spoke to recommended that Bill and I each get an individual policy as opposed to a couple's policy. Together they cost only slightly more. However, if one of us were to become ill, we would have a lower amount out-of-pocket before coverage kicked in.

✔ **Stop-loss limit:** After you meet the deductible, the company pays a percentage, usually 50% or 80%, up to another amount, called the stop-loss limit. After you exceed that amount, they pay 100% of additional expenses (up to any limits on single illness or your lifetime limit). The lower your stop-loss limit, the less you pay out-of-pocket.

✔ **Canada and Mexico:** Oftentimes prescriptions are less expensive in Canada or Mexico. Do some comparison shopping because the costs vary by medication. One RVer with no health insurance successfully took her treatment for breast cancer in Mexico because it was more affordable. It was comparable to U.S. procedures, not an alternative treatment.

Things to check in a policy

For an article which appeared in *Escapees* magazine, Alice Zyetz interviewed two Texas insurance agents, David Loring and Roger Thomas (since retired). Their advice for RVers seeking health insurance coverage is summarized here:

✔ **Lifetime coverage:** Make sure your policy has a lifetime coverage of at least five million dollars.

✔ **Coverage where you travel:** Buy a quality plan that provides coverage everywhere you travel. Be sure you have coverage in other countries if you travel outside the United States. If you are working or spending time in a location away from the state where your policy was written, remember that the amount allowed for a doctor's visit or procedure is based on the usual rates for the home area, not where you receive treatment. In a high cost area you will have to pay the difference.

✔ **Rating:** Find out the insurance company's A.M. Best rating, an impartial assessment based on a company's financial stability and ability to pay claims. *(www.ambest.com)* Ask the company for its rating.

✔ **Be a shopper:** Compare the different plans. Make sure the coverage is in plain English. Ask questions.

✔ **Fees to agent:** A reputable insurance broker can be invaluable in understanding the "fine print" of your policy. However, don't pay a "policy origination" fee to an agent. There may be a small dollar fee to process the paperwork, but nothing else.

✔ **Deductible**: Check to see how the deductible is written. Some companies will have your deductible start over for each new illness. Instead, it should start again each year.

✔ **Pre-existing conditions:** Be clear about the definition of a pre-existing condition. A good company will describe it as a condition "for which you have received treatment, medication, or advice in the past six months."

A bad company may define it as a condition that manifested itself for a particular time before the policy began. For example, you have coverage as of February 1 and visit the doctor on February 3. Cancer is discovered that may have been growing for more than six months. The plan could label this as a pre-existing condition, even if you had no knowledge of it.

✔ **Evaluate coverage:** Don't just compare premiums. Carefully evaluate the coverage. A low premium may indicate poor coverage.

Check with the State Insurance Department in your state to make sure this company is regulated there. Horror stories abound where an out-of-state company has either jacked up premiums or dumped members who file substantial claims and the state insurance commission could do nothing about it. (Check **Resources** for the Georgetown University Institute for Health Care Research and Policy Web site for contacts for each state's insurance department. Insurance companies, where permitted, play games to get rid of policy holders that cost them money.)

Make sure you have a proper address in the state where you have coverage. One RVer couple had been covered in Oregon prior to hitting the road. The insurance company continued their coverage when they began full-time RVing and agreed to bill them through their mail forwarding company in another state. When one of them had a major claim, the insurance company balked at paying, saying the couple no longer had an address in Oregon. They were able to rectify this, but were lucky. Of course the company didn't raise any objections until a claim was actually filed.

No health insurance

If you do not have health insurance, there are a few resources and ideas that can help you get affordable treatment:

- ✔ **Check into state programs.** You may be eligible. Some states provide free mammograms and pap smears to women that meet age and income qualifications.
- ✔ **Planned Parenthood** provides some free and low-cost tests to women.
- ✔ **Health fairs** are another source of free and low-cost tests as well as useful health information. We have seen them sponsored by a variety of businesses, including a chain of supermarkets.
- ✔ **Clinics run by a nurse practitioner** may be less expensive for routine tests or minor illnesses and injuries.
- ✔ **Many hospitals will work with you** to pay your bill, through no-interest loans or a payment plan. Always attempt to negotiate a lower amount. This is often successful, particularly if you can pay the balance off.

Unless you need immediate emergency treatment, in most cases, you can take time to do research before having a procedure. This is true even in the case of cancer. By checking prices of

> **In most cases, you can take time to do research before treatment.**

physicians and hospitals, you can save a great deal of money.

DeAnna's Story

At a fairly young age, DeAnna found herself suffering painful arthritis in her knees. Doctors advised her she would need knee replacement surgery on both knees soon. At such a young age, there is a good chance you will need a second knee replacement operation in your lifetime and the second one usually doesn't work as well. DeAnna was also without health insurance.

She began researching. A librarian told her about the U.S. News and World Report annual July issue that rates hospitals. She contacted hospitals that had high ratings in orthopedics, and was then referred to orthopedic surgeons who practiced there.

A friend then told her about partial knee replacement and the doctor who operated on her. From there DeAnna found a Web page of the procedure, called Repicci II, or unicompartmental knee joint replacement. The site gave listings of doctors who do the procedure as the main part of their practice. The doctors she found through the hospital ratings did not do this procedure as frequently, preferring total knee replacement. DeAnna felt, in the long run, she'd be better off having the partial done first, since she will likely need a full knee replacement in the future.

Next she researched prices. The cost of the surgeons ranged from $4,000 to $8,000 for one knee. DeAnna found a doctor who does 150 of these procedures each year and would do each knee for $2,000, since she was having both done. He also helped her obtain the Medicare rate for the hospital, X-rays, lab and anesthesia.

Some of the steps DeAnna took:

✔ **Contacted her network** of RVing and other friends to see if they had any knowledge that could help her.

✔ **Research, research.** She used the librarian and the Internet.

✔ **Contacted hospitals** about charges and payment plans. Usually a person in Billing is designated to handle special problems and would know of any financial assistance. (For example, I found out that a Utah hospital has a source for no-interest loans to pay off hospital bills.)

✔ **Check out the hospital** to see if it is accredited. Find out when it was evaluated and talk to the infection control nurse about what their "infections in surgery" rating is.

✔ **Take time to research.** Remember, unless it is a matter of life or death, even if you have cancer, you have time to research. DeAnna was surprised at how many people simply do what their doctor or HMO recommends without doing any research. RVers often have the flexibility to go wherever they can get the best treatment or best price.

OTHER FINANCIAL CONSIDERATIONS
A few other issues may also have a financial impact.

Unemployment
If you work sufficient time and have sufficient earnings, you could be eligible for unemployment compensation. You can collect unemployment payments from a state even if you are no longer physically there. If you decide to apply, contact the unemployment office nearest to where you are now located (in any state) and they will help you determine if you are eligible and who to contact if another state handles your case. (Or check the Web site of the state where you will collect it.) In many states, you file your weekly or biweekly report via telephone and checks are deposited directly into your account.

> **You may be eligible for unemployment.**

Investments
The Securities Investor Protection Corporation (SIPC) and the National Association of Investors Corporation (NAIC) teamed up to survey investors in 2001, reporting that 85% failed a "survival" quiz gauging their awareness of what to do in times of market downturns and other financial difficulties. This is a complex field.

If you will be obtaining part of your income from investments, or planning to use that income or principal for later years, I recommend you consult with a licensed, practicing professional who understands the unique needs of RVers. According to Dave Loring, licensed financial consultant, the time to consult with this advisor is in the planning stage, before going on the road full-time. Says Dave, "Your advisor should integrate investments, financial planning and estate planning concerns so you preserve, as well as increase your funds for your retirement years." Look for an independent agent who is a member of both the National

Association of Security Dealers (NASD) and (SIPC). These organizations should be listed right on their business cards. You should not have to pay for advice and it never hurts to get a second opinion.

ATM fees and other expenses

Avoid ATM fees: Getting charged $1.50 or more each time you get cash from a "foreign" (not your bank's) ATM can make a big dent in your account over the course of a year. You can avoid these fees by:

✔ **Credit unions:** Use an ATM at a credit union. Only 50% charge a fee as opposed to 94% of banks.

✔ **Cash back:** Get cash back using your debit card at point-of-sale terminals at grocery stores and other retail stores.

✔ **Alliances:** If you use a credit union or small bank, see if they are a member of an alliance where customers do not get charged fees at other member banks.

✔ **Online banking**: Only 11% of Internet banks charge customers to use another institution's ATM. Some even reimburse customers for a limited number of foreign ATM charges.

✔ **Debit card:** You should be able to go into a bank or credit union and use your debit card to get a withdrawal with no fees. Check with your bank to see if they will assess any fees on the other end.

✔ **Brokerage account:** If you have an account with Charles Schwab and maintain a certain balance, there is no service charge for using your ATM card to make a cash withdrawal inside the bank or credit union.

OTHER EXPENSES

To enjoy RVing, you need to be at a point in your life where material things aren't as important. If you need your "stuff" or have to keep acquiring "things" you probably aren't going to be happy RVing for very long. It is a different mind set. Many RVers do keep things in a storage unit somewhere, but they are usually past acquiring more things.

Purchases

Purchasing knickknacks doesn't mean as much as experiencing a location. Besides, space is limited in an RV and who wants to dust knickknacks? Photos preserve the memory and take up much less space, and could even be stored on your computer.

Clothes

Both a change in lifestyle and lack of space will probably trim your clothes budget. Casual clothes are the rule on most seasonal jobs. Some employers provide uniforms or at least shirts. You might save a few dressier clothes, but most of us find ourselves weeding these out of our closets after not using them in years.

Admissions and entrance fees

Initially you may spend more on admissions and entrance fees when you first hit the road. You naturally want to see some of this country. You'll probably find these decreasing over time as your pace slows down. When you arrive in an area, check the newspaper for coupons, or ask at the visitor center or chamber if they have discount coupons. Members of Good Sam, AARP, or automobile clubs get discounts on certain attractions. Museums or attractions may offer free days or discounts. In San Diego's Balboa Park, for example, each museum has free admission one day a month.

If you have some idea of your travels, request state or regional travel planners. Festivals, fairs, parades and other events can add enjoyment to your visit and give you a real flavor of the area and are usually inexpensive. (See **Appendix 1** for state contact information.)

Ideas for saving money from working RVers

✔ Buy prepaid phone cards. Shop for the best price, as they vary widely.

✔ Get cash when shopping, rather than using an ATM.

✔ Exchange services, such as sewing or repairs, or barter for a site during off-season.

✔ Check discard bins or give-away shelves at libraries for good reading materials.

✔ Work in places you want to visit. Save travel time and expenses.

✔ Stay out of debt. If you don't have lots of money going out, you don't need a lot coming in.

✔ Eat at home.

✔ When you eat out, go to the late lunch specials or breakfast.

✔ Check credit card bills carefully to make sure charges are accurate.

✔ Review insurance policies regularly to make sure you don't encounter expenses you thought were covered or that you aren't paying for coverage you don't need.

Key points

👍   **There are many ways to reduce expenses on the road.**

👍   **The change in lifestyle is a money-saver in some budget categories like clothing.**

👍   **There are many free or low-cost activities and places to stay that can help control your budget.**

He who waits for the roast duck to fly into his mouth
must wait a very, very long time.
Chinese proverb

Chapter 24
Lifestyle considerations

The ranks of full-time RVers, once the province of older, retired couples, are becoming diversified. Single men and women, families, and the physically challenged are also out on the road. There are some issues we face, or may face, at one time or another as we travel. The first is perhaps most critical to sticking with the full-time RV lifestyle.

YOUR NEW COMMUNITY

A difficult aspect of becoming a full-time RVer can be that you lose contact with people who were once your friends. Long distance relationships are hard to maintain and many people won't want to do that. Writing letters is hard to keep up. E-mail can keep you in touch, but you may have limited access much of the time. RVers find they have less in common with friends who choose to stay in one place.

> **It is important to build a new community.**

It is important to find or build a new community. It can be lonely traveling by yourselves from place to place. Contacts you meet on the road can become your new community. If you seem to have a connection with someone you meet, stay in touch. When you are traveling or in your off season you may be able to meet up.

For Bill and me, the Boomer BOF (Birds of a Feather group) of the Escapees RV Club is our primary community. As the name implies, it caters to the younger RVer, though the group has no age restrictions. We stay in touch by a newsletter, Internet bulletin board, e-mail and letters. We also belong to the Workers on the Road BOF. This group shares work and moneymaking information through a quarterly electronic newsletter. We also participate in RV working forums and discussion groups. We meet working RVers at our jobs and on the road. More recently, I've acquired RVing Internet friends whom I've never met in person. If you are new to this lifestyle, you'll find the vast majority of RVers are more than willing to help out a fellow RVer.

Other clubs like FMCA or Good Sam have rallies and chapters with chances to make lasting friends and form a community. If you belong to and use membership parks, you'll run into the same people over time.

WORKING TOGETHER

Many of the jobs or moneymaking opportunities could find you spending a lot of time on the job with your spouse or partner. Then you come home to your RV and spend more time in a small space.

RV workers Jack and Sylvia worked as a "team" in maintenance, primarily janitorial, at one state park. It was an adjustment working together as well as living together. At an RV dealership, they worked for the same employer and were in the same building but not always together. Advises Sylvia, "The first step is to identify what's happening, then make the decision not to let it affect your relationship."

> **I need a "Jaimie Day."**

Kay Peterson, who along with husband Joe Peterson founded Escapees RV Club, gives talks at Escapades about the full-time lifestyle. A blessing for us was to hear her talk about "Kay Days." Telling Joe she needed a "Kay Day" was a signal to Joe she needed a day to herself. She would go do something she wanted to do: shopping, go to the library or the movies. Needless to say, when I feel like I need some space, I tell Bill I need a "Jaimie Day." He knows I mean I need some time alone. I have a great time and come back recharged.

THE SOLO WORKER

Not everyone travels as a couple. Even in the case of a couple, both may not work. Even though many ads seem to be advertising for couples, there are plenty of jobs and moneymaking opportunities for the solo worker.

Many RV parks advertise for couples. If they provide a site, they get two workers per site, which is more cost-effective for them. However, if the situation is one that interests you, don't hesitate to approach the owners. An employer may require that you work so many hours for your site. You may have to work the full amount, where a couple would split it. And this may be negotiable.

The majority of jobs and moneymaking opportunities described in **Section III** apply to the single worker.

✔ RV worker April travels on her own. She has gotten many jobs in RV parks and public campgrounds and has picked apples in Washington. Couples picking apples earned more, but she was still hired.

✔ RV worker Phyllis often works in RV parks, though her husband is on disability and is unable to work. She prefers working as an activity director and has had no problem getting jobs.

✔ RV volunteer Jerry has volunteered in several national forests.

✔ RV volunteer Betty worked for her site and use of the facilities at a clothing-optional resort.

$ **RV writer: Joei Carlton Hossack** has been on the road since 1989. She and her husband traveled by RV through Great Britain, Europe, and parts of Africa. In 1992, during their travels, her husband died at the young age of age 52. Joei has continued traveling. She has worked on three archaeological digs in England and has traveled solo through Turkey, the Greek Islands and Cyprus. She also drove her RV to Alaska. Joei supports herself through writing and speaking about her adventures and has written four books. She is also a columnist for the *Gypsy Journal*.

A number of groups for singles provide activities where singles can meet up and travel with other singles. (See **Resources.**) Use these groups as opportunities to network for job information.

TRAVELING WITH FAMILIES

You may run across families traveling together full-time in their RV. Often the children are homeschooled. There are resources for the homeschooler and groups providing curricula, support and assistance. Other RVers with families make it a point to stay in one location for the school year. Still others enroll their children in a variety of schools as they travel.

Traveling with young children would make it difficult for both parents to work unless they had different schedules or had affordable child care available. Resort areas and concessionaires in national parks have positions with evening shifts in food service, security, and retail.

We have worked in a couple of towns where pre-teens and teens were welcome additions to the work force. Busing tables, pet walking, and yard work were a few ways enterprising young people made money.

If parents have a business, such as selling items at shows, children can be involved in all aspects of the business. Judith Waite Allee in *Educational Travel on a Shoestring* describes how her daughter learned to interact with customers, fill out order forms and make change as they traveled with the family photography business. *(www.DreamsOnAShoestring.com)* Some organizations seeking volunteers welcome families as well.

> **Jeff and Susan travel with daughter Samantha and have worked at Disney World.**

Shelley Zoellick provides information on traveling, working and homeschooling children at her Families on the Road Web site. A poll she conducted at her Web site found that 25% of families are or will be financing their RV travels through finding temporary jobs along the way, while 17% have an RV home business. *(www.familiesontheroad.com)*

It is a good idea to advise your employer you are traveling with children if you will be staying onsite in case there are restrictions. Some RV parks are adults-only parks also. The employer may be able to accommodate families scheduling parents on different shifts. Jeff and Susan travel with their daughter, Samantha. They have worked at Disney World several winters and have been able to work different shifts so their daughter is never alone.

$ **RV worker: Brandy** began traveling with her children many years ago. Says Brandy, "Working on the road takes no special skills or talents, except flexibility." Her accounts of the few times she had difficulty finding jobs show determination as well. Once in Seattle she had spent a week looking for a job and was still not working. She decided on the job she wanted and approached the owner. He told her there were no openings. She said, "That's okay, but I'm going to work for you." Wednesday she went back; he still had no openings. She reminded him she was going to work for him. Friday she stopped by again to let him know she was still interested. Monday, the same thing happened, and she told him not to forget her. On Thursday she went back again. The owner said she was so persistent, she must really need a job and want to work there, so he hired her. Months later when it was time to leave, he told her he was glad she kept trying and offered her a job if she was ever back in town.

THE DISABLED RVER

Individuals with disabilities are discovering something wonderful: They no longer have to stay at a "fixed" home from which to work. With the advent of the RVing industry offering more accessible features on their units like wider doorways, wheelchair lifts, and barrier-free floor plans, more and more wannabe travelers are able to hit the road. With an increasing number of parks and campgrounds becoming modem friendly, working from the road via the Internet has become an viable lifestyle for RVers. Additionally, with the ongoing development of computer-assisted technology, more and more individuals are opting for work on the open road.

Hope Sykes, writer and volunteer, found out quickly that RVing and the Internet offered a rewarding lifestyle and global network when a sudden illness struck. She is a firm believer that the RVing lifestyle along with Internet access opens a world of possibilities and taps into the depths of the imagination. To her, there are several keys to success: get an affordable rig that meets your needs, network, and build up your skills by volunteering, if your résumé doesn't have the impact that you would like. She also encourages anyone with questions about accessible RVs to contact the Handicapped Travel Club. (*www.handicappedtravelclub.com*) She shares her experience below.

Hope's story

After RVing over 200,000 miles throughout the U.S. and Canada over the years and fully expecting no lifestyle changes, I noticed a dramatic transformation in myself one morning: I had trouble getting up and was in pain. Not long after that, I progressed to using a cane. Fortunately, a recent operation has improved my condition but I want to share with you some of the things that I'm learning.

Most importantly, I'm learning not to be afraid of what life hands us and that there are often ways to continue the enjoyable RV lifestyle and to be productive. That's how my writing took a more serious turn and I can honestly say that I've never enjoyed working, learning, and traveling more after this deep reflection.

"That can't always be," you say. You're right. I'm the first to admit that things aren't always rosy, but with the availability of accessible RVs and the Internet, I've found out that many individuals can actually have the dream job that they've always wanted with a future not so filled with barriers.

Even during my most difficult times, I found that with an RV and occasional Internet hook-ups, I could work from where I wanted. A beach. A forest. With a view of a lake. Yes, I was much slower than my colleagues at times, yet I seized this opportunity to decide upon what was really important in my life.

Through the RVing lifestyle, quality time with my family has been a reality. Reaching out globally via the Internet was possible at any hour when hook-ups were available and I have developed fulfilling relationships with my colleagues who are from practically any place on the planet.

I also strived to have a work area set up as I like it; where I could learn and read to my heart's content. And, instead of spending wasted hours using my more limited energy reserves on cleaning and maintaining a large house on a fixed foundation, I've been productive and working with a passion on things that I really love to do.

Getting started

Here's are suggestions for getting started. If you are currently working for a company that caters to telecommuting (working from home via computer), ask if the company would allow you to continue your job while you are on the road. For more about telecommuting, check **Resources.**

If you work on a number of projects for different clients, you may find that you only need occasional hook-ups for data uploads to an employer and can meet other communication needs by cell phone or through a calling card. For Internet access, plan ahead and see what parks offer the modem access you need. *(www.southpoint.com)*

Hope's advice

Once you are able to free yourself of many of the barriers, an interesting thing happens — you'll begin to dream. Suddenly your mind begins to think things like:

✔ I could do that.
✔ I wonder what would happen if I...
✔ Why doesn't someone come up with...

You might start taking a few notes here and there or even keeping a journal. You begin to set your own pace. You discover things (lots of things) that you love to do. Perhaps you begin to understand that you really do have some of those talents that people had been telling you that you had all along. You used to brush off those comments. Now you reflect upon them. Hmmm. Remember what they said? "Gee, I wish that I could be good at that like YOU." Yes, you do remember. Maybe your friends weren't just trying to be nice after all.

I know, this probably won't happen overnight. It took me some time to get this far and I'm still working on it daily. So how do you get from there to here? Mostly, it takes some planning.

> **Work for while and then take some time off ...**

Pulling up roots and looking for work isn't so new these days. Companies seem to be handing out pink slips or merging or going out of business at a steady rate so few of us have really any job security. Temporary workers and independent contractors are becoming more popular in the corporate world. That's where having a mobile lifestyle can be a real plus — work for a while and then take some time off, see another part of the country, or take a telecourse during a break. Remember: This is supposed to be your dream career.

If you feel that your skills aren't as sharp or your résumé is a little thin, you might want to think about doing some virtual volunteering first by using the Internet. For great resources on the topic, you'll want to visit the Virtual Volunteer Project online at *(www.serviceleader.org)*.

Here's just a partial list of ideas from the center:

✔ Conduct online research
✔ Provide professional consulting
✔ Translate a document into another language
✔ Make sure a Web site is accessible for the disabled
✔ Design an agency's newsletter or brochure
✔ Help with language instruction
✔ Try distance learning: train volunteers in a subject via the Internet

Who wouldn't want some of these valuable skills on their résumé? From here, it is easier to then pursue the possibility of telecommuting where you work for a company from "home." Maybe you feel confident enough to start your own business.

If you are looking for some tools and resources to make yourself more marketable, stop by disAbility.gov at *(www.disability.gov)*. Look at the section called "Self-Employment" and once you are there click on "Profiles of Entrepreneurs." If you are beginning to have a sudden attack of I-Can't-Do-This, read some of the "Success Stories" at that section before you make your final decision.

Before you sign off from the Internet, take a look at a new virtual community for the disabled called I Can at *(www.icanonline.net)*. They have an Internet channel devoted to employment topics and their "Career Center" offers guidance on everything from preparing a proper résumé and exploring telecommuting to finding exemplary employers.

Indeed, the RVing lifestyle can offer more flexibility than you ever could have imagined. When looking for additional employment resources, don't forget to check out other Web sites and leads which may cover areas beyond your current location. You are in a unique opportunity where you have a choice of going to a job or having it come to you. Remember that your new backyard is as big as the whole outdoors.

Protection from discrimination

The Americans with Disabilities Act (ADA), enacted in 1990, is a comprehensive civil rights law for people with disabilities. The Department of Justice enforces the ADA's requirements in three areas: the employment practices of state and local government; programs, services and activities of state and local government; and public accommodations and commercial facilities. Under the Act, you have the right to ask your employer for reasonable accommodations for your disability, like extra breaks or an adjustable desk. Small employers are exempted from these regulations.

TRAVELING AND WORKING WITH PETS

Working RVers who travel with pets will encounter employers and park owners who do not permit pets. National Parks have restrictions on pets running loose in the park, though workers with their own RVs can usually have pets if they keep them on leash. Make sure the employer is aware of your pets prior to accepting the position. It could be quite costly for both of you if it turns out they cannot or will not allow your pets on premises. If you have multiple pets or large dogs and have trouble getting a position, you might try visiting a potential employer as a guest. Let them get to know you and your pets. If your animals are well behaved, kept on a leash, and you clean up after them, the employer may relax the rules for you.

> **Make sure the employer is aware of your pets prior to accepting a position.**

Solo with horses: Carol loves to trail ride. She sold her home and her business in Florida and travels the USA with two horses, a dog and a cat. As she travels, she locates places to ride and work ahead before moving on. She uses the Internet, first looking up the state, then searching the site for equine usage places. At one job on a ranch in Texas, she worked between 20–24 hours/week for her full hookup site, laundry, and some meals. She did mostly miscellaneous repairs, mowing and painting. Working about four hours a day left her plenty of time to ride. She often trailered the horses out to other areas to ride and explore.

Key points

  ✍   **Individuals can successfully find work on the road.**

  ✍   **There are work and volunteer opportunities for disabled RVers.**

  ✍   **Advise your employer if you are traveling with children or pets if you will be staying onsite or if their care will impact your job.**

"Life is not a dress rehearsal."
Joe Lacey, Escapees RV Club member

Chapter 25
Conclusion

Congratulations! You have all the tools to successfully find the job you desire. You can find jobs that meet your criteria for pay, location, duties, and good employers. You should have dozens of ideas too, on how you can earn or make money on the road. Put that together with the résumé you created and your job search skills, and you are on your way to new adventures.

Keep up your **Job Notebook.** You never know when you'll need a different job or be ready for a change. One of the joys of this lifestyle is trying new things and seeing new places. Take advantage of your mobility and flexibility while you have time. Circumstances could change and that opportunity could fade away. When you need or want to make a change, your **Job Notebook** and this book will have invaluable resources.

Web sites are notorious for changing or disappearing. If you cannot open a Web site listed in **Resources,** please advise me. I will post updates to **Resources** and new information at RV Hometown. *(www.rvhometown.com)* I would love to hear about your work experiences too. Please feel free to send me an e-mail at *CalamityJaimie@escapees.com.*

This is your life and your time. Now it is time to write your own stories. I hope to hear from you!

SECTION V. APPENDICES

Appendix 1
State tourism offices

Alabama Tourist Bureau
800/ALABAMA
www.touralabama.org

Alaska Division of Tourism
907/929-2200 x201
www.dced.state.ak.us/tourism

Arizona Office of Tourism
866/298-3795
www.arizonaguide.com

Arkansas Department of Parks and Tourism
800/NATURAL
www.arkansas.com/vacation_kit

California Office of Tourism
800/TO-CALIF
www.gocalif.ca.gov/state/tourism/tour_homepage.jsp

Colorado Tourism Board
800/COLORADO
www.colorado.com

Connecticut Tourism
800/CT-BOUND (282-6863)
www.tourism.state.ct.us

Delaware Tourism Office
866/2-VISITDE (284-7483)
www.visitdelaware.com

Florida Division of Tourism
888/7-FLA-USA
www.flausa.com

Georgia Dept of Industry
800/VISIT-GA (847-4842)
www.georgia.org/tourism

Hawaii Visitor & Convention Bureau
800/600-1623
www.gohawaii.com

Idaho Travel Council
800/464-2924
www.visitid.org

Illinois Tourist Information
800/2CONNECT
www.enjoyillinois.com

Indiana Tourism Division
800/ENJOY-IN
www.in.gov/enjoyindiana

Iowa Department of Tourism
888/472-6035
www.traveliowa.com

Kansas Tourism Division
800/2-KANSAS
www.travelks.org

Kentucky Depart. of Travel
800/225-TRIP
www.kentuckytourism.com

Louisiana Tourism Office
800/33-GUMBO
www.louisianatravel.com

Maine Tourism Division
1/888-624-6345.
www.visitmaine.com

Maryland Office of Tourism
800/634-7386
www.mdisfun.org

Massachusetts Division of Tourism
800/227-MASS
www.massvacation.com

Michigan Travel Bureau
888/78-GREAT
www.travel.michigan.org

Minnesota Office of Tourism
800/657-3700
www.exploreminnesota.com

Mississippi Div. of Tourism
800/WARMEST (927-6378)
www.visitmississippi.org

Missouri Division of Tourism
800/877-1234
www.missouritourism.org

Montana Travel Bureau
800/VISIT-MT (847-4868)
www.visitmt.com

Nebraska Travel/Tourism
877/NEBRASKA
www.visitnebraska.org

Nevada Tourism Commission
800/NEVADA-8
www.travelnevada.com

New Hampshire Travel
800/FUN-In-NH (386-4664)
www.visitnh.gov

New Jersey Tourism
800/VISITNJ
www.state.nj.us/travel

New Mexico Tourism
800/733-6396 ext.0643
www.newmexico.org

New York Travel Information
800/CALL-NYS
www.iloveny.state.ny.us

North Carolina Tourism
800/VISIT-NC
www.visitnc.com

North Dakota Tourism
800/HELLO-ND
www.ndtourism.com

Ohio Office of Tourism
800/BUCKEYE
www.ohiotourism.com

Oklahoma Tourism Depart.
800/652-OKLA (652-6552)
www.travelok.com

Oregon Tourism Division
800/547-7842
www.traveloregon.com

**Pennsylvania State Travel
Bureau**
800/VISIT-PA
www.experiencepa.com

Rhode Island Dept. of Tourism
800/556-2484
www.visitrhodeisland.com

South Carolina Tourism
888/SCSMILES
www.discoversouthcarolina.com

South Dakota Div. of Tourism
800/SDAKOTA
www.travelsd.com

Tennessee Depart. of Tourism
800/836-6200
www.state.tn.us/tourdev

Texas Tourist Agency
800/88-88-TEX
www.traveltex.com

Utah Travel Council
800/200-1160
www.utah.com

Vermont Travel Division
800/VERMONT (837-6668)
www.travel-vermont.com

Virginia Division of Tourism
800/321-3244
www.virginia.org

Washington Tourism Division
360/725-5052.
www.tourism.wa.gov

West Virginia Tourism
800/255-5982
www.callwva.com

Wisconsin Division of Tourism
800/423-8747
www.travelwisconsin.com

Wyoming Travel Commission
800/225-5996
www.wyomingtourism.org

*Those who say it cannot be done should not
interrupt the person doing it.
Chinese proverb*

Appendix 2
National Park Service Offices

National Park Service
Headquarters
1849 C St. NW
Washington, DC 20240
202/208-6843

Alaska Area Region - NPS
2525 Gambell St. Rm 107
Anchorage, AK 99503
907/257-2687

Northeast Region - NPS
U.S. Custom House
200 Chestnut St., 5th Fl
Philadelphia, PA 19106
215/597-7013

Midwest Region - NPS
1709 Jackson St.
Omaha, NE 68102
402/221-3471

National Capitol Region - NPS
1100 Ohio Dr., SW
Washington, DC 20242
202/619-7256

Intermountain Region - NPS
12795 Alameda Pkwy
Denver, CO 80225
303/969-2500

Southeast Region - NPS
100 Alabama St., SW
1924 Bulding
Atlanta, GA 30303
404/562-3100

Pacific West Region - NPS
One Jackson Center
1111 Jackson St., Ste 700
Oakland, CA 94607
510/817-1300

Appendix 3
U.S Forest Service Offices

U.S. Department of Agriculture
U.S. forest Service
National Headquarters
PO Box 96090
Washington, DC 20090-6090
202/205-8333

Region 1 - Northern
200 E. Broadway
PO Box 7669
Missoula, MT 59807
406/329-3511
www.fs.fed.us/r1

Region 2 - Rocky Mountain
740 Simms St.
PO Box 25127
Lakewood,CO 80225-0127
303/275-5350
www.fs.fed.us/r2

Region 3 - Southwestern
333 Broadway, SE
Albuquerque, NM 87102
505/842-3192
www.fs.fed.us/r3

Region 4 - Intermountain
32425th St.
Ogen, UT 84401
801/625-5306
www.fs.fed.us/r4

Region 5 - Southwest
1323 Club Dr.
Vallejo, CA 94592
707/562-8737
www.fs.fed.us/r5

Region 6 - Pacific Northwest
PO Box 3623
333 SW First Ave.
Portland,OR 97208-3623
503/808-2468
www.fs.fed.us/r6

Region 8 - Southern
1720 Peachtree Rd., NW
Atlanta, GA 30309
404/347-4177
www.southernregion.fs.fed.us

Region 9 - Eastern
310 Wisconsin Ave., Ste 500
Milwaukee, WI 53203
414/297-3600
www.fs.fed.us/r9

Region 10 - Alaska
Federal Office building
PO Box 21628
Juneau, AK 99802
907/586-8806
www.fs.fed.us/r10

Appendix 4
State Parks

For each system of state parks, address, phone and contact for volunteer programs are listed. If a specific Web page or volunteer coordinator could not be identified, general information is listed instead. You can always contact an individual state park to find out how to apply as a campground host or find out their needs for volunteers for other tasks. Seasonal employment information is listed where available.

Alabama State Parks
Promotions Section
64 N. Union St.
Montgomery, AL 36130-1452
334/242-3154
E-mail: *parkspr@dcnr.state.al.us*
Web site: *www.dcnr.state.al.us*
Notes: Volunteer campground hosts for one month or more. Singles or couples. Call or write for application form or ask at individual parks.

Alaska State Parks
550 W 7th Ave, Suite 1380
Anchorage AK 99501-3561
907/269-8708
E-mail: *volunteer@dnr.state.ak.us*
Web site: *www.dnr.state.ak.us/parks/vip/index.htm*
Notes: Apply Oct 1 through April 1. Many types of positions, some have stipend. If you would like to receive a paper copy of the Alaska State Parks Volunteer Catalog, contact the Volunteer Coordinator at the above address. Please be sure to include a complete postal address.

Arizona State Parks
Arizona State Parks Human Resources Office
1300 W. Washington
Phoenix, Arizona 85007
602/542-6922 or 602/542-6900

For volunteer opportunities, call 602/542-7152, or
e-mail *volunteer@pr.state.az.us* for information.
Web site: *www.pr.state.az.us/employment/hrmain.html*

Arkansas Department of Parks and Tourism
Department S06PT
One Capitol Mall
Little Rock, Arkansas 72201
888/AT-PARKS (V/TT)
Job Line: 501/340-3993
E-mail: *natural.jobs@mail.state.ar.us* Attn: Dept. S06PT
Web site: *http://arkansasstateparks.com*
Notes: Contact the park of your choice. An RV site may not be
included. Some parks participate in the Good Sam program.
Seasonal employment information:
www.arkansas.com/employment/default.asp

California State Parks
Interpretation and Education Div.
PO Box 942896
Sacramento, CA 94296-0001
916/653-9069
Web site: Volunteers in parks
http://parks.ca.gov/allpages/default.asp?page_id=886
E-mail: *vipp@parks.ca.gov*
Seasonal employment information:
http://parks.ca.gov/allpages/default.asp?page_id=847
Notes: A variety of volunteers are needed. Contact the volunteer
coordinator of the district you are interested in or call the above
number for a volunteer packet. Apply early. Approval process includes
background checks and fingerprinting.

Colorado State Parks
1313 Sherman St., Room 618
Denver, CO 80203
303/866-3437
Web site: *http://parks.state.co.us/home/*
E-mail: *jane.burns@state.co.us* for volunteer brochure.

Notes: Look under "quick finder:" for individual parks. Under "Jobs" find seasonal both jobs and volunteer opportunities listed there.

Connecticut Department of Environmental Protection
State Parks
79 Elm Street
Hartford, CT 06106-5127
860/424-3200
Seasonal employment information:
http://dep.state.ct.us/fss/hr/seasonal/seasonal.htm
Notes: Some campgrounds use volunteer campground hosts, others do not. Contact individual park.

Delaware Department of Natural Resources & Environmental Control
Division of Parks & Recreation
Attn: Greg Abbott
89 Kings Highway
Dover, DE 19901
302/739-3197
Web site: *www.destateparks.com/Volunteers/index.asp*
Notes: Download volunteer form at Web site
Seasonal and contractual job opportunities:
www.destateparks.com/know/work/seasonal.htm

Florida State Parks
Coordinator of Volunteer Services
Bureau of Operational Services
Division of Recreation and Parks
3900 Commonwealth Blvd., MS 535
Tallahassee, Florida 32399
850/245-3098
Web site: *www.floridastateparks.org/information/volunteer.htm*
Call for an application. Apply to individual parks.

Georgia State Parks and Historic Sites
Volunteer Program
205 Butler St. Suite 1352

Atlanta, GA 30334
Web site: *www.gastateparks.org/volunteer*
Volunteer Resources Coordinator: *ChuckG@mail.dnr.state.ga.us*
Volunteer Coordinator direct line: 404/656-6533
Notes: Find volunteer opportunities at Web site. Online form to apply also. Contact above for more information on volunteering.

Hawaii State Parks
Department of Land and Natural Resources
Division of State Parks
P.O. Box 621
Honolulu, HI 96809
808/587-0307
Web site: *www.state.hi.us/dlnr/dsp/dsp.html*
Notes: Click on volunteering for information. Several agencies use volunteers.

Idaho State Parks
PO Box 83720,
Boise, ID 83720-0065
208/334-4199
Web site: *www.idahoparks.org/about/volunteering.html*
Notes: Campground hosts, interpretive, maintenance, visitor center, special projects volunteers.

Illinois State Parks
Illinois Department of Natural Resources
Lincoln Tower Plaza
524 S. Second St., Room 500
Springfield, IL 62701-1787
Call 217/785-4963
Web site: *http://dnr.state.il.us/legislation/volunteer*
E-mail *jjohnson@dnrmail.state.il.us*
Notes: Variety of positions, as well as clerical. Positions listed at Web site, apply online.

Indiana State Parks
Campground Host/Volunteers in Parks program
Indiana Department of Natural Resources
Division of State Parks and Reservoirs
402 W. Washington Room W298
Indianapolis, IN 46204
800/622-4931
Volunteer coordinator: Ginger Murphy, Chief Interpreter,
Phone: 317/232-4143
Web site: *www.in.gov/dnr/* Click on Parks and Destinations (State
Parks), then Other Info, then Brochures. Find Volunteering in Indiana
State Parks and Reservoirs. Contact the property manager at the park
you are interested in.
For intermittent employment opportunities, go to
Web site: *www.in.gov/dnr/humanres/sitelist.htm*
Available intermittent positions in the Dept. of Natural Resources
include Naturalist Aide, Natural Resources Attendants, Timber
Technicians, Engineering Assistants, Laborers, Clerical Assistants,
Security Officers, Housekeepers and Lifeguards

Iowa Department of Natural Resources
Keepers of the Land
502 E. 9th Street
Wallace State Office Building
Des Moines, IA 50319-0034
515/281-0878
Web site: *www.iowadnr.com/volunteer/index.html*
Lists volunteer positions and volunteer enrollment form.

Kansas Department of Wildlife and Parks
512 SE 25th Ave.
Pratt, KS 67124-8174
316/672-5911
Notes: Contact individual state park for needs and application. Also
participate in the AmeriCorps program, a volunteer program that will
pay a living allowance and give a grant for college once you have
completed the required hours.

Kentucky Department of Parks
Capital Plaza Tower
500 Mero Street, Suite 1100
Frankfort, KY 40601-1974
800/255-7275
Web site: *www.parks.ky.gov* for list of parks.
Notes: There are about 12 different ways to volunteer. Each park
recruits and operates their own volunteers

Louisiana Office of State Parks
Campground Host Coordinator - Outreach Section
P.O. Box 44426
Baton Rouge, LA 70804-4426
Toll free 888/677-1400
E-mail: *parks@crt.state.la.us*
Web site: *www.crt.state.la.us/crt/parks* Click on volunteer and
employment opportunities.
Notes: Minimum 4 weeks commitment, 24-hours/week. Shirt or vest
supplied. Write or call for application. For other volunteering in state
parks, contact individual parks.

Maine State Parks
Gloria M. Allen, Coordinator
Maine Volunteers in Parks
Maine Department of Conservation
Bureau of Parks and Lands
107 State House Station
Augusta, Maine 04333-0107
Telephone: 207/624-6079
Web site: *www.state.me.us/doc/parks/volunteer/volunteer.html*
E-mail: *gloria.m.allen@state.me.us*
Notes: Many types of volunteers needed.

Maryland State Parks
Maryland Department of Natural Resources
580 Taylor Ave Annapolis, Maryland 21401.
410/260-8100
Web site: *www.dnr.state.md.us/volunteer*

E-mail: *metvolunteer@dnr.state.md.us* or via phone at 410/514-7914
Seasonal employment *www.dnr.state.md.us* Click on Job Openings.

Massachusetts Department of Environmental Management
Division of Forests and Parks
251 Causeway St., Ste 600
Boston, MA 02114-2104
617/626-1250
Contact individual units.
Web site: *www.state.ma.us/dem/forparks.htm*
Seasonal interpretation jobs:
www.state.ma.us/dem/programs/interp/INTERP.HTM

Michigan State Parks
Parks and Recreation
Mason Building, Third Floor
P.O. Box 30257
Lansing MI 48909
517/373-9900
Web site: *www.michigan.gov/dnr/0,1607,7-153-10366_10871---,00.html*
Notes: Campground hosts, Piping Plover Patrol, seed collection and others needed. Apply online.

Minnesota Department of Natural Resources
DNR Information Center
500 Lafayette Road #36
St Paul, MN 55155-4040
Anne DuFresne, Volunteer Coordinator: 651/297-1449
For DNR Info: *www.dnr.state.mn.us/volunteering/index.html*
Notes: Volunteer opportunities listed at Web site. You can also contact a unit directly.
Seasonal jobs: *www.dnr.state.mn.us/jobs/openings.html*

Mississippi State Parks
Mississippi Department of Wildlife, Fisheries and Parks
1505 Eastover Drive
Jackson, MS 39211-6374

Phone: 601/432-2400
Web site: *www.mdwfp.com/parks.asp* Contact individual parks.
Seasonal employment: *www.mdwfp.com/careers.asp* Contact individual parks.

Missouri Department of Natural Resources
Volunteers in Parks (VIP) Program
Division of State Parks
PO Box 176
Jefferson City, MO 65102
800/334-6946 for information
Web site: *www.mostateparks.com/volunteer.htm* for volunteer application and information.
For employment as a ranger check:
www.mostateparks.com/rangers/index.html
Notes: Volunteers serve as interpreters, park aides, trail workers and campground hosts. Four-week (consecutive) stay minimum. Full hookup RV site.

Montana Department of Fish, Wildlife and Parks, Division of Parks
1420 East Sixth Avenue
P.O. BOX 200701
Helena, MT 59620-0701
406/444-2535
Volunteer coordinator: Debbie Cheek in the Helena headquarters at 406/444-4701 or call local park.
Web site: *www.fwp.state.mt.us/parks/volunteer.asp*
Notes: Campground hosts, naturalists, visitor center attendants, archaeological volunteers, special projects. Application online.

Nebraska Game and Parks Commission
2200 North 33rd Street
Lincoln, Ne. 68503
402/471-0641
Web site: *www.ngpc.state.ne.us/parks/programs/vip/vip.asp*
Request an application: *ngpc@ngpc.state.ne.us*

Nevada State Parks
1300 South Curry St.
Carson City, NV 89703
775/687-4384
Web site: seasonal employment and volunteering:
www.state.nv.us/stparks/job.html
For volunteer brochure and application, contact
stparks@parks.state.nv.us

New Hampshire Division of Parks and Recreation
PO Box 1856
172 Pembroke Rd
Concord, NH 03302
Phone: 603/271-3556
E-Mail: *nhparks@dred.state.nh.us*
Web site: *http://nhparks.state.nh.us/*
E-mail: *Vol-NH@excite.com* Office of Volunteerism
Seasonal employment opportunities: Call 603/436-1552 for
information.

New Jersey Department of Environmental Protection
Division of Parks and Forestry
501 East State Street, PO Box 404
Trenton, NJ 08625
For more information: 800/843-6420 or 609/984-0370
Volunteers in Parks program -contact any park office
www.state.nj.us/dep/forestry/intropark.htm
E-mail for seasonal employment: at *gerry.davies@dep.state.nj.us* Hire
approximately 600 seasonals. Applications available in February.

New Mexico State Parks
1220 St. Francis Dr.
Santa Fe, NM 87505
505/476-3391
Web site: *www.emnrd.state.nm.us/nmparks/* Click on Volunteer or
Employment Opportunities. Online volunteer form plus information
on program.

Notes: Several different types of volunteers sought.
Employment: *www.emnrd.state.nm.us/nmparks/PAGES/Employmt/
Jobs.htm* or 505/476-7777. Jobs listed online at New Mexico State
Personnel Office Web site.

New York State Parks
Albany, New York 12238
518/474-0456
Web site: *www.nysparks.state.ny.us/info//* - Camper Assistance Program
(CAP), their volunteer program. Contact parks directly.
Employment: *www.nysparks.state.ny.us/jobs/*

North Carolina State Parks
1615 Mail Service Center,
Raleigh, NC
919/733-4181.
Web site: *http://ils.unc.edu/parkproject/explore/volunteer.html*
E-mail: *parkinfo@ncmail.net*
Notes: Numerous types of volunteers needed. Contact the Volunteer
Manager at the park you are interested in.
Find seasonal employment opportunities at
http://ils.unc.edu/parkproject/explore/employseas.html

North Dakota Parks and Recreation Dept.
1835 Bismarck Expressway
Bismarck, ND 58504
701/328-5357
Web site: *http://www.ndparks.com/sitemap.htm*
E-mail: *npettys@state.nd.us*
Notes: Find Campground Host program, Volunteers in Parks, and
Employment on this page. Usually volunteer for four weeks, 30-hours/
week though it can be extended. Receive full hookup plus annual ND
State Park pass.

Ohio State Park Resorts
1952 Belcher Drive, Building C
Columbus OH 43224-1386

614/265-6561
E-mail: *dnrmail@dnr.state.oh.us*
Web site: Describes volunteer opportunities. Apply online.
Seasonal employment: *www.dnr.state.oh.us/jobs*
Resorts state parks operated by Xanterra Parks and Resorts.
www.coolworks.com/ohspr/default.htm. 800/282/7275

Oklahoma State Parks
15 N. Robinson, Suite 100
Oklahoma City, OK 73102
405/521-3411
Web site: *www.touroklahoma.com/Pages/stateparks/stateparks.html*
E-mail: *mcossey@otrd.state.ok.us*

Oregon State Parks
OPRD
Suite 1
1115 Commercial St NE
Salem OR 97301-1002
Toll-free: 877-225-9803
E-mail: *volunteer.info@state.or.us*
Web site: *www.prd.state.or.us/volunteer.php*
Apply online.
Employment: *www.prd.state.or.us/jobs.php*

Oregon Dept of Fish and Wildlife
Volunteer Host Program
7118 NE Vandenberg Ave.
Corvallis, OR 97330-9446
541/757-4186
Web site: *www.dfw.state.or.us*
Notes: Link to both paid and volunteer jobs. Duties could include stocking and feeding fish, visitor contact, maintenance, carpentry, habitat projects, clerical.

Pennsylvania State Parks
Bureau of State Parks
PO Box 8551

Harrisburg, PA 17105-8551
888/PA-PARKS
Web site: *www.dcnr.state.pa.us* See "quick links" for volunteering and jobs.
Notes: Several different types of Conservation Volunteer opportunities. Call above number or contact state park directly.
Concession opportunities:
www.dcnr.state.pa.us/stateparks/business

Rhode Island State Parks
Division of Parks & Recreation
2321 Hartford Ave
Johnston, RI 02919-1719
Phone Number: 401/222-2632
Web Address: *www.riparks.com*
Volunteering: Do not have a volunteer program at this time, but you might be able to offer your services at an individual park.
Seasonal employment: *www.riparks.com/employment.htm*

South Carolina State Park Service
1205 Pendleton Street
Columbia, SC 29201
803/734-0156
1-888-88-PARKS
Web site for employment and volunteer opportunities:
www.discoversouthcarolina.com/stateparks/employment.asp
Notes: Many types of volunteers are needed, including campground hosts. Contact the State Parks for a volunteer application. Submit completed application to the park of your choice.

South Dakota Division of Parks and Recreation
Volunteer Coordinator
523 East Capitol Ave.
Pierre, SD 57501
605/773-3930
www.sdgfp.info/parks/Index.htm
E-mail for more information: *SDParksVolunteers@state.sd.us*

For volunteering at Custer State Park:
www.custerstatepark.info/CSPvolunteer.htm
Notes: positions can include campground hosts, naturalist assistants, and visitor center attendants. Apply online. Custer has paid seasonal positions and a concessionaire.

Tennessee Department of Environment and Conservation
State Parks and Recreation
401 Church Street
Nashville, TN 37243
888/891-8332
Web site: *www.state.tn.us/environment/parks/index.html* for list of parks and volunteer opportunities.

Texas Parks and Wildlife
4200 Smith School Rd.
Austin, TX 78744
800/792-1112 , ext. 4415; 512/389-4415
Web site:
www.tpwd.state.tx.us/park/admin/spout_prog/volinfo.htm
E-mail: *kevin.good@tpwd.state.tx.us*
Seasonal employment opportunities:
www.tpwd.state.tx.us/involved/jobvac/job.htm
Notes: Contact the park of your choice or write, call or e-mail the above contact information. Several different types of volunteer opportunities available. See Web site.

State of Utah Natural Resources
Division of Parks and Recreation
1594 West North Temple St., Ste. 116
Box 146001
Salt Lake City, UT 84114-6001
801/538-7220
Volunteer coordinator: 801/537-3445
Web site: *http://parks.state.ut.us/parks/volunter.htm*
Notes: Positions/duties can include camphosts, plus docents, golf course marshal, visitor center/gift shop, trail maintenance and patrol, OHV and PWC safety education, assist curator of collections, park

maintenance and general park operations. Call or write for an application.

Vermont State Parks
103 South Main Street
Waterbury, VT 05671-0601
802/241-3655
E-mail: *parks@fpr.anr.state.vt.us* for information.
Web site: *http://www.vtstateparks.com/htm/employment.cfm* for volunteer and seasonal employment applications.

Virginia Department of Conservation and Recreation
203 Governor Street, Suite 213
Richmond, VA 23219-2094
800/933-PARK
Web site: *www.dcr.state.va.us/parks/volnteer.htm*
E-mail: *camphost@smyth.net* or call 276/646-8009 for an application or more information.
Notes: A variety of opportunities. Campground and park host programs for RVers. See site for more information and list of parks needing hosts.

Washington State Parks and Recreation Commission
7150 Cleanwater Lane
PO Box 42650
Olympia, WA 98504-2669
360/902-8583 for application/volunteer packet.
Web site: *www.parks.wa.gov/volunteer.asp*
E-mail: *volunteers@parks.wa.gov* Include your mailing address.
Seasonal jobs: *www.parks.wa.gov/jobs.asp* Hire Park Aides.
Notes: Send application to individual parks or one of the regional offices. Off-season volunteers/hosts needed in some parks. Volunteers needed for park projects (mainly maintenance and construction), cleanup projects, and interpretative center projects. Specialized skills sought in archaeology, computer skills, boating education, trade show volunteers, executive skills, marine guides, and public affairs. Participants in the Senior Environmental Corps for those age 55 and older share skills in a variety of projects.

West Virginia State Parks
Parks and Recreation
Volunteer Coordinator
1900 Kanawha Blvd., E.
Building 3, Room 709
Charleston, WV 25305-0314
304/558-2764
800/CALL-WVA
Web site: *www.wvstateparks.com/community/volpark.htm*
E-mail: *parks@westvirginia.com*
Notes: Volunteer park host program for RVers.

Wisconsin State Parks
Bureau of Parks and Recreation
P.O. Box 7921
Madison WI 53707-7921
Web site: *www.dnr.state.wi.us/org/land/parks/voljobs/volseek. html*
For information: Calll 608/264-8958
Seasonal jobs: *www.dnr.state.wi.us/employment/*
Notes: Several types of volunteers. Find volunteer application online.
Send completed application to park of your choice or the address
above.

Wyoming State Parks and Historic Sites
Human Resources
231 Central Ave., 4th Floor
Cheyenne, WY 82002
307/777-6303 307/777-7010 or *spcr@state.wy.us*
Write or call for information and application for volunteer program.
Seasonal employment information:
http://wyoparks.state.wy.us/seasonal%20employment.htm

Notes

"A life isn't significant except for its impact on others."
Jackie Robinson

Appendix 5
State revenue offices and tax information

A quick comparison chart of State Individual Income Tax rates at the
Federation of Tax Administrators Web site:
http://www.taxadmin.org/fta/rate/ind_inc.html

Alabama Department of Revenue
http://www.ador.state.al.us

Alaska Tax Division on Line
http://www.tax.state.ak.us
(No state income taxes)

Arizona Department of Revenue
http://www.revenue.state.az.us

Arkansas Department of Finance and Administration
http://www.accessarkansas.org/dfa
http://www.state.ar.us/dfa/taxes/movingto.html (information for new
residents)

California Franchise Tax Board
http://www.ftb.ca.gov

Colorado Department of Revenue
http://www.revenue.state.co.us/main/home.asp

Connecticut Department of Revenue Services
http://www.ct.gov/drs

Delaware Department of Finance, Division of Revenue
http://www.state.de.us/revenue/default.shtml

Florida Department of Revenue
Information for new residents:
http://sun6.dms.state.fl.us/dor/taxes/new.html

To speak with a Department of Revenue representative, call Taxpayer Services, Monday through Friday, 8 a.m. to 7 p.m., ET, at 800/352-3671 (in Florida only) or 850/488-6800.

Georgia Department of Revenue, Income Tax Division
http://www2.state.ga.us/departments/dor/inctax

Hawaii State Department of Taxation
http://www.state.hi.us/tax/tax.html

Idaho State Tax Commission
http://tax.idaho.gov/index.html

Illinois Department of Revenue
http://www.revenue.state.il.us

Indiana Department of Revenue
http://www.in.gov/dor

Iowa Department of Revenue and Finance
http://www.state.ia.us/tax/elf/eservice.html

Kansas Department of Revenue
 http://www.accesskansas.org/living/taxes.html

Kentucky Revenue Cabinet
http://www.revenue.state.ky.us

Louisiana Department of Revenue
http://www.rev.state.la.us

Maine Revenue Services
http://www.state.me.us/revenue/

Maryland - Comptroller of Maryland
http://www.comp.state.md.us/

Massachusetts Department of Revenue
http://www.dor.state.ma.us/

Michigan Department of Treasury
http://www.treas.state.mi.us/

Minnesota Department of Revenue
http://www.taxes.state.mn.us/

Mississippi State Tax Commission
http://www.mstc.state.ms.us/taxareas/individ/main.htm

Missouri Department of Revenue, Taxation and Collection
http://www.dor.state.mo.us/tax/

Montana Department of Revenue
http://www.discoveringmontana.com/revenue/css/default.asp

Nebraska Department of Revenue
http://www.revenue.state.ne.us/

Nevada Department of Taxation
http://tax.state.nv.us/
(No state income tax)

New Hampshire Department of Revenue
http://www.state.nh.us/revenue/index.htm
(Taxes interest, dividends, inheritance)

New Jersey Division of Taxation
http://www.state.nj.us/treasury/taxation/index.html

New Mexico Taxation and Revenue Department
http://www.state.nm.us/tax/

New York Department of Taxation and Finance
http://www.tax.state.ny.us/

North Carolina Department of Revenue
http://www.dor.state.nc.us/

North Dakota State Tax Department
http://www.state.nd.us/taxdpt/

Ohio Department of Taxation
http://www.state.oh.us/tax/

Oklahoma Tax Commission
http://www.oktax.state.ok.us/

Oregon Department of Revenue
http://www.dor.state.or.us/

Pennsylvania Department of Revenue
http://www.revenue.state.pa.us/revenue/site/default.asp

Rhode Island Division of Taxation
http://www.tax.state.ri.us/

South Carolina Department of Revenue
http://www.sctax.org/

South Dakota Department of Revenue
http://www.state.sd.us/revenue/revenue.html
South Dakota has no personal or corporate income tax.

Tennessee Department of Revenue
http://www.state.tn.us/revenue/

Texas Comptroller of Public Accounts
http://www.cpa.state.tx.us/taxinfo/taxtypes.html
No state income tax. See above for other types of taxes including inheritance.

Utah State Tax Commission
http://incometax.utah.gov/

Vermont Department of Taxes
http://www.state.vt.us/tax/

Virginia Department of Taxation
http://www.tax.state.va.us/

Washington Department of Revenue
http://dor.wa.gov/
No state income taxes

West Virginia State Tax Department
http://www.state.wv.us/taxdiv/

Wisconsin Department of Revenue
http://www.dor.state.wi.us/

Wyoming Department of Revenue
http://revenue.state.wy.us/
No personal income taxes

Notes

"He [or she] who is overcautious will accomplish little."
J.C.F. von Schiller

Appendix 6
State motor vehicle and
driver's license bureaus

Alabama Department of Public Safety, driver's licenses
http://www.dps.state.al.us
Alabama Department of Revenue, motor vehicle registration
http://www.ador.state.al.us/motorvehicle/index.html

Alaska Department of Administration, Division of Motor Vehicles
http://www.state.ak.us/local/akpages/ADMIN/dmv

Arizona DOT, Motor Vehicles Division
http://www.dot.state.az.us/MVD/custservices.htm

Arkansas Department of Finance and Revenue, Office of Motor
Vehicles & Drivers Services
http://www.state.ar.us/dfa/motorvehicle/index.html

California Department of Motor Vehicles
http://www.dmv.ca.gov/dmv.htm

Colorado Department of Revenue, Motor Vehicle Group
http://www.mv.state.co.us/mv.html

Connecticut Licensing Information Center
http://www.ct.gov/dmv/site/default.asp

Delaware Division of Motor Vehicles
http://www.delaware.gov/yahoo/DMV

Florida Department of Highway Safety and Motor Vehicles
http://www.hsmv.state.fl.us/index.html

Georgia Dept of Motor Vehicle Safety
http://www.dmvs.ga.gov.

Idaho Division of Motor Vehicles
http://www.itd.idaho.gov

Illinois Secretary of State
Information for new residents:
http://www.sos.state.il.us/services/new_residents.html

Indiana Bureau of Motor Vehicles
http://www.in.gov/bmv

Iowa Department of Transportation
http://www.dot.state.ia.us

Kansas Department of Revenue, Division of Motor Vehicles
http://www.accesskansas.org/living/cars-transportation.html

Kentucky Transportation Cabinet
http://www.kytc.state.ky.us/mv/
Click on Vehicle Regulation

Louisiana Office of Motor Vehicles
http://omv.dps.state.la.us/

Maine Bureau of Motor Vehicles
http://www.state.me.us/sos/bmv

Maryland Motor Vehicle Administration
http://www.mva.state.md.us/

Massachusetts Registry of Motor Vehicles
http://www.state.ma.us/rmv/

Michigan Department of State, Driver and Vehicle
http://www.michigan.gov/sos

Minnesota Department of Transportation
http://www.dot.state.mn.us/cars.html

Mississippi State Tax Commission
Motor vehicle registration:
http://www.mstc.state.ms.us/mvl/rules/main.htm
Department of Public Safety
Driver's license: http://www.dps.state.ms.us/

Missouri Department of Revenue, Motor Vehicle and Driver Licensing
http://www.dor.state.mo.us/mvdl/drivers/forms/

Montana Department of Justice, Motor Vehicle Division
http://www.doj.state.mt.us/default.asp

Nebraska Department of Motor Vehicles
http://www.nol.org/home/DMV

Nevada Department of Motor Vehicles and Public Safety
http://nevadadmv.state.nv.us/index.htm

New Hampshire Department of Safety, Division of Motor Vehicles
http://www.state.nh.us/dmv/index.html (Biennial report)

New Jersey Motor Vehicle Services
http://www.state.nj.us/mvc

New York Department of Motor Vehicles
http://www.nydmv.state.ny.us

North Carolina Division of Motor Vehicles
http://www.dmv.dot.state.nc.us

North Dakota Department of Transportation/ Driver, Vehicle, Fleet Services
http://www.state.nd.us/dot

Ohio Bureau of Motor Vehicles
http://www.state.oh.us/odps/division/bmv/bmv.html

Oklahoma Tax Commission Vehicle registration:
http://www.oktax.state.ok.us/mvhome.html
Oklahoma Dept of Public Safety -Drivers licenses:
 http://www.dps.state.ok.us/dls/

Oregon Driver and Motor Vehicle Services
http://www.odot.state.or.us/dmv/index.htm

Pennsylvania Department of Transportation
http://www.dmv.state.pa.us/

Rhode Island Division of Motor Vehicles
http://www.rilin.state.ri.us/Statutes/TITLE31/INDEX.HTM

South Carolina Department of Motor Vehicles
http://www.scdps.org/dmv/

South Dakota Department of Transportation
Driver licenses: http://www.state.sd.us/dps/dl
Vehcile registration: http://www.state.sd.us/drr2/motorvehicle/index.htm

Tennessee Department of Safety, Motor Vehicle Services
http://www.state.tn.us/safety/nav2.html

Texas Department of Public Safety
Driver license: http://www.txdps.state.tx.us/geninfo.htm
Vehicle registration: http://www.txdot.state.tx.us

Utah Division of Motor Vehicles
http://www.utah.gov/living/newcomers.html

Vermont Department of Motor Vehicles
http://www.dmv.state.vt.us/dmvhp.htm

Virginia Department of Motor Vehicles
http://www.dmv.state.va.us

Washington Department of Licensing
http://www.wa.gov/dol/

West Virginia DOT Division of Motor Vehicles
http://www.wvdot.com/6_motorists/dmv/6G_DMV.HTM

Wisconsin DOT Division of Motor Vehicles
http://www.dot.wisconsin.gov/drivers/

Wyoming Department of Transportation
http://wydotweb.state.wy.us/

Notes

*"Every thought, decision, and action moves you
closer to or further from achieving your goals -
Everything counts!"*
The Goals Guy at www.goalsguy.com

Appendix 7
Janice's grocery shopping list

When my husband, Gabby, and I became full-time RVers in the mid-1980s, a situation occurred that was totally unexpected: Grocery shopping in a different market, in a different city every time supplies were needed.

Now, I knew I wasn't on a different planet and many stores are laid out in a similar fashion. Nonetheless, I became frustrated with my usual style of keeping a grocery list. I had to come up with a better method than simply jotting down an item on a piece of scrap paper whenever I thought it was needed and ending up with a list that jumped from one type of product to another.

What I designed was a list with headers in alphabetical sequence by shape or style of items. For example, the first column of the list is titled, Boxes, followed by Cans. Next I have columns for Dairy, Freezer, Fruits, Jars, Meats, Starches, Vegetables, and last, Miscellaneous, such as cleaning products, paper goods or pharmaceutical supplies.

Now, when I run out of, say, cereal, that item is written down in the Box column. If I happen to have a coupon for that product, an asterisk is plugged in next to the item, and the coupon is immediately attached to the list.

Once my list is full (or near-full), it automatically becomes market day no matter where we are. The list, with coupons attached, and a pen, accompany me. As I cruise each aisle, I simply shop by shape. No more scanning a piece of scratch paper from top to bottom each time I come to a new item on the shelf. When each product goes into the shopping cart, it is crossed off the list and I don't have to look for it again. A quick glance down each column indicates whether the columns are complete, and, of course, when they are, shopping is done.

Sharing the list

The way the list is made up, it can be split down the middle and if there are two of you shopping, each of you can take half the list and shopping is accomplished in half the time.

If you stick to what is on the list, you'll avoid impulse buying, and consequently, save even more money. I've shared the list with friends and have been told they are still using this method after making changes to suit their own shopping needs.

One added suggestion is to permanently add the names of your favorite products and the chain that carries them. Listing the city wouldn't hurt.

Another way to save time and money is to prepare master lists of your favorite company or holiday meals. Reverse the shopping procedure by circling only those items you need.

For me, this is shopping made simple and is a system that has worked well for us for many years. Now, if we could only remember where we parked the car in that strange parking lot.

Author's note: Janice Lasko shared her grocery shopping list with me in 1994. This list was a lifesaver the two seasons we worked at Bull Frog marina at Lake Powell, Utah. We shopped four hours away in Grand Junction every four to six weeks. If we forgot something, we were out of luck until the next trip. The little grocery at the marina was expensive and had few items we needed. I kept the list handy and immediately wrote down anything we ran out of or would need on the next trip.

Since I was planning meals for a month or more, I would list my menu on the back and as I decided on a meal, I would record any ingredients I needed in the appropriate column. That way I didn't plan lasagna and get home with no ricotta cheese.

Our boss was able to make a refrigerator available for us to freeze bread and meat. We were able to supplement our diet with fresh fruit and vegetables locally. We ate once or twice a week at the concessionaire dining room, which had an excellent salad bar. Fellow workers shared produce from their gardens and fruit trees planted in the housing area produced peaches and apricots.

To take into account my shopping patterns, I modified the headings Janice used slightly to the ones you see on the following page. Feel free to do the same.

FRUIT/ VEGETABLES	BOXES/ JARS	CANS	PASTA BEANS	BAKING/ SPICES	BREADS/ MEAT	DAIRY/ FROZEN	HOUSEHOLD /MISC/WLMT
					HEALTH FOOD		

Menu/notes

Appendix 8
Budget worksheet

(Per month)	Now	Full-timing
RV payment/housing	$ _____	$ _____
Food, including restaurants	$ _____	$ _____
Health		
Medical insurance	$ _____	$ _____
Other medical expenses	$ _____	$ _____
Camping Fees		
Membership parks & campground fees	$ _____	$ _____
Transportation		
Fuel	$ _____	$ _____
Insurance, incl. towing	$ _____	$ _____
License & reg.	$ _____	$ _____
Maintenance	$ _____	$ _____
Communication		
Telephone and Internet	$ _____	$ _____
Mail service	$ _____	$ _____
Other		
Clothing	$ _____	$ _____
Gifts	$ _____	$ _____
Laundry	$ _____	$ _____
Life insurance	$ _____	$ _____
Memberships- clubs	$ _____	$ _____
Federal/state taxes	$ _____	$ _____
Propane	$ _____	$ _____
TV/satellite	$ _____	$ _____
Misc.	$ _____	$ _____
Total	$ _____	$ _____
	X 12 = _____/yr	x12=_____/yr

Notes

Appendix 9
Stephanie Bernhagen's
Budget worksheet

This worksheet will help you evaluate your expenses today, help you determine what your expenses will be in the full-timing lifestyle and help you make a decision if you have enough money or will need to work on the road. The categories listed are typical categories, but may not include all of your expenses, so don't forget to add your unique expenses. Be sure all your dollar amounts are for the same period, i.e. monthly, quarterly, or annual.

	TODAY	FULL-TIMING
Camping		
· **Campground Fees**	$_____	$_____
· **Membership Fees**	$_____	$_____
Clothing		
· **Laundry**	$_____	$_____
· **New Clothing**	$_____	$_____
Communications		
· **Phone**	$_____	$_____
· **Calling Card**	$_____	$_____
· **Postage**	$_____	$_____
· **Mail Service**	$_____	$_____
· **Internet Access**	$_____	$_____
· **Message Service**	$_____	$_____
Entertainment		
· **Cable/Satellite TV**	$_____	$_____
· **Admission Fees**	$_____	$_____

- **Movies** $_____ $_____
- **Books/CDs/**
    Newspapers $_____ $_____
- **Crafts/Hobbies** $_____ $_____
- **Entertaining Others** $_____ $_____
- **Other** $_____ $_____

Fuel
- **Towed/Tow** $_____ $_____
- **Motorhome** $_____ $_____

Food
- **Groceries** $_____ $_____
- **Dining Out** $_____ $_____

Health
- **Health Insurance** $_____ $_____
- **Dental Insurance** $_____ $_____
- **Vision Insurance** $_____ $_____
- **Prescription**
    Insurance $_____ $_____
- **OTC Drugs** $_____ $_____
- **Out of Pocket**
    Medical Expenses $_____ $_____
- **Long-term Health** $_____ $_____

Home/Vehicle Insurance
- **Homeowners** $_____ $_____
- **Renters** $_____ $_____
- **Vehicle** $_____ $_____
- **RV** $_____ $_____
- **Road Service** $_____ $_____

Housing/RV
- **House Mortgage** $_____ $_____
- **Property Taxes** $_____ $_____

- **Home Owners**
  Dues $_____ $_____
- **Home**
  Maintenance $_____ $_____
- **Rent** $_____ $_____
- **RV Loan** $_____ $_____
- **RV Maintenance** $_____ $_____
- **RV Registration** $_____ $_____

Pets
- **Food** $_____ $_____
- **Veterinarian** $_____ $_____
- **Kennel** $_____ $_____

Savings
- **RV/Vehicle**
  Replacement $_____ $_____
- **Medical**
  Deductible $_____ $_____
- **Property Purchase** $_____ $_____
- **Care Facility** $_____ $_____
- **Burial** $_____ $_____

Taxes
- **State** $_____ $_____
- **Federal** $_____ $_____

Utilities
- **Electric** $_____ $_____
- **Propane** $_____ $_____
- **Natural Gas** $_____ $_____
- **Sewer/Water** $_____ $_____
- **Other** $_____ $_____

Vehicle

- **Loan** $_____ $_____
- **Registration** $_____ $_____
- **Maintenance** $_____ $_____

Work

- **Work Related Expenses** $_____ $_____

Miscellaneous

- **Storage Unit** $_____ $_____
- **Gifts** $_____ $_____
- **Life Insurance** $_____ $_____
- **Other** $_____ $_____

	TODAY	**FULL-TIMING**
Total Expenses	$_____	$_____

The following one-time expenses will deplete your savings. Be sure to account for one-time expenses and subtract them from your savings before you determine what you can earn on your savings. (Unless you plan to raise additional money for these expenses before making the purchase.)

FULL-TIMING

One-Time Expenses

- **RV Purchase Without Loan** $_____
- **Vehicle Purchase without Loan** $_____
- **Solar Panels** $_____
- **Heater** $_____
- **RV Accessories** $_____
- **Initial Membership Costs** $_____
- **Other Expenses** $_____

	TODAY	**FULL-TIMING**
Income		
· **Investments**	$_____	$_____
· **Interest**	$_____	$_____
· **IRA, 401K, etc.**	$_____	$_____
· **Pension**	$_____	$_____
· **Social Security**	$_____	$_____
· **Work**	$_____	$_____
· **Other**	$_____	$_____

	TODAY	**FULL-TIMING**
Total Income	$_____	$_____

Budget notes

*"Find a job you love and add five days to
every week."*
H. Jackson Brown

Appendix 10
Three RV worker stories

In this appendix we have stories of the work experiences of three RV workers. They are expanded to give you some ideas of the variety available and more details on how some working RVers have put it all together.

In the first story, Bill and I share how we targeted a specific geographical area to work in and fulfilled our Alaskan dream. Normally we prefer to apply to national parks. However, to work in Alaska, we were willing to work for another employer and make less money. We share the many resources we used to put together a geographic job search.

In the second story, Janice Lasko, editor of *Escapees* magazine, recounts their fascinating work history. Their preference is working in cold locations because they love to ski. They have held some unique positions while doing what they love.

Finally, Lou Schneider shares a variety of work experiences he has had on the road. He obtained his Commercial Driver's License so he could make more money on the road.

PUTTING IT ALL TOGETHER:
OUR ALASKA DREAM COME TRUE
When you have a specific destination or location where you want to work, and that is the overriding factor for your employment choice for the season, it is time to use all you've learned about finding jobs. You may not be as concerned about the type of job as the location so the important thing is to get job offers. How we got jobs in Alaska is a review of the many techniques we have covered. If you too would like to work in Alaska, see the resources we used in **Resources (Appendix 10).**

Traveling and working in Alaska had been one of my dreams for years. Five years after hitting the road, we focused on finding summer jobs in Alaska.

Getting a job in Alaska isn't difficult; employment opportunities are plentiful. Cruise lines bring myriads of tourists to ports along the Inside Passage. Many tourists visit the main part of Alaska — Anchorage, Denali and Fairbanks — in RVs or on tours connected with their cruise package. Holland America and Princess also have land-based operations, hotels and bus tours in several locations.

Skagway, where we worked, adds about a thousand seasonal workers to its year-round population of 700. Major employers include White Pass & Yukon Route Railroad, National Park Service, Princess Tours, Gray Line Tours, Skagway Street Cars, Westmark Hotel, and Temsco Helicopters. Retail stores also hire.

Wages are generally higher in Alaska, but that is offset by the cost of getting there and the higher cost of living. Weather and extended daylight are factors too. The panhandle of Alaska, along the Inside Passage, is coastal rainforest. Annual rainfall varies from 30" in Skagway, to over 150" in Ketchikan. Summer temperatures are generally cool, though occasionally temperatures can reach 90 degrees. Long daylight hours make it difficult for some people to sleep.

> **Wages are generally higher in Alaska**

We began searching for potential summer employers in November. We applied to just about any employer so we would have definite jobs before heading north. Since Seattle to Skagway is 1,800 miles and over 2,400 miles to Anchorage, travel is a big expense.

Housing

Make sure you have housing or an RV site lined up before you leave. We had heard that RVers parked the whole summer at Wal-Mart or Fred Myers and were told by an employer in Juneau that we could park at the Fred Myers the whole summer. We later found out that was not allowed. We interviewed with a Denali concessionaire who could not provide an RV site nor a place to park our RV if we stayed in their housing. He suggested a boondocking area about 20 miles away, but we were not comfortable with that option since we could not check it out beforehand.

RV parks may be limited. In Skagway, at the time, only one of the three RV parks had a monthly rate. The park was expensive and we were packed in like sardines. We found that most Skagway employers who provided RV sites or employee housing charged their employees rent.

Be alert to camphosting opportunities. Page and Ardith acted as campground hosts in an Anchorage campground during off hours in exchange for a site. They still had time for full time jobs. The next year they were able to park at the RV dealership where they worked. Halfway through the season, Bill got the job camphosting at the NPS campground in nearby Dyea. We eliminated rent from our budget and had a gorgeous, quiet setting for the rest of the summer.

Ron and Val contacted Halsingland Hotel in Haines, and lined up jobs in their RV park. Their paid positions came with site, plus many other perks like free and discounted tours and transportation. A bonus for Ron — great fishing!

> **Make sure you have housing or an RV site lined up before you leave.**

Bill had fun helping visitors pan for gold at Liarsville (and telling lies!) and I gave talks and tours as a ranger at Klondike Gold Rush National Historical Park. For two summers, we took advantage of free and discounted prices offered by tourist attractions to "summer locals" at the beginning of each season. On weekends, we explored nearby Alaska, British Columbia and the Yukon Territory. We kayaked in Glacier Bay and panned for gold near Dawson City.

For us the scenery, wildlife, and history made our summers in Alaska a dream come true.

Other tips

✔ **Start early:** Begin in November or December prior to the summer you are targeting. Some employers fill their positions very early.

✔ **Express your interest** even if there are no current openings. A former employee may not come back.

✔ **Keep in contact** with employers you would really like to work for. The more contacts you have with a potential employer, the more likely you are to be remembered for that last minute opening.

✔ **Apply to many employers:** Don't put all your eggs in one basket. You can always turn down a job offer; if you didn't apply, it may be too late.

✔ **Network:** Now is the time to go back through your **Job Notebook** and see if you have any notes that would help you. Contact everyone you know who might have knowledge of jobs in this area. As you talk to employers or the Chamber of Commerce, ask them if they know of anyone else who might be hiring.

WHISTLE WHILE WE WORK BY JANICE LASKO

I knew I was in for a fair amount of traveling when my husband Gabby proposed in early 1971 saying, "Let's fly to Jamaica to be married." We were living a good distance from Kingston, in Marina del Rey, California.

It took nearly one year of preparation and corresponding with the Magistrate of Home Affairs to gather the proper documentation. We finally married in Kingston at the Magistrate's home and honeymooned on the island in December 1971. There were three people in attendance at the celebration: the Magistrate, who performed the ceremony; his son, who doubled as our photographer and witness; and the Magistrate's housekeeper, who was the second witness, played the appropriate wedding march and served the celebratory champagne. It was intimate and special.

We have since traveled to Europe on several occasions, Mexico at least

> **"We began traveling in an RV with a bang."**

a half dozen times, taken cruises and island-hopped in the Pacific and Caribbean. One summer we self-crewed a sailboat with two other couples around the British Virgin Islands. These trips would be preludes to our eventual ease into full-time RVing because we felt RVing would be the best way to see North America in depth via the back roads.

Although I say we eventually eased into full-timing, I should mention we began traveling in an RV with a bang. In 1982 we had already sold our home and had quit high-pressure jobs in the city. Gabby was a construction contractor and I was part of the exciting world of advertising in the Los Angeles area. We moved into our vacation condo in a ski resort community in the California High Sierras, promising ourselves to take only fun jobs and work just enough to support our favorite hobbies — skiing, windsurfing and traveling.

Hitting the road full time

That all changed when one day in 1985 we saw a used class-A motorhome for sale, test drove it and bought it. (The motorhome really wasn't for sale; we just kind of talked the owner into selling it to us.) Our first trip was a whopping 17 miles from our condo, and each time we thought of something we had forgotten to bring with us, we simply drove back home to pick it up and then returned to our campsite. We have become much more organized and have subsequently realized one of the biggest advantages to traveling in a motorhome is having all of our stuff with us all the time.

We eventually extended our distances and found we were spending more time in our motorhome traveling than we were in our fixed dwelling. That's when we began to think about traveling on a full-time basis. We wondered if it could be done and whether others sold everything, abandoned family and friends and hit the road for good. Our condo sold in less than one week and closed escrow by the second week. So, whether others did or didn't go on the road full-time, that's what we wanted to do and did. We soon learned we were not alone.

> **"Full-time traveling is a way of life, not a permanent vacation."**

We also discovered that full-time traveling is a way of life, not a permanent vacation. New restaurants are fun, but not three times a day. Laundry, shopping and cooking still must be accomplished and the rig needs to be cleaned on a regular basis, although it only takes about one hour to do a thorough job. Most importantly, vehicle maintenance takes a high priority. All these things can't wait to be taken care of as usually happens at the end of a vacation.

Eventually we realized we wanted and needed to divide our attention between our hobbies, traveling and maintaining an income that would allow us to remain living on the road. So we became the opposites of snowbirds (those who follow the sun and camp in southern climates all winter). We didn't run from the snow for the Sun Belt each winter. That way we could find jobs in order to pursue and support the expensive sport of snow skiing.

Winter work

I'm an early-blooming baby boomer. Gabby is 18 years my senior and, I must add, in excellent condition. He prides himself on skiing anywhere from 50 to 100 days each season. In spite of his white hair, we are thrilled at the acceptance we've both had when applying for work.

Did I say work? That's right. We found that, in order to stay ahead of the financial game and remain on the road, the word "work" would have to reenter our vocabulary and become part of our lives again. As a result, we have added some unusual and extremely interesting skills to our experiences on the road, which come second to the people we've met and the friends we've made. Another benefit of working in this lifestyle is the network of people who are doing what we do and who share job possibilities. In a sense, one job has led to another in different parts of the country and sometimes with the same friends.

For instance, one winter season we sold lift tickets at a ski resort in Oregon. One of the couples we met also worked at the resort and were camped near us in the same RV park. We have remained in touch with this couple ever since, traveled together on several occasions and worked with them again, selling Christmas trees in central California one year, and in Texas a few years later. By the way, the perks for that ticket-selling job were numerous. In addition to a salary, there was a company bus from town to the mountain, which gave our truck a much-needed rest that winter, free skiing and a locker at the base of the mountain to store our ski gear. And that gave us oodles of extra storage space in the rig that season. We were finished selling lift tickets by 11:00 a.m. and were on the hill skiing by noon, following a discounted meal on the mountain.

Preparing the Christmas tree lots and subsequent three to four weeks of tree sales was physically demanding. However, that turned into a plus for us because the physical labor conditioned us for the slopes. Since we were through selling trees by Christmas day, we looked for the best snow conditions in the country and drove our fifth-wheel trailer to the area as quickly as possible to set up for the rest of the winter. More than one season found us back in Mammoth Lakes, California, our former home base. It was a simple task to procure jobs amongst former neighbors and be working by mid-January. One year Gabby went into show business in Mammoth candy counter at the local theater. Then one of his coworkers led him to a desk clerk position at a motel in town.

> **"One year Gabby went into show business..."**

We stayed past the winter that season, which gave Gabby the opportunity to work in the maintenance department of the motel.

That same year I was a nanny (nicknamed by the youngsters 'Janny the Nanny') for a four-year-old and his sister, just 13 months his junior. Being a close-knit town, word spread, and there were days when I was taking care of seven children, all under the age of six. It was exciting to watch these youngsters grow and mature as winter turned to summer and eventually autumn. Their mom and dad owned a restaurant, and from time to time I'd fill in as a hostess in the best pizza house in town. The drawback with this job was the growing attachment to the children. After eight months, it definitely was time to move on.

> **"Short visits are better than no visit at all."**

We have stayed in touch with another couple we met when we first began to travel via RV and have met up with them all over the country 42 times, some planned, other times by sheer good fortune. The shortest visit was under one hour when they happened to see our parked rig from the highway while on their way to a new job in the next state. Our motto is, "in this lifestyle, short visits are better than no visit at all." Well, this couple interested us in working for a company that produces RV park guides with area maps pinpointing local businesses. Although we didn't work for the company too long, we were rewarded with a supportive home-office staff and the ability to remain on the move, seeing new, as yet unexplored towns, in addition to complimentary campsites, plus, of course, that oh-so-thrilling-to-receive commission check.

Time for work and play

An added challenge to our job hunting is to leave the days free to ski and play. One season I did data entry for a catalog company filling Thanksgiving and Christmas gift orders. Being willing to work the 4:00 p.m.-to-midnight shift meant time-and-a-half and sometimes double-time pay. The company provided a data entry/computer training course at no expense to new employees and superior fruit items at the end of each shift that didn't quite meet top-quality standards for shipment to customers.

One interesting time found Gabby and me sharing the rig for a mere four hours a day. Gabby was the night-shift bartender for a ski resort and didn't arrive home until midnight. I awoke at 4:00 a.m. to provide

50 radio stations with ski and weather conditions. When I was done by 9:00 a.m., I would fetch Gabby, we'd ski a few hours together and start over. Again, we were provided a salary as well as free skiing.

We have both enjoyed the challenge of waiting tables in various restaurants and have also worked in several RV parks in Texas, California, Idaho and Alabama. At these parks we maintained a balancing act of taking reservations, checking guests in and out, cleaning the bathrooms, running a grocery store, shoveling snow out of the RV parking sites and skimming leaves out of the swimming pool. Five days a week in Alabama, I even taught line dancing (now that is not work, it's just plain fun). Maintenance of the grounds at one park gave me the opportunity to freshen up a nine-foot totem pole on a miniature golf course with a new coat of paint while Gabby helped install water, sewer and electric hookups to 10 new sites.

> **"We were provided a salary as well as free skiing."**

For working in RV parks we were rewarded with a free campsite, salary, cost-of-living allowance, and, if we stayed one full year at the park in Idaho, a rather princely bonus. We stayed beautiful ski resort of Sun Valley.

As fun and challenging as these jobs were, time seemed to stretch slowly and it became difficult for us not to pick up and go whenever someone pulled out a map or began talking to us about their travel plans.

The jobs are out there almost for the taking. It's just a matter of attitude and willingness and honesty. We try to let our prospective employer know we are interested only in seasonal, part-time employment. This avoids hard feelings when we suffer from "hitch-itch" and begin poring over maps, something we can do for hours on end.

Motorhome or 5ᵗʰ wheel?

By 1987 we switched from that used motorhome to a new truck and fifth-wheel trailer, which served us well for five years, followed by a second fifth-wheel (same truck). We were delighted with the space the single, 17-foot slide-out provided, which was half the length of the rig. Actually, we were not looking for another new rig, but our latest purchase was a brand-new motorhome. We decided we could always work to pay it off, which is exactly what we are doing.

The latest job offer came from the Escapees RV Club when I was asked to be editor of *Escapees* magazine, produced in Livingston, Texas, national headquarters of the Escapees RV Club. The magazine is a bi-monthly publication for the serious RVers. We had no intention of set-tling down to such a challenging commitment, but another lesson we've learned is to never say never to anything, even sitting in one place, be-cause you never know what it may lead to. Only recently I was given the opportunity to continue as *Escapees* magazine editor, but editor-on-the-go. Now, I have my cake and can eat it, too, as we travel and I edit. Gabby has a slice of the pie, too, as he worked this winter in an inn as maitre d' at a ski mountain, Taos Ski Valley in New Mexico.

There are advantages to each type of recreational vehicle, and what works for us seems to change as we age. All we ask is plenty of storage space for our bulky winter clothes and ski gear, as well as the bicycles and golf clubs. (The windsurfing equipment was donated to a younger generation of our family long ago.)

Sticking to a budget

Because I keep copious records, we are able to account for every penny spent, by category, since day one. The categories are (1) campsites, (2) gas and truck maintenance, (3) groceries, (4) restaurants, (5) telephone, (6) laundry, and (7) gifts, museums, and entertainment. Fixed and unknown expenses, such as campground memberships, dues, insurance, medical, and dental are kept in a separate file. I analyzed six months of working versus six months on the

> **"We've traveled over 235,000 miles since 1985."**

road and found the cost of living to be slightly less while traveling. When we work, I adjust our budget higher, but we are also careful not to fall into the trap of spending what we earn. We try to live frugally so we can rebuild our surplus and be back on the road.

Although we've traveled over 235,000 miles since 1985, when look-ing back, sometimes it seems we've been working more than traveling. But that's okay with us. It turned out better than we originally planned. We first thought we'd RV for two years, see it all and settle down again permanently. We didn't count on becoming so passionate about this way of life; we've discovered it's fun to settle for a short period of time and then hit the road again. No matter which role we're in, we are always looking forward to something new.

The years are whizzing by. We have cut our skiing back to roughly 15 or 20 days a year, and have even slowed down on crisscrossing North America in the RV. If the day comes when we are forced to hang up the keys, maybe we'll do it in some snowbird-type RV park where we can line dance, play cards, golf, take an occasional bike ride or even an airplane trip. But best yet, we'll always look forward to a vacation in any RV. If planned and timed right, the RVer can catch, for example, the Calgary Stampede, the Hot Air Balloon Festival in New Mexico, the Fryeburg Fair in Maine, and then pick up Autumn's burst of fall colors throughout New England. Well, the list of famous events and small, local festivals goes on. The more we see, the more we learn there is to see.

> **"We would not have missed this myriad of job opportunities for the world."**

We would not have missed this myriad of job opportunities for the world. Each one has led to discovering a part of our country, a heritage, a way of life that would have remained alien to us had we locked ourselves into that old lifestyle of fixed dwellings and job commuting. We have learned that work is certainly not a four-letter word; it is a means to an end, and never have we faced so many stimulating choices. It's no wonder we have reason to whistle while we work.

For more information about the Escapees RV Club, see **Resources.**

LOU SCHNEIDER'S WORKING TALES

My work career was as a radio engineer, installing and maintaining broadcast transmitters and all of the related technical equipment. I had been doing this since I was 16 and decided it was time to try something new.

Two years ago I quit my job and started full-timing at age 45. A couple of years prior to this, I moved into my RV and lived in a nearby RV park while I worked. The park rent was much less than what I had paid to rent an apartment, so I put the difference into savings. When I was ready to make the break, my rig was paid for and I had a nice little nest egg.

The first thing I did was get my Class A Commercial Drivers License (CDL). I always wanted to drive a big rig. I'd seen several classified ads from Swift Trucking Company offering CDL training, so I talked to their recruiters and told them I was exploring career options. They said

I could pay for the school up front and not be under any obligation to work for them, but if I did they would reimburse my tuition. So I spent three weeks at the school, then said, "No thanks," after I got my license.

There is an acute shortage of CDL drivers and I found job opportunities are plentiful. While spending last winter in Quartzsite, Arizona, I noticed a truck assembly plant near the California state line. I made some inquiries and applied to the company that had the contract to deliver the new trucks to customers. I was promptly hired, even though I had no commercial driving experience. The assembly plant builds both CDL and non-CDL trucks, and there was a desperate need for drivers with a CDL to deliver the larger trucks. These trucks had 24 foot van bodies, a GVWR over 26,000 lbs., dual drive axles and air brakes. Unloaded they drove about the same as a smaller truck. The pay for delivering these was almost twice as much as delivering a non-CDL truck.

> **"There is an acute shortage of CDL drivers."**

I only delivered a couple of trucks while in Quartzsite, but the money more than covered my living expenses for the three months I stayed there.

Temporary agency

Later I was in Sacramento and signed up with a temporary agency, Link Staffing. I told them that although I had a Class A license I didn't want to drive anything larger than a Class B truck until I gained more experience. Even so, they kept me as busy as I wanted at $10-15 per hour.

The agency would call the day before an assignment, which I was free to accept or reject. Usually I would report to work at a warehouse or distribution center where there would be a loaded truck waiting. I would follow another truck to a destination or be given a map and sent out on my own. All of these were local deliveries within a 50-mile radius. At the end of the day I would return to Link's office, where they issued a check on the spot. I did this for six weeks, and when I left I was told I could start any time I wished. Link has offices in other major cities and my records could be transferred to any of them.

Tomatoes

My goal was to find a something I could do for four to six months and earn enough money to carry me through the rest of the year. I came close when I started driving the tomato harvest. I applied to a seasonal trucking company and got a job driving a full Class A rig, a tractor towing two flatbed trailers carrying tubs full of tomatoes. The loaded weight was 80,000 lbs. Drivers are paid based on the delivered weight and mileage traveled, and I was able to average $850 to $1,000 per week. The only disadvantage was it was a 7-day per week job. Once the harvest starts it doesn't let up for two to three months.

> **"They issued a check on the spot."**

I would report to the terminal in the morning, check out the truck, then head south with a set of empty trailers. At the field I would drop off the empty trailers, hitch up a loaded set, then take the load to the cannery. After dropping the loaded trailers at the cannery, I'd get another empty set and repeat the process. Each leg of the process took one to two hours, so I was able to deliver two or three loads each day.

Don't burn your bridges

After a month I was looking forward to the end of the harvest and returning to the Arizona desert for the winter. That's when I discovered the value of not burning my bridges.

My former boss in radio installation left the company I had worked for about the same time I began driving the tomato harvest. He took a similar position across town at another group of radio stations and quickly discovered there was a backlog or work, including installing several transmitters. He contacted me via e-mail and asked if I would be willing to help him out at consultant rates.

The pay was too good to pass up — $75 per hour for three to four weeks of full time work. So I left the trucking company with the understanding I could return and finish out the harvest after I had finished installing the transmitters. I never did go back.

I was asked to take a full-time position, and negotiated an arrangement that allows me to travel for extended periods of time plus gives me an ongoing income for the foreseeable future.

I'm classified as a full-time employee so I get company benefits like health insurance and retirement. But I get substantially more annual vacation than standard company policy. While this year the company has a backlog of work and I will only get off two weeks per quarter, in the next year, I will work about six months of the year. I'll work one or two months, then get the same amount of time off. While I am off, the company will continue paying my health insurance and I'll continue to participate in the retirement plan.

Two things I've learned

✔ Keep your eyes open for employment possibilities. They are everywhere.
✔ Don't overlook the possibility of continuing to work in the career field you are leaving.

It's been an interesting ride so far!"

Notes

"If you don't make a total commitment to whatever you're doing, then you start looking to bail out the first time the boat starts leaking. It's tough enough getting that boat to shore with everyone rowing, let alone when a guy stands up and starts putting his life jacket on."
Lou Holtz

Section V. Resources
Listed by chapter

General resources:
BOOKS ON HOW TO FULL-TIME RVING
- *Complete Guide to Full-Time RVing: Life on the Open Road*, Bill and Jan Moeller. Trailer Life Books.
- *Home is Where You Park It*, Joe and Kay Peterson, RoVers Press. *(www.escapees.com)*
- *Movin' On*, Ron and Barb Hofmeister, R&B Publications. *(www.movinon.net)*
- *Survival of the RV Snowbirds*, Joe and Kay Peterson, RoVers Press. *(www.escapees.com)*
- *Over the Hill: An Ethnography of RVing Seniors in North America* by Dorothy Ayers Counts and David Reese Counts. Results of a study of full-timing. (Amazon.com) New edition March 2001.
- *Take Back Your Life! Travel Full-Time in Your RV,* Stephanie Bernhagen, Bernham-Collins. *(www.rvhometown.com)*
- **Nick Russell's** account of their first year as full-time RVers. *Meandering Down the Highway. (www.gypsyjournal.net)*

BOOKS ON WORKING ON THE ROAD
- *Road Work: The Ultimate RVing Adventure* by Arline Chandler *(www.workamper.com)* Newly revised 2002.
- *Travel While You Work,* by Joe and Kay Peterson. RoVers Press *(www.escapees.com)*
- *Work Your Way Across the USA: You Can Travel and Earn a Living too!* Nick Russell, Publishing Partners. *(www.gypsyjournal.net)*

RV PUBLICATIONS
- *RV Companion:* written by RVers for RVers. Both print and Web-based editions. *(www.rvcompanion.com)* Print subscriptions $15/year. Subscribe online, by mail or fax. PO Box 174, Loveland CO 80539, 888/763-3295.
- **RV club membership** in RV clubs includes a subscription to their print magazine.

RV ELECTRONIC MAGAZINES (e-zines)

- *RV Lifestyle:* Semimonthly ezine edited by this author. Subscribe by sending an e-mail to *RVLifestyle-subscribe@listbase.net.* Then add *RVLifestlye@listbase.net* to your address book.

CHAPTER 1: WHAT DO YOU BRING TO THE JOB MARKET?

- **Taking a look at yourself:** A number of books have been written to assist you in looking at your life, deciding on goals for your life or job, and how to achieve them.
  - *What Color is My Parachute:* Richard Bolles' classic book on looking at what careers are a match.
  - **Barbara Sher's books:** All her books are helpful, especially *I Could Do Anything if I Only Knew What It Was,* and *It's Only Too Late If You Don't Start Now.*
  - *Finding Your Perfect Work:* Paul and Sarah Edwards. Geared for finding self-employment that works for you. Discover your personal style, then find a match.
  - **Look also:** The Career section of a bookstore or library should have these and other helpful references.

CHAPTER 3: HOW MUCH MONEY WILL YOU NEED?

Budgeting and financial management

- **Bankrate.com** has a number of useful financial calculators. At the "Home Page," click on "calculate." *www.bankrate.com*
- "**Managing Your Money** While Living on the Road is a Breeze," by Lucy Lazarony at Bankrate.com. *www.bankrate.com/brm/news/auto/20010507a.asp*
- **Bloomberg University** offers free online courses in investing and retiring rich. Help your retirement funds grow. Start with Investing 101. *(www.bloomberg.com/analysis/univ/index.html)*
- **BudgetYes!** A personal financial program designed to develop a customized money plan to meet your goals. *(www.stretcher.com/resource/bkstor/ord-form.htm)* or call 954/772-1696 to order.
- **Escapees RV Club:** Discussion forum/RVing on a Budget. *(www.escapees.com)*

- **North Dakota State University** *NDSU Extension Service.* Taking Charge of Family Finances: Family Money Manager. *(www.ext.nodak.edu/extpubs/yf/fammgmt/he222w.htm)*
- *Over the Hill: An Ethnography of RVing Seniors in North America* by Dorothy Ayers Counts and David Reese Counts. Elaborates on their 1993 study on what RVers spend. The March 2001 edition contains a new section on working RVers and an additional resource section.
- **Quicken** money management program. User-friendly for those with minimal computer skills. There are five versions of the software available. *(www.quicken.com)* Available at office supply stores.
- *Take Back Your Life! Travel Full-time in an RV,* by Stephanie Bernhagen. See Chapter 2, on finances and determining how much you will need, and Appendix A, a budget form for comparing your expenses on and off the road, will help determine how much money you need. The budget categories Bernhagen suggests are a good place to start. *(www.rvhometown.com)* See also **Appendix 9**.

Benefits

- **Benefits Check Up** is the nation's first 50-state (including the District of Columbia) online service to provide public benefit screening. Ranging from health coverage to supplemental income to help in paying utility bills, there are millions of older adults who could benefit from a wide array of public programs if they knew about them and how to apply for them. *(www.benefitscheckup.org)*
- **Medicare benefits:** Check benefits and find out about supplemental policies and prescription drugs. Call 800/633-4227 to speak to a customer service representative. *(www.medicare.gov)*
- **Social Security benefits:** Check "Retirement" to determine how to best take those benefits. Information also on Disability and other benefits. *(www.ssa.gov)*
- **AARP** has information on these topics at *(www.aarp.org)* social security. Other related topics as well.

Buying an RV

- **RV Consumer Group:** Before you buy an RV, check *(www.rv.org)* The Court of Public Opinion includes consumer problems with various rigs. Worth joining to get rating information on RVs.

- **RV Safety Web site:** Recall notices, towing laws, plus ratings of RV accessories. Useful articles. *(www.rvsafety.com)*
- **Used RV prices:** If you are considering buying or selling your RV, check prices at *(www.nadaguides.com)*. Complete an appraisal report by inputting model and features. Lemon check by VIN number.
- **RV Buyers Guide:** If you haven't purchased an RV, read the articles on things to consider, particularly about weight. Overloading your RV is one way to wear it out more quickly. *(www.rvbg.com)*

Income tax, financial planning, estate planning

- These professionals are familiar with the unique issues RVers face. All are members of the Escapees RV Club.
  - **Dave Loring:** Licensed financial consultant. Free consultation, no charge for placement or management of investment. 800/260-1615. 146 Rainbow Dr., #4650, Livingston, TX 77399-1046.
  - **Alfred Lutz:** Attorney. Tax preparation for all 50 states. Wills and trusts for all except Louisiana. Will give phone advice generally without charge. 530/398-4143. PO Box 128, Macdoel, CA 96058. *Alutz@cot.net*
  - **Carol Richards:** Attorney in Livingston, TX. Specializes in wills, estate planning. 936/327-5764.

Insurance - RVs

- **Foremost Insurance:** Call 800/527-6136 to find a local agent; 800/262-0170 for quote. *(www.foremost.com)*
- **Good Sam VIP Insurance:** For members. 800/234-3450 for membership information. *(www.goodsamclub.com)*
- **Progressive Insurance Company:** Mention RV club affiliations. 800/776-4737 or *(www.progressive.com)* for quote.
- **RV Alliance America:** Mention RV club affiliations. 800/521-2942. Quick quote at *(www.rvaa.com)*.
- **Note:** If you belong to an RV club like Escapees, Good Sam, or FMCA, you may be eligible for a discount on an insurance policy based on your membership.

Membership campgrounds

- **NAM:** Before buying into a membership campground, check the

National Association for Members Web site to see if it is experiencing problems. *(www.natlassoc.com)*

CHAPTER 5: HOW EMPLOYERS AND FAMILY CAN REACH YOU: GETTING MAIL AND PHONE CALLS ON THE ROAD.
Cellular service providers - national
- **AT&T Wireless:** 800/290-4613 (sales), 800/888-7600 (customer service) and *(www.attwireless.com)*.
- **Verizon:** 800/2-JOIN-IN. *(www.verizonwireless.com)*

Federal Express
- **Federal Express locations:** Pick up your package at a Federal Express location. Free service. Inquire at a Federal Express drop off location or see *(www.fedex.com)*. "Locations,"then "Advance Search Options- hold at location." Customer service is 800/463-3339.

United Parcel Service:
- **UPS:** Pick up your package at a UPS location. It must be one of the centers, not a retail location. Call 800/742-5877 to check.

Voice mail
- **Voice Mail Connect:** Check at Web site to see whether or not you have any messages. Save a call if no messages. For a description and demonstration, go to *www.voicemailconnect.ws*. Click on Information for an explanation and demonstration. E-mail: *Support@voicemailconnect.ws*. You can also contact Customer Service at 760/602-3050.
- **Cellular service:** Voice messaging is usually included.
- **RV clubs:** Escapees RV Club and FMCA have voice mail service.

Zip Codes and toll-free directory
- **USPS zip code** lookup at 800/275-8777 and *(www.usps.com)*. Find general delivery zip code for a city. Type "General Delivery" on the delivery address line for lookup.
- **AT&T Toll-free directory:** Call 800/555-1212. *(www.tollfree.att.net)* Also White and Yellow pages online.

CHAPTER 6: HOW TO USE A COMPUTER IN YOUR JOB SEARCH

Computers for RVers

- *Camping on the Internet:* Book by Loren Eyrich covers choosing a computer, setting up a computer in your rig, and using the Internet. Excellent for those with little or no background in computers or using the Internet. Cottage Industries. 800/272-5518. Also at Amazon.com

Computer education

- **Senior Net** has 160 learning centers in 36 states and provides adults 50+ with education in computer technology. 121 Second St., 7 Fl., San Francisco, CA 94105, 415/495-4990. *(www.seniornet.org)*
- **Online courses:** *(www.ecollege.com)*. Customers & Programs, Degree & Certificate Search. Lists various programs.
- **Gateway computers:** Online learning courses.(Fee charged.) *(www.learnatgateway.com)* Stores also offer classes and free clinics. Look up stores at *(www.gateway.com)* or call 888/852-4821.

E-mail on the road

- **Discussion Forums:** InternetbyCellPhone@yahoogroups.com and InternetbyWiFi@yahoogroups.com. Sign up at *(http:// groups.yahoo.com)*.
- **AOL** has several plans. Light usage plan provides 3 hours of time, including the Internet, is $4.95 per month with additional time $2.50 per hour. See *(www.aol.com)* or call 888/265-8002 to get a copy of the software. Customer service: Windows users : 888/346-3704. Macintosh users: 888/265-8007.
- **AT&T Wireless:** Add ATT&T Pocketnet to your AT&T wireless plan. Three plans from $6.99/mo. At *(www.attwireless.com)* go to Wireless Internet.
- **PocketMail:** Information on devices and service plans *(www.pocketmail.com)*. Customer service can be reached at: 925/454-5066.
- **Earthlink** has a low-usage plan for $9.95/month for 10 hours, additional hours are $1.00. Call Dialup Sales at 800/395-8425. *(www.earthlink.net)*

- **Free Web-based e-mail:** *(www.hotmail.com)* and *(www.yahoo.com)* are two popular services. Sign up at Web sites.

Wireless technology

- **WiFi Planet:** *(www.wi-fiplanet.com)* Information and tutorials on this technology. See also Discussion Forums under E-Mail on the Road.
- **Full-timer Communication Web site:** Options for calling cards, cellular service and Internet connections. *(www.full-timer.com)*
- **Traveling with laptop computers:** See *(www.roadnews.com)* for articles and advice.
- **Roadwirer columns:** Find at *(www.roadtripamerica.com)* under Dashboarding.

CHAPTER 7: HOW TO PREPARE RÉSUMÉS AND COVER LETTERS FOR WORKING ON THE ROAD

Résumés

- **AARP:** "Résumés really do count!" publication. Order by e-mailing *member@aarp.or*g or by writing to AARP, 601 E Street, NW, Washington, DC 20049. Request publication D17024. Includes sample functional, chronological and electronic résumés. Free.
- **Damngood.com:** A thorough Web site with résumé tips, advice plus other resources is Yana Parker's *(www.damngood.com)*.
- *Dynamic Cover Letters* by Hansen and Hansen is a complete book about cover letters. Available from Ten Speed Press, 800/841-2665 or Amazon.com. For more information see *(www.quintcareers.com/dcl.htm*l*)*. Job/career Bookstore section has more books on getting a job.
- **Resumania:** Under Career Tips, good advice for résumés from *Job Hunting for Dummies®, 2nd edition.* Lots of lines included in résumés and cover letters that did *not* help the job-seeker. Good for a laugh. You'll be more careful after reading these bloopers. *(www.resumania.com)*
- **7-Step Résumé Sampler program:** Walks you through seven steps to create your résumé and cover letter. List of power words. Also tips on interviewing and negotiating. While geared for students entering work force, it is worth taking a look. *(www.7step-resumesampler.com)*

- *You Shoulda Listened to Your Mother: 36 Timeless Success Tips for Working Women* by Alice Zyetz. Chapter on résumés elaborates on functional vs chronological résumés, strong words, do's and don'ts.

CHAPTER 8: HOW TO DO A JOB SEARCH
Publications for finding RV-related or seasonal jobs
- *The Caretaker Gazette*, PO Box 4005-M, Bergheim, TX 78004 830/336-3939. E-mail: *caretaker@caretaker.org* ; Web site: *(www.caretaker.org)*. Subscription is $29/year.
- *Workamper News*, 709 W. Searcy St., Heber Springs, AR 72543-3761. 800/446-5627.E-mail: *info@workamper.com*; Web site: *(www.workamper.com)*. Subscription is $25/year for basic; $37 for WorkamperPlus subscription.

Campground directories See Resources for Chapter 14.

Networking
- **Workamper Viewpoint forums:** Good place to find out about employers and work-related issues. For *Workamper News* subscribers. Register at *(www.workamperviewpoint.com)*
- *You Shoulda Listened to Your Mother* by Alice Zyetz. Chapter on networking and informational interviews. (Amazon.com)
- **Other resources:** Discussion group on Working on the Road at Escapees RV Club Web site at *(www.escapees.com)*. Escapees members can also join the Workers on the Road BOF (Birds of a Feather interest group). Information in *Escapees Magazine* and at the Web site.

CHAPTER 9: HOW TO USE THE INTERNET TO FIND WORK
Campgrounds with phone/modem hookups
- **Southpoint.com:** *(www.southpoint.com)* Click on RV Campgrounds, then scroll down to "Directory of Campgrounds with Instant Phone Hookups at the Site."

Job search - how to use the Internet
- **Job Hunters Bible:** *(www.jobhuntersbible.com)* by Richard Bolles, author of *What Color is Your Parachute*. Worth a look. An excellent resource to using the Internet for job hunting, plus links.

- **The Riley Guide:** *(www.rileyguide.com)* Comprehensive gateway to job search sites, including conventions and trade shows of specific occupations and job-specific agencies. Link to key job search sites.

Job search - Web sites with seasonal jobs
- **Coolworks:** *(www.coolworks.com)* Over 60,000 seasonal positions.
- **Job Monkey:** *(www.jobmonkey.com)* Seasonal positions. Bookstore has books on jobs and careers.
- **Jobs in Paradise:** *(www.jobsinparadise.com)* Oriented more towards college-aged kids but there are some possibilities. Listed by types of jobs, i.e. resorts, mountains.
- **Seasonal employment:** *(www.seasonalemployment.com)* lists summer and winter seasonal employers, several concessionaires at national parks.
- **Summer Jobs:** *(www.summerjobs.com)* Lists jobs by state. Look under "More world-wide jobs."
- **Workamper News:** Some postings. "Subscription Plus" includes weekly Hotline e-mail updates, Awesome Applicants résumé data base along with your print subscription. Post situation wanted ads. *(www.workamper.com)*

Job search - Web sites with some seasonal jobs
- **America's Job Bank:** Over 1,000,000 jobs. Links to state employment service sites. Search by job category and/or zipcode. *(www.ajb.org)*
- **Career Builder:** *(www.careerbuilder.com)* Features jobs from 75+ career sites, personalized job hunting tools, skills certification, and articles. Access to more than 3 million jobs on the Internet.
- **Monster Jobs:** *(www.monster.com)* Some 50,000 listings
- **Hot jobs:** *(http://hotjobs.yahoo.com)* Search by type of job, location or company. Highly rated site.

Newspapers on the Web
- **Abracat jobs:** *(www.abracat.com/c2/jobs/search/index.xml)* Database or over 200,000 jobs, updated daily by 700 newspapers. Search by geographic area or key word like "seasonal."
- **Newspaper Association of America:** *(www.newspaperlinks.com)* Links to most newspapers. Or search their Bonafide Classified Ads site *(http://bonafideclassified.com)*

- **Newspaper links:** *(www.abyznewslinks.com)* Search by state, then city.

CHAPTER 10: HOW TO INTERVIEW AND GET RESULTS
Interviewing

- *Getting in shape for your next job interview,* Your Career Information Resource, AARP Order from AARP, 601 E Street, NW, Washington, DC 20049 or send an e-mail to *member@aarp.org* requesting publication D17025. Free.
- **Wetfeet.com:** Many articles on interviewing in *(www.wetfeet.com)*. You can do other research on jobs hunting at the site too.
- **Job Search Web sites:** Most have articles with tips on interviewing.
- *You Shoulda Listened to Your Mother* by Alice Zyetz. Chapter on preparation for interviewing. (Amazon.com)

CHAPTER 11: HOW TO NEGOTIATE FOR BETTER COMPENSATION
Negotiation

Check the Job Search Web sites listed in Chapter 9 for articles on negotiation.

CHAPTER 13: LEGAL AND TAX CONSIDERATIONS
State and federal income tax

- **AARP** produces a "State Personal Income Tax Comparisons" chart as well as booklets by region itemizing personal income tax, sales tax and property tax relief programs for each state. Free. Order from AARP, 601 E Street, NW, Washington, DC 20049, call 800/424-3410, or send an e-mail to *member@aarp.org*. The regional publications are items numbered AC2410 (Midwest), AC2412 (Northeast), AC2415 (Southeast), AC2414 (Southwest), and AC2413 (West). States can change their tax codes at any time so check with the state revenue office for the latest information. **Appendix 5** has Web sites.
- **Federation of Tax Administrators:** Compare state tax rates for income tax, sales tax and others. *(www.taxadmin.org/fta/rate/ tax_stru.html)*

CHAPTER 14 HOW TO FIND JOBS WITH A CAMPSITE
Campground directories
- **Go Camping America:** ARVC's campground information online at: *(www.gocampingamerica.com)*
- *Military RV, Camping & Outdoor Recreation Areas Around The World: Directory of Military RV Parks and Camps.* Order from Military Living Publications, P.O. Box 2347, Falls Church, VA 22042-0347. 703/237-0203 or at *(www.militaryliving.com)* under Books. Web site includes RV/camping links.
- *Trailer Life Directory:* Online at *(www.tldirectory.com)*. Order the directory in print or on CD at site or check magazine.
- *Wheelers RV Resort and Campground Guide*: Directory can be purchased at many RV dealers and suppliers. Order online at *(www.wheelersguides.com)* or click on "search" to locate campgrounds. 800/323-8899.
- *Woodall's Campground Directory*: Purchase at RV dealers and suppliers, campgrounds or bookstores, or online at their Web site. Or, contact Woodall Publications at 888/226-7328. Find a searchable directory online at *(www.woodalls.com/campsrch.cfm)*.

Campground guides: jobs
- **Wheelers Resort and Campground Guide,**1310 Jarvis, Elk Grove Village, IL 60007Telephone: 800/323-8899; fax: 847/981-0106. E-mail: *gwheelers@yahoo.com*. Web site: *(www.wheelersguides.com)*

Christmas tree sales
- **National Christmas Tree Association:** At their Web site *(www.realchristmastrees.org)* select "find a tree near you." From there, choose a state to obtain a list of tree farms and retail lots.

Site-sitting
- **Publications:** *Caretaker Gazette* and *Workamper News.*
- **Homesitters on Wheels**, 5200 Torrey Pines Court, Carmichael, CA 95608. 800/214-7488. E-mail: *sitters@homesitters.net*; Web site: *(www.homesitters.net)*
- **Starkey International:** Household management certification and placement of house couples. 800/888-4904. *(www.starkeyintl.com)*

Training

- **Escapees RV Club:** Training for members interested in becoming managers, assistant managers, hosts, activity directors for one of their RV parks. Contact Escapees RV Club. *(www.escapees.com)*
- **National Association of RV Parks and Campgrounds** (ARVC) training program: *(www.arvc.org)* and click on Educational Opportunities. ARVC, 113 Park Avenue, Falls Church, VA 22046 703/ 241-8801. *arvc@erols.com* Or, call the Oglebay Division of Continuing Education at 800/624-6988, Ext. 4019, in Wheeling WV, where the course is held.

  A 42-hour, two-year program is conducted for one week each year. The course is designed for park owners, operators and managers and covers a wide array of management and operations topics including finance and administration, marketing, customer service, recreation programming, maintenance, personnel management, retail and food service operations and more. The course is held at Oglebay Resort, WV. Earn CPU credits and credits toward ARVC's Certified Park Operator (CPO) certification.
- **British Columbia Lodging & Campgrounds Association** Professional certification, based on national standards established by the Canadian Tourism Industry, for campground operators. 209 - 3003 St. John's Street Port Moody, BC V3H 2C4, 888/923-4678Email: *info@bclca.com* *(www.bclca.com/education/occupational_certification.htm)*

CHAPTER 15: HOW TO GET JOBS TRAVELING IN YOUR RV

Caravans

- **Fantasy Caravans**, PO Box 95605, Las Vegas, NV 89193-5605. Call 800/952-8496. *(www.fantasyrvtours.com)*
- **Other caravan companies:** look for ads in RV magazines. Check at RV shows for their booths. If you take a caravan, talk to the wagonmaster about job opportunities and whom to contact.

Carnivals and circuses

- *Carnival and Circus Booking Guide:* List of carnivals and circuses. While intended for booking circuses, contact information will be useful for finding a job. $10 from 800/407-6874 or at *(www.amusementbusiness.com)*. Click on shopping cart.

- **Circustuff:** Circus companies, links to circuses and related sites. *(www.circustuff.com)*
- *Workamper News* often has a carnival or circus advertising under 'multiple locations." *(www.workamper.com)*

Mystery shoppers

- **Genesis Group, Inc.:** Find information and apply at *(www.genesisgrp.com)*. Genesis Group, Inc., 1300 114th Ave. SE, Suite 220, Bellevue, WA 98004. 877/363-3945. Email: *info@speedmarkweb.com*.
- **Mystery Shoppers Providers Association:** 2695 Villa Creek Dr., Ste 260, Dallas, TX 75234. 972/406-1104. *Info@mysteryshop.org*. Search for assignments by state. *(www.mysteryshop.org)*
- **National Center for Professional Mystery Shoppers, Inc.:** *(www.justshop.org)* Non-profit referral service. Many links.
- **Fabjob:** An electronic, downloadable book is available at the site for $25.95. *(www.fabjob.com/mysteryshopper.asp)*

RV transport companies

- *How to Get Paid $50,000 a Year to Travel (Without Selling Anything)* by Craig Chilton. Describes the Road Rat® lifestyle and lists over 4,000 manufacturers in the U.S., Canada, Europe and Australia, plus RV transporter companies. *Workamper* bookstore.
- **Other resources:** *Workamper News* usually has a listing for at least one company. Talk to dealers at RV shows or contact manufacturers for names of companies they contract with. Look at RV America's Web site, *(www.rvamerica.com)* under Resources/Employment-RV Deliveries for a list of professional delivery services.

Dog show judging

American Kennel Club (AKC): Becoming a judge is a long process and takes experience showing dogs. The AKC also hires field personnel that go from show to show. AKC Job-Line: 919/852-3896. See Inside AKC at *(www.americankennelclub.com)* For information on selling products at dog shows and other shows, see Chapters 20 and 21.

Manufacturer's reps

- **MANA** (Manufacturer Agents National Association), 23016 Mill Creek Road, P.O. Box 3467, Laguna Hills, California 92654. *(www.manaonline.org)* E-mail *MANA@manaonline.org*
- **UAMR** (United Association of Manufacturers' Representatives),P.O. Box 986, Dana Point, California 92629. 949/240-4966. *(www.uamr.com)*

Pipeline Technicians

- **Southern Cross**, PO Box 2168, Norcross Ga 30091-2168. 404/441-0403. *(www.southerncrosscorp.com)*

Site guides - selling

- **AGS**, PO Box 790, Port Angeles, WA 98362. 800/245-9666. E-mail: *mike@agspubl.com*.
- **Southeast Publications**, 4360 Peters Road, Fort Lauderdale, FL 33321. 800/832-3292. *(www.rvingusa.com)*
- **Other leads:** Fairgrounds and towns sometimes have similar maps. Look on the map for the name of the company that produces it.

CHAPTER 16: HOW TO GET JOBS WITHIN THE RV INDUSTRY

Camping World - jobs

- **Camping World**, PO Box 90018, Bowling Green, KY 42102, Job line: 877/612-JOBS, ext. 488. *(www.campingworld.com/jobs)*

Mechanic certification

- **National Institute for Automotive Service Excellence**, (ASE certified mechanics)13505 Dulles Technology Drive, Suite 2 Herndon, Virginia 20171-3421 Toll-Free Information Line: 877/ASE-TECH, *(www.asecert.org)*. ASE certification tests measure technicians' knowledge of diagnostic and repair skills necessary for competent job performance.

Training

- **Camping World RV Institute**, 134 Beech Bend Rd., Bowling Green, KY 42101. *(www.cwrvi.com)* The complete Service Technician training is nine weeks long, or take individual units. 800/356-0311. E-mail: *rvi@campingworld.com*

• **The National RV Technical Institute:** Offers certified RV Technician training through a number of community and technical colleges around the U.S. Sponsors are Recreation Dealers Association (RVDA) and the Recreation Vehicle Industry Association (RVIA). Certification is independent of training, but the training at Camping World and RVIA is designed to help prepare the applicant for the test. For information on locations for training, contact RVIA at 703/620-6003, ext. 355. Check their Web site *(www.rvia.org)*, under RV Technician Training. Or write to: National RV Technical Institute, PO Box 2999, 1896 Preston White Dr., Reston, VA 22090-0999.

  For information on the The RVDA certification program and testing, see *(www.rvda.org)*. E-mail *techcert@rvda.org* or call 703/591-7130.

• **Escapees RV Club** training for park managers and activity directors. See **Resources**, Chapter 14.

CHAPTER 17: HOW TO GET SEASONAL FEDERAL JOBS

Federal agencies
Army Corps of Engineers

• **Bid on contracts:** Contact individual districts to get information and to be notified about upcoming solicitations. Look at "Where we are" at *(www.usace.army.mil)* for District information.
• *Camping With The Corps of Engineers* by S. L. Hinkle. Lists all COE campgrounds. (Online RV bookstores and Amazon.com)
• *Workamper News:* The September/October issue each year lists projects soliciting bids as well as projects seeking volunteers. 501/362-2637. *(www.workamper.com)*

BLM

• **Internet:** BLM has a Web site for nationwide and worldwide seasonal positions at *(www.blm.gov/careers)*. At USAJOBS, sort by agency. *(www.usajobs.opm.gov)*

Fire towers
- **Web sites:** Lists fire towers, links to agencies that employ workers and volunteers. *(www.firetower.org)* and *(www.firelookout.org)*

National Park Service
- **Internet:** At USAJOBS *(www.usajobs.opm.gov)*, sort by agency. Look for temporary positions. Some seasonal positions found at *(www.sep.nps.gov)*. (USAJOBS will refer you to this site when applicable.)

USDA Forest Service
- **Web site:** The USDA Forest Service has a page at their Web site giving information about jobs with the Forest Service. In an alternative program, many of their jobs are required to be posted locally and at the local state employment office. Check *(www.fs.fed.us/ fsjobs)* for more information. Look at Web site for "Fire Hire" positions. These include paid positions as lookouts for fire towers.
- **Other:** Check USAJOBS, *(www.usajobs.opm.gov)*, sort by agency (Department of Agriculture). Contact the specific forest ahead of time to be put on the mailing list for their employment package. Check also with the state employment office. This way you won't miss an opportunity or deadline.
- **Senior Community Service Employment Program:** Designed for low-income workers over 55-years of age. Contact Forest Service Headquarters of the specific forest, or write for more information to U.S. Dept. of Agriculture, Forest Service, Human Resources Program, PO Box 96090, Washington, DC 20090.
- **Regional offices** can supply you with a map and listing of the forests in their region plus other employment information.(See **Appendix 3**)

Federal jobs-find job announcements
- **Internet:** *(www.usajobs.opm.gov)* You can search by agency, state or work series. Most, but not all, seasonal/temporary positions are grade-5 or lower. Some common temporary positions are: visitor use assistant, ranger, fee collector, maintenance worker, motor vehicle operator, forestry technician, and archaeologist, range technician.

- **Automated Telephone System:** Call 478/757-3000 or TDD 478/744-2299.
- **Touch Screen Computer Kiosks:** Located in OPM offices and in many Federal office buildings nationwide.
- **Contact the agencies** that you are interested in working for specific application instructions.

OF-612 Federal job application and résumé
- **Software:** Purchase and then download a program to complete your OF-612 application or government résumé using Word or Word-Perfect at *(www.fedquest.com)*. $29.95 for download.
- **Obtain a copy:** You can print out a copy of the OF-612 at *(www.opm.gov/forms/html/of.asp)*. The OF-510, which includes requirements for your application or résumé, can be found here too. I do recommend purchasing software if you will be applying to more than one position.

Getting your first federal job
- **Student Conservation Association (SCA).** Volunteer positions, internships, paid postions. Receive housing, small stipend, money towards tuition and experience. Provides conservation service in national parks, refuges, forests and urban areas in all 50 states. *(www.thesca.org)* 603/543-1700.
- **Other:** See Chapter 22 on volunteering.

CHAPTER 18: HOW TO GET JOBS WORKING IN THE OUTDOORS
Helicopter jobs
- **Just Helicopters:** Lists jobs for helicopter pilots and mechanics. *(www.justhelicopters.com)*
Variety of job opportunities
- **Coolworks:** *(www.coolworks.com)* Check the following categories: National Parks, State Parks, Older and Bolder, Jobs for RVers, Jobs on Water, and Other Cool Work for possible jobs in the outdoors. Several NPS concessionaires are listed here.

- *Workamper News: (www.workamper.com)* See **Resources,** Chapter 8, for address and subscription information. Print edition has ads for forest service concessionaires and other types of jobs listed in Chapter 18.

Other job sources

- **NPS concessionaires:** There are over 500 NPS concessionaires. Find out concessionaire information for a park by contacting NPS there. If a park does not have any concessionaires, ask for names of "gateway" or nearby cities. Ccontact the chamber of commerce or tourist/visitor center for lists of employers. Information about park locations and contact information can be found at *(www.nps.gov).*
- **Forest Service concessionaires:** Contact USDA Forest Service regional or a specific forest headquarters to find out who operates their campgrounds. Contact information for regions and specific forests can be found at *(www.fs.fed.us).* (See also **Appendix 3.**)
- **Operate a concession in a national forest:** Contact the individual forest(s) you are interested in. When a concession comes up for bid, the forest will first publish a prospectus and solicit bids. Contracts run from 1-5 years. Find contact information at *(www.fs.fed.us).*
- **State and county concessions:** If you have an area in mind, contact state and county parks to find out names of any concessionaires.
- **Firefighter support:** State and federal forests may contract out fire-fighting support services. Your best bet is to check with an individual forest to find out the contractor.
- **PA State Parks:** Bid on concessions in Pennsylvania State Parks. *(www.dcnr.state.pa.us/stateparks/business)*

State and city parks

- See **Appendix 4** for contact information for state parks.
- **Other:** Look at Coolworks.com and *Workamper News.*

CHAPTER 19: HOW TO GET A JOB AT RESORTS AND TRAVEL DESTINATIONS

Amusement parks

- **International Association of Amusement Parks and Attractions:** (IAAPA) *(www.iaapa.org)* See Links for lists of related Web sites.

IAAPA, 1448 Duke Street, Alexandria, VA 22314. Telephone: 703/
836-4800. E-mail: *iaapa@iaapa.org*
- **Other:** Check *Workamper News* and Coolworks.com for jobs.

Bed and Breakfasts
- **Professional Association of Innkeepers International** (PAII) has
  books, training. Join to be listed as an innsitter, which is circulated
  to all PAII members. P.O. Box 90710, Santa Barbara,California,
  93190. 805/569-1853. E-mail: *info@paii.org*. Web site:
  (www.paii.org)
- **Other:** Find jobs working for a B&B by contacting directly or
  through local help wanted classified ads.

Casinos
- *American Casino Guide* for $13.95 plus s/h lists details of more
  than 600 casinos in 300 states, including riverboat and Indian
  facilities. Their Web site at *(www.americancasinoguide.com)* includes
  links to casino Web pages and often employment information. For
  some casinos, you can apply right online or download an application. Call 954/989-2766 to order the latest edition, or order online.
- **Non-dealer positions:** Go to the casino personnel office or check
  local help-wanted ads.

Cruise lines/maritime jobs
- **Find cruise lines:** Check at Coolworks *(www.coolworks.com)* under
  Alaska and Jobs on the Water. Search for individual cruise lines.
  Check at their Web sites or call their toll-free numbers. For dance
  host positions, contact individual cruise lines.
- **Maritime jobs:** *(www.maritimejobs.com)* Find concessionaire posi-
  tions on cruise ships such as beauty shops, gift shops, massages.
  Also work in ship's casinos, Alaska fishing boats or processing.

Dude ranches
- **The Dude Ranchers' Association,** PO Box 2307, Cody, WY 82414.
  Telephone: 307/587-2339. *(www.duderanch.org)* Obtain a directory
  of member ranches or access online. For $10, you can place an
  employment-wanted ad directly in their biweekly newsletter.

- **Guest Ranches of North America,** P. O. Box 191625, Dallas, TX 75219-8503. 214/467-9444. *(www.ranchwork.com)* Employment openings of member ranches by state. Post your employment-wanted ad at no charge.
- *Workamper News:* Find some listings in the print publication.

Overseas work

- **Transitions Abroad Magazine:** Articles and advertisements for working overseas. Many are open only to students who can obtain a student visa, as countries often restrict foreigners from seeking employment in their countries. (That is not to say you can't find work in another country.) At *(www.transitionsabroad.com)* look under "Work" for categories like: Work Abroad Resources, Short-term Work Abroad, Internship Programs, Volunteer Programs, and Teaching English Overseas. Copies available at newsstands.
- **Peace Corps:** Volunteer in other countries for two years, plus three months training. Receive stipend plus $6,000 when you return. 800/424-8580. *(www.peacecorps.gov)*
- **Work at Antarctica:** Many support workers are hired by Raytheon Polar Services. Most work from October to February. Take a look at their Web site at *(www.polar.org)*

Resorts

- **Coolworks:** *(www.coolworks.com)* Lists resort jobs.
- **Resorts and Lodges:** *(www.resortsandlodges.com)* Sorted by area and resort types.

Resorts/attractions that hire RV workers

- **Wall Drug,** 510 Main Street, PO Box 401, Wall, SD 57790. 605/279-2175. *(www.walldrug.com)* Check for employment information at Coolworks. *Workamper News* may carry an ad.
- **Disney World Jobline:** 407/828-1000. They like to hire RVers. RV site not included. (Jobline for Disneyland is 818/558-2222.)
- **Branson, Missouri:** Order a travel planner from the Chamber of Commerce plus find a list of shows, attractions, and RV parks at*(www.explorebranson.com)* or call 800/214-3661.

- **Silver Dollar City:** *http://sdcprops.silverdollarcity.com* or e-mail *employment@silverdollarcity.com.* 417/338-8122
- **Adventureland Park:** Located in Des Moines, Iowa, this amusement park hires upwards of 200 Workampers. 800/532-1286 or e-mail *hr@adventureland.com.* Web site: *(www.adventureland-usa.com)*

Ski resorts
- **Go Ski:** *(www.goski.com)* lists ski resorts all over the world. Under USA, search by region or state for ski resort. Obtain contact information, or link to resort's Web site. Find employment opportunities at individual Web sites.
- **Skiing the Net:** *(www.skiingthenet.com)* is also a source for ski jobs. Listed by job category, employer and End of the Season.
- **Coolworks:** *(www.coolworks.com)* has a "ski jobs" category.

CHAPTER 20: HOW TO FIND TEMPORARY JOBS AND WORK AT SPECIAL EVENTS

Computer assignments (short-term), high-tech assignments
- **Resources for short-term computer jobs:** Check *(www.dice.com)* and *(www.net-temps.com)*.
- **Contract Job Hunter:** Specializes in job openings for *serious* contractors and consultants in engineering, IT/IS, and technical disciplines. Print magazine available. Web site subscription $20/year. *(www.cjhunter.com)* E-mail: *staff@cjhunter.com.* Contract Job Hunter is a service of: C.E. Publications, Inc., P.O. Box 3006, Bothell, WA 98041-3006. Phone: 425/806-5200.
- **Directory of Contract Service Firms:** Find agencies at C.E. Publications Web site at *(www.ceweekly.com)*. Links to both Contract Job Hunter and the online directory.
- **National Technical Employment Service** (NTES) *(www.ntes.com)*. Also has contract listings. Links to information on cost-of-living, government contract, special events.
- **Other:** Check Internet job sites, local classified ads, and temporary agencies.
- **U.S. Register of Technical Service Firms:** Available from National Technical Employment Services at *(www.ntes.com)*. Download your

resume, subscribe to Hotflash with more than 500 positions a week. Telephone: 256/259-6837.

Motorsports/NASCAR

- *Workamper News:* Check *(www.workamper.com)* for ads in this sport as well as the print publication.
- **Other leads:** Contact tracks that have NASCAR events for job openings during races. At *(www.nascar.com)* click on Races, then Schedule to find a list of upcoming races, dates and track.

Road construction - flagging

- **Flaggers:** Flaggers on DOT road construction sites must be certified. The course and job openings can often be found through the Laborers' International Union of North America. In some areas, certification may be offered at local community colleges. Check Yellow Pages of local telephone books for labor organizations or talk to personnel at a road construction company to find out they how obtain their temporary workers.

Special events

- **Clark's Flea Market Book:** Cost is $5. Order at 904/626-2133.
- **Special Events Directory:** The most complete source for North American fairs, craft shows, festivals, indoor & outdoor shows is available for $168 plus shipping. Order online or call 609/953-9544. *(www.eventcrazy.com)*
- **Directory of North American Fairs, Festivals and Expositions:** Published by Amusement Business, 49 Music Square West, Nashville, TN 37203. 800/745-8922. *(www.amusementbusiness.com)*
- **International Association of Fairs and Expositions (IAFE):** *(www.fairsandexpos.com)* Click on Find a Fair to locate fairs and expositions by state. Check dates, employment opportunities.
- **Trade Show News Network:** Web site listing trade shows. Sort by type, date or location. *(www2.tsnn.com)* ASD/AMD Trade Shows:. Calendar of trade shows in Las Vegas and other locations for vendors. View and purchase merchandise to sell. *(www.merchandisegroup.com)* Resale number/tax identification number required to attend.

- **Wholesale merchandise:** Do a computer search for "wholesale merchandise." One Web site is *(www.pubdisco.com)*, which sells a comprehensive directory.
- **Other:** Check for jobs at special events at Internet job sites, local classified ads, and temporary agencies.

Temporary agencies

- **National Association of Temporary and Staffing Services:** (NATSS) At Web site search for temporary agencies and contact information under "Job Seek." Search by area, type of work and whether you are looking for a temporary position, temporary to permanent or permanent position. *(www.staffingtoday.net)*
- **Temping.com:** *(www.temping.com)* This free service allows you to search for temporary staffing agencies and positions by geographic area. Good article, "Twelve Tips for Successful Temps." Click on Articles under "For Applicants."
- **Specialty agencies** place accountants and financial personnel, medical personnel, and others. Larger cities may have agencies that specialize in labor- or construction-type positions. Look in the Yellow Pages and Help Wanted ads in Sunday newspaper.
- **Nation-wide agencies:** May offer employees benefits and the ability to transfer records from one office to another:
  - **Adecco:** Over 5000 offices in 59 countries. Health insurance, paid holidays and vacation, 401K program. *(www.adecco.com)*
  - **Manpower:** Provides jobs that are full-time, part-time, long-term positions with career potential, or short-term assignments. Advertise that they "provide the most complete set of benefits available in the industry." Over 1,000 online training course through their Global Training Center. *(www.manpower.com)*
  - **Kelly Services:** *(www.kellyservices.com)* 2,200 offices in 25 countries.
- **Sunshine Enterprises:** Find a job detasseling corn for three weeks at *(www.corn-jobs.com)*
- **ReserveAmerica** hires call center reservation agents in Ballston Spa, NY, Madison, WY, and Rancho Cordova, CA. ReserveAmerica, P.O. Box 199, Ballston Spa, NY 12020. Email resume to: *csacala@reserveamerica.com* or Fax to: 518/884-9576 (Attention:

Human Resources. Mention position you are applying for.) *(www.reserveamerica.com)*

CHAPTER 21: HOW TO OPERATE YOUR OWN BUSINESS ON THE ROAD

Performing

* **School assemblies:** Resource for making money by putting on assembly programs in schools. *How to Make Money Performing in Schools: Definitive Guide to Developing, Marketing and Presenting School Assembly Programs* by David Helflick. (Amazon.com)
* **RV parks:** Contact individual RV parks to arrange an exchange of services or pay for performing.
* **Workamper Entertainers:** A service of S-O-S Consulting, a division of *Workamper News*, designed to bring entertainers together with employers who seek talented acts for their venues. Workampers can be included in the talent pool and have their audio or video talent sampling posted at the Web site. 866/450-6113. *(www.s-o-sconsulting.com).* Click on Workamper Enterainers.

Photography

* **Photographer's Market:** Updated each year. Thousands of markets like magazines, advertising agencies and stock photography agencies. Published by Writers Digest Books. Available at bookstores or at online bookstores. *(www.writersdigest.com)*

Self-employment resources

* *422 Tax Deductions for Businesses and Self-employed Individuals,* by Bernard B. Kamoroff, C.P.A. Useful information for small business owners and independent contractors.
* **Are you an entrepreneur?** Excellent checklist by Robert Sullivan, author of *The Small Business Start-up Guide.* Entrepreneurial aptitude test. *(www.thealternativebookshop.com/busn0001.html)*
* **Chambers of Commerce:** Check with the Chamber of Commerce where you plan to register your business for local resources for assisting businesses. You may find funding sources, support groups and opportunities for networking when you are in that area.

- *Entrepreneur Magazine:* One of the magazines geared to small business owners. Web site has numerous articles on starting and growing a business, electronic newsletters. Find magazine at newsstands or subscribe at Web site. *(www.entrepreneurmag.com)*
- **How to Form a Corporation**, LLC, or Partnership in ..." Guides by W. Dean Brown for each state leading entrepreneurs through the incorporating process in their own state. Includes necessary forms and step-by-step instructions. Available through the Independent Publishers Group at *(www.ipgbook.com)*.
- **National Association for the Self-Employed (NASE):** Resources for the self-employed. Includes discounted services, legal issues, and health insurance. *(www.nase.org)*
- **Service Corps of Retired Executives Assoc. (SCORE):** A resource partner with the U.S. Small Business Administration. Dedicated to aiding in the formation, growth and success of small businesses nationwide. *(www.score.org)* Offers e-counseling, workshops and other information.
- **U.S. Small Business Administration (SBA):** Government agency that helps small businesses. Find a local office. Helps with financing and other aspects of getting started in your own business. Obtain a *Small Business Resource Guide* or Start-Up Kit from your local office, or download it from the Web site. *(www.sba.gov)* Write for free booklet on SBAs programs and services to: U.S. Small Business Admin., 409 Third St., S.W., Washington, DC 20416.
- **SBA resources for women:** Office of Women's Business Ownership of the Small Business Administration has a free packet of information of interest to women. *(www.sbaonline.sba.gov/financing/special/women.html)*. See also *(www.onlinewbc.gov)*. Directory of local Women's Business Center at Web site .

Seminars and public speakers

- **National Speakers Association:** Provides professional development, a Certified Speaking Professional (CSP) designation program, plus other resources. Find local chapters. NSA, 1500 S. Priest Dr., Tempe, AZ 85281. 480/968-2552. *(www.nsaspeaker.org)*
- **Toastmasters International:** Toastmaster clubs meet in 70 countries worldwide to help people improve their communication skills and lose their fear of public speaking. Find local chapters in White Pages

of the local telephone book or contact the headquarters at Toastmasters International, PO Box 9052, Mission Viejo, CA 92690, 949/858-8255. Look also at *(www.toastmasters.org)*.

- **Fabjob.com Guide to: Become a motivational speaker** by Tag Goulet E-book or CD available at *(www.fabjob.com)*.
- **Hot Tips for Speakers:** Book by Rob Abernathy and Mark Reardon on how to get ideas across to an audience with maximum effect possible. Available through the Independent Publishers Group at *(www.ipgbook.com)*.

Sales
- **See Special Events**, Chapter 20.

Telecommuting
- American Telecommuting Association. Resources for the telecommuter. 1-800-ATA-4-YOU *(www.knowledgetree.com/ata.html)*
- **Find postings:** *(www.tjobs.com)*

Windshield repair
- **Startup kits:** Contact Gene and Kathy Thaden for information on starting your own windshield repair business at123 Rainbow Dr., #2352, Livingston, TX 77399-1023. 515/360-9444. Or e-mail at *ekthaden@pocketmail.com* with your contact information.
- **Other:** See business opportunity magazines for franchises.

Web-based businesses
- **Bryce and Lisa Jackson's Webworker.com** has information about affiliate sites for the beginner. Includes information on selling on eBay. *(www.webworker.com)*
- **See also:** magazines and books geared to this at a bookstore or newsstand.

Writing and publishing
- **Writer's Market:** A Writers Digest book listing thousands of markets and useful advice for writers. Also, *Writer's Online Marketplace* for Internet markets. The monthly magazine, *Writer's Digest*, is an

excellent resource for writers too. See *(www.writersdigest.com)*. Magazine available at newsstands.

- **Internet newsletters:** Several electronic newsletters provide invaluable information for those wanting to sell articles or publish books and e-books. A few of my favorites are:
  - **Publishing Poynters:** Dan Poynter is known as the guru of self-publishing. Subscribe at *(www.parapublishing.com)*.
  - **NAWW Weekly:** National Association of Women's weekly e-zine. Subscribe at *(www.naww.org)*.
  - **Writing World:** A world of writing information. Moira Allen's e-zine. Subscribe at *(www.writing-world.com)*.
  - **Funds for Writers:** Paying assignments, grants. Subscribe by sending an e-mail to *FundsforWriters-subscribe@yahoogroups.com*
- *Well-Fed Writer* : *Financial Self-Sufficiency as a Freelance Writer in Six Months or Less* by Peter Bowerman. How to make good money copywriting. (Workamper bookstore, RV Hometown.com)

CHAPTER 22: HOW TO HELP THE BUDGET BY VOLUNTEERING

Volunteer opportunities - volunteer Web sites/publications

- **The RVing Volunteer:** Information about volunteering by Hope Sykes. *(http://rvcompanion.com/newsflash/rv_vol_072001.htm)*
- **American Hiking Society:** *Get Outside.* Purchase at AHS, Get Outside, 1422 Fenwick Lane, Silver Spring, MD 20910. 301/ 565-6704. Booklet is $10.95 plus shipping. Purchase book at Hiker's Store. View sample listings online. *(www.americanhiking.org)*
- **Escapees RV Club:** See volunteer pages at *(www.escapees.com)*
- **Family Matters:** *(www.pointsoflight.org)* Look under Programs. Excellent resource for families looking for a volunteer project.
- **Habitat for Humanity:** To find a local affiliate, call 229/924-6935, ext. 2551 or 2552. Ext. 2446 will connect you to RV-Care-A-Vanners. Also find affiliates and information about international needs at *(www.habitat.org)*.
- **Passport in Time:** Obtain a copy of PIT Traveler from Passport In Time Clearinghouse, PO Box 31315, Tucson, AZ 85751-1315. 520/722-2716. *pit@sricrm.com. (www.passportintime.com)*

- **Random Acts of Kindness:** *(www.actsofkindness.org)* Free resources especially useful for parents who are homeschooling or want a project idea. Lots of good ideas for all for short ways to help out.
- **RV Hometown:** See volunteering pages at (*www.rvhometown.com*).
- **Servenet:** *(www.servenet.org)* find volunteer projects by zip code.
- **Service Corp of Retired Executives:** (SCORE). Volunteer to help small business owners succeed. *(www.score.org)*
- **Volunteer Match:** Search for short and long term volunteer opportunities by zip code at (www.volunteermatch.org), a large database with all kinds of opportunities.
- **Idealist:** *(www.idealist.org)* is a database of nonprofits both nationwide and worldwide, including volunteer opportunities. Search for positions that match your interests.
- **Volunteer America:** Links to many public agencies and volunteer experiences at *(www.volunteeramerica.net)*.

Virtual volunteering
- **Netaid.org:** *(www.netaid.org/volunteer)* Volunteer internationally without leaving home. Use your computer to write grants, fund raise or Web design.
- **Virtual Volunteering Project:** *(www.serviceleader.org/vv)*

Volunteer vacations
- **American Hiking Society:** *(www.americanhiking.org)* Volunteer vacations are $60.
- **Archaeological Fieldwork Opportunities Bulletin:** Comprehensive listing about almost 300 excavations and field schools throughout the world with openings for volunteers and students. Updated yearly. Order from (www.oxbowbooks.com) or 800/791-9354. Searchable database at *(www.archaeological.org/ webinfo.php?page=10015)*
- **Earth Watch Institute:** *(www.earthwatch.org)* An international nonprofit organization. 4,000 members volunteer their time and skills to work with 720 research teams each year on Earthwatch field research projects in over 50 countries all around the world. Programs are 1-3 weeks. 800/776-0188; *info@earthwatch.org*.

- **Global Volunteers:** *(www.globalvolunteers.org)* Two-three week programs, most of fee is tax deductible. Non-profit, non-sectarian organization. Call 800/487-1074.
- **Trash Tracker:** Write Glen Canyon National Recreation Area, Trash Tracker, PO Box 1507, Page, AZ 86040. 928/608-6200.
- **Volunteer vacations:** *Volunteer Vacations : Short-Term Adventures That Will Benefit You and Others* by Bill McMillon, Edward Asner.

International volunteer opportunities

- **Cross-Cultural Solutions:** A non-profit organization that sends volunteers abroad to provide humanitarian assistance with our Volunteer Work Programs in China, Ghana, India, Peru and Russia. *(www.crossculturalsolutions.org)* Fees are associated with each program, however you can obtain a fund-raising kit. 800/380-4777.
- *The International Directory of Voluntary Work:* (7th Ed) by Louise Whetter, Victoria Pybus. Vacation-Work. Available at Amazon.com.
- **International Habitat for Humanity:** (see above in Volunteer section for contact information.)
- **Mercy Ships:** *(www.mercyships.org)* or write to PO Box 2020, Garden Valley, TX 75771-2020. 800/MERCYSHIPS.
- **Student World Traveler:** *(www.studenttraveler.com)* has working and volunteering positions overseas. Search by country.
- **Transitions Abroad:** *(www.transitionsabroad.com)* (See **Resources** Chapter 19.)
- **Volunteer Abroad:** *(www.volunteerabroad.com)* One of largest directories on Internet.
- **World Teach:** A nonprofit organization that sends people to teach in various countries. One year, six months, and summer prorams. Fees cover airfare and living allowance. Financial assistance is available. B.A. degree required or its equivalent, except for China. They try to place couples. *(www.worldteach.org)* World Teach, c/o Center for International Development Harvard University, 79 JFK Street, Cambridge MA 02138. 800/4-TEACH-0 (483-2240).

CHAPTER 23: HOW TO REDUCE EXPENSES

Camping - free or reduced cost

- **BLM Long term visitor areas (LTVAs):** Buy an LTVA pass from the BLM Yuma Field Office located at 2555 E. Gila Ridge Road in Yuma, 85365-2240 *(http://www.az.blm.gov/yfo/outrec.htm)* Phone: 928/317-3200, and BLM El Centro Field Office, 1661 South Fourth Street, El Centro, CA 92243P: 760/337-4400. *(http://www.ca.blm.gov/elcentro/)*

Health insurance

- **AARP:** "Health Insurance Options for Midlife Adults: Finding and Keeping Coverage," AARP Publication. Free. Order from AARP, 601 E Street, NW, Washington, DC 20049 or send e-mail to *member@aarp.org* requesting publication D17025. Check *(www.aarp.org)* for more information.
- **Department of Labor:** Pension and Welfare Benefits Administration of the DOL has information and brochures on health benefits and COBRA. *(www.dol.gov/ebsa)*
- **Georgetown University Institute for Health Care Research and Policy:** Find information about insurance protections in all 50 states. The Web site has a list of all state insurance departments, with contact names, phone numbers and Web addresses. Call 202/687-0880 to consult *Consumer's Guide to Getting and Keeping Health Insurance*, or visit the Web site *(www.healthinsuranceinfo.net)*
- *U.S. News and World Report*: Annual ranking of best hospitals in the U.S. July issue. Also at their Web site *(www.usnews.com)*. Look under Rankings and Guides. Search the data base by specialty or geographic area. Related articles.

Investments

- **Licensed financial consultant:** Dave Loring offers free financial planning consultations for Escapee RV Club members and other RVers. 800/260-1615.
- **Securities Investor Protection Corporation (SIPC):** Articles on protecting yourself against investment fraud, links to regulatory agencies. *(www.sipc.org)*

- **Department of Labor: Pension and Welfare Benefits Administration** has articles and information on investments as it relates to pensions. *(www.dol.gov/ebsa)*

Lose your credit cards
- **What to do:** Besides calling the credit card company, notify the anti-fraud departments of the major credit bureaus:
  - **Equifax** 800/525-6285
  - **Experian** (formerly TRW) 800/879-3752
  - **Trans Union** 800/680-7289
  - **Social Security Administration-** Fraud line at 800/269-0271

Chapter 24: Lifestyle considerations

Disabilities
- **Access-Able Travel Source:** *(www.access-able.com)* Information on accessible attractions and HTC-identified accessible RV parks.
- **Americans with Disabilities Act (ADA):** For more information, go to *(www.usdoj.gov/disabilities.htm)*. Information line: 800/514-0301
- **Disability.gov** has links to the federal government's resources and services. *(www.disabilityinfo.gov)*
- **Enabled RVer:** Hope Sykes at *(http://maxpages.com/enabledrver)*
- **Handicapped RV Club:** *(www.handicappedtravelclub.com)* Lists accessible RV campgrounds and other useful resources. More information at the Web site .
- **RV America** has a list of manufacturers of accessible RVs. *(www.rvamerica.com/data/rvdisable.htm)*
- **Virtual community** for the disabled at *(www.icanonline.net)*. See Employment.
- **Virtual Volunteer Project:** *(www.serviceleader.org)* Includes online tutoring and mentoring.

Family travel
- *Educational Travel on a Shoestring* by Judith Waite Allee and Melissa L. Morgan. Order from the publisher at Harold Shaw Publishers, 2375 Telstar Drive #160, Colorado Springs, Co 80920. 719/590-4999, or at *(www.dreamsonashoestring.com)*.

- *Homeschooling on a Shoestring* also by Allee and Morgan. Resources at Web site for parents homeschooling their children.
- **Families on the Road:** Shelley Zoelick's Web site. See article index and resources. *(www.familiesontheroad.com)*

RV Clubs

- **Escapees RV Club**, 100 Rainbow Dr., Livingston, TX 77355, 888/757-2582. *(www.escapees.com)* "Sharing the RV Lifestyle." Provides services for full-time RVers. Find Boondocking Etiquette letter under "What's Hot" at the Escapees Web site (See Action Items).
- **Family Motor Coach Assoc.:** *(www.fmca.com)* FMCA, 8291 Clough Pike, Cincinnati, OH 45244 800/543-3622
- **Good Sam Club:** 800/234-3450. *(www.goodsamclub.com)*

Solo travelers

- **Loners on Wheels (LOW)**, P.O. Box 1060-WB Cape Girardeau, MO 63702. 888/569-4478. For information and a sample newsletter, e-mail lonersreply@clas.net. *(www.lonersonwheels.com)*
- **RVing Women**, PO Box 1960, Surprise, AZ 85378-1960, 888/557-8464. *(www.rvingwomen.com)* E-mail: *rvingwomen@juno.com*
- **Wandering Individuals Network, Inc. (WIN)**, PO Box 6068, Pahrump, NV 89041-6068. Request a sample newsletter at winofc@hotmail.com. *(www.rvsingles.org)*
- *The Woman's Guide to Solo RVing* by Jaimie Hall and Alice Zyetz. Pine Country Publishing. Available in eBook or CD at *(www.rvhometown.com* and *www.rvtravelingtales.com)*.
- **Joei Carlton Hossack:** Order her books from Amazon.com or call 800/472-0438. *Restless From the Start; Everyone's Dream Everyone's Nightmare; Kiss This Florida, I'm Outta Here;* and *A Million Miles From Home,* and *Alaska Bound and Gagged.*

APPENDIX 10: THREE RV WORKERS' STORIES

Alaska job search

- **Coolworks:** Start with *(www.coolworks.com)*. Click on Alaska for links to a variety of employers.
- **Alaska's Division of Tourism:** *(http://www.dced.state.ak.us/oed/toubus/visinfo.cfm)* Find links to, and addresses of, city visitor

bureaus and chambers of commerce under Other Sources For Information. Call 907/929-2200, ext. 201, for a free vacation planner or see *(www.travelalaska.com)*. Ron and Val saw Halsingland Hotel advertised, sent in their resumes and were hired.

- **Alaska Campground Owners Assoc.:** Fax resume to 907/333-1016. They make resumes available to member campgrounds.
- **Internet search:** Search for Alaskan cities by name. Chamber of Commerce will list potential employers and RV parks.
- **Federal seasonal jobs:** For seasonal jobs with federal agencies check *(www.usajobs.opm.gov)*. Limit your search to Alaska.
- **Classified sections**: Many newspapers can be found on the Internet. Ardith and Page checked out employment ads in Anchorage prior to heading north. (See **Resources,** Chapter 9.)
- **Volunteer:** Volunteers needed for Alaska State Parks. Look at Coolworks or call 907/269-8708. Contact federal agencies around the first of the year for summer volunteer positions.
- *Workamper News:* Look under Alaska listings.

Additional resources/notes

*"Get a good idea and stick with it. Dog it, and
work at it until it's done and done right."*
Walt Disney

Index —Job list

A

Act as a booking agent for a circus - *Ch 15*

Activity director or recreation leader - *Resorts Ch 19*

Activity director for club RV parks - *Ch 16*

Adventure/recreation tours: jobs like raft guide, stable hand, tour leader, reservations staff, cashier, mechanic, maintenance worker, driver, loader or packer - *Resorts Ch 19*

Aids or technicians in archaeology, biological, hydrological, lands, range, real estate and surveying - *USFS Ch 17*

Airport driver - *Dude ranch Ch 19*

Archaeological assistance - *State volunteering Ch 22*

Artist or craftsperson: painting, beading, photography, weaving, jewelry etc. - *Own business Ch 21*

Assistant on archaeological digs - *Federal volunteering Ch 22*

Attractions host/hostess, tickets host/hostess - *Disney Ch 19*

B

Badges - *Own business Ch 21*

Baggage handling for cargo aircraft - *Temporary Ch 20*

Bartender - *Casinos Ch 19*

Bike rental clerk, mechanic - *RV park Ch 14*

Blackjack dealer - *Casinos Ch 19*

Bookkeeper - *Ch 16*

Bookkeeping/orders - *Non-profit Ch 18*

Brake assists - *Own business Ch 21*

Breakfast preparation - *B&B Ch 19*

Bus driver/guide - *Cruise/land tours Ch 19*

Bus maintenance and cleaning worker - *Cruise/land tours Ch 19*

Business consultant - *Own business Ch 21*

C

Cafeteria worker - *Wall Drug/similar Ch 19*

Campground hosting, which can include a variety of tasks - *State volunteering Ch 22*

Campground worker - *Amusement/theme parks Ch 19*

Campground host - *Federal volunteering Ch 22*

Campground host - *Concessionaire Ch 18*

Campground host - *State parks Ch 18*

Campground host at military Fam camps - *Federal volunteering Ch 22*

Campground hosts - *NF concessionaires Ch 18*

Campsite construction - *State volunteering Ch 22*

Canoe rental clerk and livery driver - *RV park Ch 14*

Caretake/work in exchange for site, extra hours for money - *Ch 14*

Caretaking ranches or other property - *Ch 14*

Carpenter and other tradesmen - *Federal volunteering Ch 22*

Cartography aid or technician - *BLM Ch 17*

Carving - *Own business Ch 21*

Census taker - *Ch. 17*

Check gas pipe lines - *Ch 15*

Child care provider or worker - *Ski resorts Ch 19*

Child care provider or worker - *Dude ranch Ch 19*

Child care- nanny - *Ch 14*

Christmas tree lot manager or helper - *Ch 14*

Christmas retail sales - *Temporary Ch 20*

Circus - *Ch 15*

Clerical, computer and fiscal help at headquarters - *State volunteering Ch 22*

Clerk or cashier selling books and other items at an NPS visitor center - *Non-profit Ch 18*

Collecting Christmas donations - bell ringer - *Temporary Ch 20*

Computer consultant, Web page designer - *Own business Ch 21*

Computer project consultant - *Contract work Ch 20*

Construction sites: paid to provide 24-hour security- *Ch 14*

Construction - carpenter, plumber, electrician - *RV park ch 14*

Construction of a Habitat for Humanity Build - *Nonprofit volunteering Ch 22*

Construction sites: mainly providing a presence - *Ch 14*

Construction work: carpentry, plumbing, electrical, sheet rock, block work - *Temporary Ch 20*

Construction worker - *Federal volunteering Ch 22*

Cook - *Wall Drug/similar Ch 19*

Cook - *Dude ranch Ch 19*

Costumed character at amusement park or clown - *Resorts Ch 19*

I

J

L

M

Office workers like secretary, bookkeeper or accountant - *RV parks Ch 14*

Office or computer work for a Habitat for Humanity affiliate - *Nonprofit volunteering Ch 22*

Office, technical and reservations: front office receptionist, reservationist - *Disney Ch 19*

Office worker - *Dude ranch Ch 19*

Office work: clerical, accounting, computers - *Temporary Ch 20*

Operator of a hunting check stations - *State parks Ch 18*

P

Paid staff for office work and RV club functions - *Ch 16*

Park or gate attendant at COE projects (bid) - *COE Ch 17*

Park aide - *State parks Ch 18*

Park guide - *NPS Ch 17*

Park at a business in exchange for night security - *Exchange Ch 22*

Parts advisor - *Ch 16*

Patrolling the backcountry - *State volunteering Ch 22*

Performer at school assemblies - *Own business Ch 21*

Personal services like hair dresser, nanny or childcare provider, computer programmer, handyman *-Resorts Ch 19*

Pet grooming - *Own business Ch 21*

Photography, updating slide collection - *State volunteering Ch 22*

Playing Santa Claus - *Temporary Ch 20*

Pool operations - lifeguard, pool cleaner - *RV parks Ch 14*

Positions in biology, archeology and other fields - *NPS Ch 17*

Post office help at Christmas - *Ch 17*

Post office temporary work - *Temporary Ch 20*

Post office contract work - *Temporary Ch 20*

Produce an electronic magazine (e-zine) - *Own business Ch 21*

Product demonstration - *Temporary Ch 20*

Professional - *Temporary Ch 20*

Propane service technician - *RV parks Ch 14*

Property caretaker - *Overseas Ch 19*

Pumpkin lot manager or helper - *Ch 14*

V

W

Index

Notes

"There is no wealth but life."
John Ruskin

Pine Country Publishing
www.RVHometown.com

Also

*RV Traveling Tales: Women's Journeys on the
Open Road*
www.RVTravelingTales.com

The Woman's Guide to Solo RVing
eBook and CD
www.RVHometown.com

RV Lifestyle Electronic Newsletter
RVLifestyle-subscribe@listbase.net

Order form

For fax orders: 561/892-2837. Send this form.
E-mail orders: CalamityJaimie@escapees.com
Postal orders: Pine Country Publishing, 127 Rainbow Dr.,
#2780, Livingston, TX 77399-1027 Telephone: 928/607-3181.
Toll-free number: 877/537-4539 #7038
Order by credit card at www.rvhometown.com

Support Your RV Lifestyle! *An Insider's Guide to Working on the Road* at **$19.95 (U.S. funds) per copy.**	
Name:	
Address:	
City:	
State and zip code:	
Number of books: @ $19.95 U.S. =	$
Media rate shipping and handling: $3.00	$
Priority Mail shipping and handling: $4.00	$
Shipping and handling for additional copies: $2.00 each	$
Texas residents add sales tax: 6.25% (Polk Cty- 6.75%)	$
Total enclosed:	$

Make checks payable to Pine Country Publishing
For Visa or Mastercard orders, complete the following:
Name as it appears on your card: _____
Card number: _____ Exp. date: _____
Check digit: (last 3 digits on back in reverse italics) _____
Telephone number or e-mail: _____
Signature: _____